THE MEAT FREE
MONDAY COOKBOOK

Foreword by Paul, Stella, and Mary McCartney

Edited by Annie Rigg

Photography by Tara Fisher

Kyle Books

For Linda, her family and our army of
dedicated believers who know we can
change things for the better.

———

Published in 2012 by Kyle Books
www.kylebooks.com

Distributed by National Book Network
4501 Forbes Blvd., Suite 200
Lanham, MD 20706
Phone: (800) 462-6420
Fax: (301) 429-5746
custserv@nbnbooks.com

First published in Great Britain in 2011 by
Kyle Books Limited
ISBN **978 1 906868 69 7**

Edited by **Judith Hannam, Vicky Orchard**
& Danielle Di Michiel
Editorial assistance by **Laura Foster**
& Estella Hung
Design **heredesign.co.uk**
Photography by **Tara Fisher**
Home economy by **Annie Rigg**
Styling by **Wei Tang**
Production by **David Hearn & Nic Jones**

Meat Free Monday Campaign is hereby identified
as the author of this work in accordance with Section 77
of the Copyright, Designs and Patents Act 1988 *except
for all recipes acknowledged on page 238

Library of Congress Control Number: 2011940444

Printed in Singapore by Tien Wah Press (Pte) Limited

A Note on Cheese

Cheese is often mistakenly thought of as always being suitable for
vegetarians. Many "hard" cheeses, however, and some blue ones, are
made using rennet, an enzyme commonly derived from the lining of
the stomach of calves. Vegetarian versions are increasingly available,
and are made with "microbial enzymes," a synthetically developed
coagulant. Soft cheeses, such as cream cheese and cottage cheese,
are manufactured without rennet. Some cottage cheeses, however,
may contain gelatin, which is derived from animal sources.
All labels should therefore be read carefully.

CONTENTS

Foreword by Paul, Stella, and Mary McCartney 6

Introduction by Claudia Tarry: The Meat Free Monday Campaign 8

Spring 12

Summer 66

Autumn 120

Winter 174

Index 228

Acknowledgments 240

FOREWORD

When I read an article regarding the 2006 report by the United Nations called *Livestock's Long Shadow*, I was mostly interested in the fact that this was coming from an organization that did not have a vested interest in vegetarianism. It's so easy for people to say "Well, you would say that, wouldn't you?" whenever a discussion of a meat-free lifestyle takes place, but here we had an organization with no such bias informing us that the meat industry was an even bigger contributor to climate change than the whole of the transport industry put together. Not only was I shocked to learn that this was so, I was pleased this was coming from a reputable source that had no vested interests in this argument.

Shortly after hearing about this report, I started writing to influential people (politicians, celebrities, musicians, etc.) to make them aware of these surprising facts. I'd also heard that there were people who were advocating the idea of not eating meat for one day of the week. It was suggested by them that if enough people followed this plan, this could have a considerable and favorable effect on our Earth's climate. In fact, the head of the Intergovernmental Panel on Climate Change, Dr Rajendra Pachauri, said: "Individuals can make a difference... by altering their diets through consuming less meat—say by giving up meat at least one day a week. Reducing meat consumption in this manner will make individuals healthier, as well as the planet." The respected charity Oxfam was also calling for a reduction in meat and dairy consumption, suggesting that replacing red meat and dairy with vegetables just one day a week could cut an individual's annual emissions by the equivalent of a 1,160-mile car trip.

We then decided as a family to launch the Meat Free Monday campaign in the UK and to try to encourage others round the world to do something similar in their own particular areas. This led to the launch of Meat Free Monday on Monday June 15, 2009, at an event in St James's Park, London, which was attended by a host of interesting and interested people who were willing to help spread the word.

It has emerged that many people like the idea because, firstly, it is not too difficult to do, and, secondly, it provides people with a positive way to do something in their own life to benefit the planet's ecology. Many people said that they already ate less meat than they previously had and many realized that they had already unwittingly adopted the idea.

There are other advantages besides being able to help with the problem of climate change. In difficult economic times, people discovered that having at least one meat-free day in their week helped their family budget. One of the things we notice is that people sometimes find the idea of a meat-free meal a little daunting, whereas, in fact, it's often quite simple to put something together. With this in mind, we have asked various people for their suggestions as to what might be a good dish for a meat-free day. We hope that you'll find them interesting and easy enough to make, and the added attraction of them being healthy and economical will hopefully entice you to try many of them.

The consequence of us all making this effort could be far-reaching for us, our children, and generations to come. Most of us understand that unless something is done and changes are made, we are going to leave an unhealthy planet for the people of the future to inherit and no doubt they will look back to this point in history and rightly say that we failed to act when things could have been altered for the better.

We feel that the vast majority of people are conscientious and would want to do something in their own lives to help secure a happier future for the generations that follow. While many suggestions offered can be quite difficult to put into practice, the idea of one meat-free day per week is something that many people find do-able and something that can be achieved relatively easily.

We hope that this publication and the recipes and ideas in it are something you will find easy enough to incorporate into your own lifestyle and that of your family. If enough of us make this move, we can make a huge difference for the better and set a new pattern for the future of this beautiful planet that we all inhabit.

THE MEAT FREE MONDAY CAMPAIGN

The McCartney family has a long history of personal interest in sustainable food—from the Linda McCartney vegetarian food range to Paul's organic farm—but it was reading a 2006 report by the United Nations Food and Agriculture Organization (FAO), *Livestock's Long Shadow*, that crystalized in Paul, Stella, and Mary's minds the global importance of making planet-friendly food choices. According to *Livestock's Long Shadow*[1], animal agriculture is currently "one of the top two or three most significant contributors to the most serious environmental problems, at every scale from local to global." On the basis of this alarming fact, the family launched the Meat Free Monday campaign in June 2009 to encourage more of us to have at least one meat-free day a week as a meaningful way of helping to slow climate change.

What is the link between livestock and the environment? Over the last 50 years, there has been a dramatic rise in the amount of meat that people are eating. Between 1961 and 2007 the world population increased by a factor of 2.2[2], but total meat consumption quadrupled, with poultry consumption increasing tenfold[3]. Due to the vast number of animals involved, the FAO estimates that livestock production is responsible for up to 18 percent of global greenhouse gas (GHG) emissions, with some estimates putting the figure as high as 50 percent. Greenhouse gases are so called because they rise into the atmosphere, trapping the sun's heat and causing what is commonly referred to as global warming.

The main culprits are carbon dioxide, methane, and nitrous oxide. Methane is caused by "enteric fermentation"—in other words, burping and farting—by cows, sheep, and goats, while nitrous oxide rises from slurry (manure) pits (primarily on pig farms) or is the byproduct of the production of fertilizers. Carbon dioxide (CO_2) is produced when rainforests are razed to the ground to make way for grazing cattle, or for growing crops to feed to farmed animals. CO_2 may get the most publicity, but the other two are much more powerful greenhouse gases: methane (CH_4) is 21 times more powerful than CO_2 and remains in the atmosphere for 9 to 14 years, and nitrous oxide (NO) is 310 times more powerful than CO_2 and hangs around for up to 114 years. What this means is that gases that are being released today will continue to degrade the climate for years to come.

As well as pumping GHGs into the atmosphere, animal agriculture sucks up massive amounts of water. The estimated 634 gallons of freshwater required to produce one 5.2 ounce (147g) hamburger would be enough for a four-hour shower[4]. Like fossil fuels, freshwater supplies are running out. The glaciers that are the source of many of the great rivers are melting due to climate change, and the Ganges, the Niger, and Yellow Rivers are drying up. As they disappear, so does the world's available water.

Reducing one's meat consumption has personal as well as planetary benefits. According to the World Health Organization, we eat considerably more protein than is considered necessary or optimal for health—mostly from animal products[5]. A meat-and-dairy-heavy diet is now being linked to some of the world's biggest killer diseases: cancer, heart disease, and stroke. A 2010 study by the Harvard School of Public Health found that as little as 1.75 ounces (50g) of processed meat a day (the equivalent of one sausage or two pieces of bacon) increases the risk of coronary heart disease by 42 percent and diabetes by 19 percent[6], while the American Cancer Society acknowledges that eating large amounts of red or processed meat over a long period of time can raise the risk of colorectal cancer, the third most common type of cancer in both men and women in the U.S. Because of its link to cancer[7], the World Cancer Research Fund recommends we: "choose mostly plant foods, limit red meat and avoid processed meat"[8].

The positive benefits of eating less meat were touted in a 2010 study carried out by Oxford University's Department of Public Health on behalf of Friends of the Earth, which found that limiting meat-eating to no more than 3 times a week could prevent 31,000 deaths from heart disease, 9,000 deaths from cancer, and 5,000 deaths caused by stroke each year[9].

If you shop and cook cleverly, Meat Free Monday could also help save you money, too. In May 2011 global meat prices hit a new record high. A number of factors including animal diseases and rising cost of feed have seen the price of meat from sheep rise 38 percent, and from cattle 20 percent, in just a year[10]. Plant proteins such as dried beans or lentils are typically cheaper than the equivalent amount of animal protein. In fact, most of the world's people eat a mostly meat-free diet made up of inexpensive commodities such as beans, rice, and corn. Less meat + more veg = save money! In the U.S., where the meat reduction message has really taken off, a survey carried out by the Food Marketing Institute and the American Meat Institute found that 36 percent of respondents said that they were purchasing less meat to help their budget[11].

It's worth mentioning that eating less meat is also a compassionate choice. In order to keep up with global demand for burgers, sausages, steaks, and nuggets, around 60 billion animals are farmed and killed each year[12]. The vast majority are raised in intensive factory farms, inside which they are crammed into small, dirty, overcrowded enclosures or cages. The life of a farmed animal is a short and unhappy one, culminating in a bloody end at the slaughterhouse.

And then there's fish: it has been estimated that if current fishing trends continue, there will be no fish left by 2048[13]. Industrialized fishing vessels with their football-field sized nets or lines of hooks a mile long trash coral reefs and ocean beds, kill and injure marine wildlife including dolphins, turtles, and sea birds, and are pushing the oceans to the brink of environmental collapse.

With so many compelling reasons to have one meat-free day each week, it should be seen as a positive, rewarding choice rather than a sacrifice. Meat Free Monday is a fun challenge with an achievable goal that will bring many benefits, while giving you the opportunity to broaden your culinary horizons along the way.

Please join this global movement for change because one day a week can make a world of difference.

[1] Steinfeld H et al, *Livestock's Long Shadow: Environmental Issues and Options*, Food and Agriculture Organization of the United Nations, Rome, 2006.

[2] *The World at Six Billion*, United Nations Department of Economic and Social Affairs Population Division, 1999.

[3] FAOSTAT online database: http://faostat.fao.org/default.aspx

[4] Hoekstra AY and Chapagain AK, *Water footprints of nations: Water use by people as a function of their consumption pattern*, Water Resource Management, 2007, 21(1): pp.35-48.

[5] World Health Organization, *Protein and amino acid requirement in human nutrition*, (WHO Technical Report Series No. 935), WHO, 2002, p.230.

[6] Hu FB et al, *Dietary fat intake and the risk of coronary heart disease in women*, NEJM, 1997, 337: p.1491.

[7] Chao A et al, *Meat Consumption and Risk of Colorectal Cancer*, JAMA, 2005, 293(2), pp.172-182.

[8] http://www.wcrf-uk.org/cancer_prevention/diet/index.php

[9] *Healthy Planet Eating*, Friends of the Earth, October 2010.

[10] *Food Outlook: Global Market Analysis*, Food and Agriculture Organization of the United Nations, June 2011, pp.39-40.

[11] *The Power of Meat 2011, An In-Depth Look at Meat Through the Shoppers' Eyes*, Food Marketing Institute and American Meat Institute, 2011, pp.12-13.

[12] FAOSTAT online database, http://faostat.fao.org/default.aspx

[13] Worm B et al, *Impacts of Biodiversity Loss on Ocean Ecosystem Services*, Science, 3 November 2006, 314 (5800), pp.787-790.

SPR I R

N G

WEEK 01

BREAKFAST

SOFT-BOILED EGGS WITH ASPARAGUS SPEARS

Cook **4–5 asparagus spears** in a large pan of boiling salted water for 3–5 minutes until tender. At the same time, boil **1 organic egg** for 3–4 minutes. Put the egg in an egg cup on a plate. Drain the asparagus and place on the plate alongside. Slice the top off the egg and season with **a pinch of salt** and some **freshly ground black pepper**. Serves 1

PACKED LUNCH

MIDDLE EASTERN TABBOULEH SALAD

Rinse **⅓ cup bulgur wheat** with cold water, then place in a bowl. Add **1¾ cups boiling water**, cover, and leave for 30 minutes. Drain well, using a sieve, and return to the bowl. Add **⅓ cup freshly chopped flat-leaf parsley**, **¼ cup freshly chopped mint**, **4 finely chopped scallions**, **¼ peeled, seeded, and finely chopped cucumber**, and **3 peeled, seeded, and finely chopped tomatoes**, and mix well. Whisk together **3 tablespoons olive oil** and the **juice of 1 lemon** and add **a pinch of salt** and some **freshly ground black pepper**, then stir into the tabbouleh. Serves 2

LUNCH

SWEET POTATO GNOCCHI WITH ARUGULA PESTO

SERVES 4

Gnocchi are little dumplings that are so light, they float to the surface when cooked. In fact, this is how you know they are done. They are usually made with regular potatoes but basing them on the sweet variety is a delicious alternative. This recipe is surprisingly quick to make and very filling. Use a classic basil pesto Genovese if you prefer.

1⅓ pounds sweet potatoes, peeled and diced
1 tablespoon butter
½ cup all-purpose flour
½ cup semolina
freshly grated nutmeg
salt and freshly ground black pepper

FOR THE PESTO
2¼ cups arugula
2 garlic cloves, crushed
3 tablespoons pine nuts
½ cup olive oil

Cook the sweet potatoes in boiling salted water for 10 minutes or until just tender. Drain and leave to cool.

Place all the ingredients for the pesto in a food processor or pound with a mortar and pestle to make a coarse paste.

Mash the potatoes in a bowl until smooth. Add the butter, flour, semolina, nutmeg, and salt and pepper. Mix to a dough. Divide the dough into four pieces and shape each piece into a long roll about ¾ inch in diameter. Cut each roll across into equal-size disks. Bring a large saucepan of salted water to a boil. Drop the gnocchi into the water in batches and cook for 3–5 minutes until they rise to the surface. Remove with a slotted spoon and keep warm while you cook the rest. Once all the gnocchi are cooked, stir in the pesto and serve.

SIDE

SPRING HERB SALAD

Gently mix in a bowl 4 handfuls of leaves: choose from what you can get/grow at home—**lamb's lettuce, sorrel (French or Buckler leaf), beet tops, or Boston**, and arrange on 4 salad plates. Make a dressing from **1 tablespoon hazelnut oil** mixed with **1 tablespoon vegetable oil, 2 teaspoons white wine vinegar**, a seasoning of **salt** and **freshly ground black pepper,** and **1 teaspoon Dijon mustard**. Dress the salad plates, and sprinkle with **fresh spring herbs** such as **dill**. Serves 4

DINNER

SPRING VEGETABLE TARTE FINE

TOM AIKENS

SERVES 4

Dishes don't get much Springier than this. A tarte fine is a thin tart with a flaky filo pastry base. It can be topped with sweet ingredients—apples are a popular option—but here it provides the base for a light cheesy sauce and a medley of vegetables and herbs. The whole thing is bursting with seasonal freshness.

1 tablespoon freshly chopped chervil
1 tablespoon freshly chopped parsley
1/4 cup crème fraîche
2 organic egg yolks
1/2 cup Gruyère, grated
6 asparagus spears, thinly sliced longwise
1 medium zucchini, thinly sliced longwise
1/2 cup fresh peas, shelled
4 tablespoons unsalted butter

8 scallions, finely chopped
3 sheets of filo pastry
12 large sorrel or spinach leaves
1 1/2 cups baby spinach leaves
2 cups arugula leaves
salt and freshly ground black pepper

Mix the chervil and parsley with the crème fraîche and egg yolks. Add half the grated Gruyère and season to taste. Set aside.

Bring a pan of salted water to a boil and prepare a bowl of ice water. When the water is boiling, add the slices of asparagus to the water, leave for 10 seconds, then plunge them into the ice water to cool. Repeat with the zucchini slices and dry both well on paper towels. Cook the peas for 2–3 minutes, then refresh them in ice water and dry on paper towels.

Place a shallow pan on low to medium heat and melt half the butter. Add the scallions, season them with salt and pepper, and cook briefly for 2–3 minutes, until just done. Transfer to a plate to cool, then mix them with the egg mixture.

Preheat the oven to 350°F. Melt the remaining butter. Take a sheet of filo, place it on a baking sheet and brush one side with butter. Place another sheet on top, brush with butter, then add the last sheet and brush with butter. Cut the filo into 4 equal rectangles, place another baking sheet on top to keep the filo flat, and bake for about 15 minutes until golden and crispy. Turn the oven down to 325°F.

Spread the scallion and egg mixture over the filo. Add the sorrel and baby spinach leaves, then season with salt and freshly ground black pepper. Add the zucchini, asparagus, and peas. Sprinkle with the rest of the Gruyère and bake for 8–10 minutes. Scatter with the arugula and serve immediately.

DESSERT

PINK RHUBARB SORBET

Cut **1 pound rhubarb** into 1-inch lengths and put into a heavy-bottomed saucepan. Add **4 tablespoons water.** Gently warm until the juices run, then stir in **1 cup superfine sugar** and the **juice of 1/2 lemon** and simmer, covered, until tender. Taste, and add more sugar if needed. Pour into a plastic container and freeze, whisking several times as it freezes to break up the ice crystals. Remove from the freezer 15 minutes before serving and leave in the fridge. Serves 4

WEEK 02

BREAKFAST
BLUEBERRY PANCAKES

Sift **2 cups all-purpose flour, 3 teaspoons baking powder, a pinch of salt** and **4 tablespoons superfine sugar** into a mixing bowl. Make a well in the middle and add **4 tablespoons melted unsalted butter, 1/2 cup organic milk, 1/2 cup buttermilk, 2 large beaten organic eggs,** and **1 teaspoon vanilla extract**. Using a whisk, gradually incorporate the wet ingredients into the dry and continue to whisk until smooth. Fold in **1/2 cup defrosted frozen blueberries**. Melt **a pat of butter** in a large frying pan over medium heat, swirling the pan so that the butter coats the bottom of the pan. Drop 4 tablespoons of the pancake batter into the hot pan and cook for 1 minute or until bubbles start to appear on the surface. Flip the pancakes over and cook the other side until golden and well risen. Remove from the pan and keep warm while you cook the remaining batter in the same way. Serve the pancakes in stacks, dusted with **confectioner's sugar, a handful of extra blueberries,** and **a splash of good-quality maple syrup**. Makes 12

PACKED LUNCH
SPICY FALAFEL WITH TAHINI SAUCE

Take **1 1/4 cups chickpeas** and soak them in cold water overnight, drain and puree finely in a food processor. Process **2 medium onions, 3 finely chopped garlic cloves,** and **3 green chiles** together with **a handful of freshly chopped parsley** and mix into the chickpeas, together with **2 teaspoons ground coriander** and **3 teaspoons ground cumin**. Add **1/2 teaspoon baking powder** and **a pinch of sea salt**. Shape the mixture into small round balls and deep-fry in **olive oil** heated to smoking point, turning until the outsides are browned. This Lebanese dish is usually served with Tahiniyeh— Tahini Sauce, made by crushing **2–3 garlic cloves** with **a little salt,** mixing in a little of the **juice of 2 lemons** and beating in **2/3 cup tahini** and a little salt to taste. You can either do this by hand or use a food processor. Dilute with the balance of the lemon juice and **a little water** until you have the consistency of heavy cream. Check the seasoning and serve with the falafel. Serves 4

LUNCH
QUINOA AND ROASTED TOMATO SALAD

SERVES 2

Quinoa, a tiny, bead-shaped grain with more protein and dietary fiber than either wheat or rice, is probably one of the world's best kept secrets. Its slightly bitter taste lends this tomato salad a refreshing piquancy that you just won't forget.

6 ripe tomatoes, halved
1/2 garlic clove, finely chopped
1 tablespoon freshly chopped parsley
3 tablespoons olive oil
salt and freshly ground black pepper

3/4 cup quinoa
1 tablespoon balsamic vinegar
1 red onion, finely chopped

Preheat the oven to 425°F. Place the halved tomatoes on a baking sheet, cut-side up. Scatter with the chopped garlic and the parsley, and drizzle with 1 tablespoon of the olive oil. Season with sea salt and freshly ground black pepper. Place the baking sheet in the oven and roast for 40 minutes until the edges begin to blacken. Meanwhile, cook the quinoa according to the package instructions, then drain well and place in a bowl. Whisk together the remaining olive oil and the balsamic vinegar, then stir into the quinoa. Last, mix in the tomatoes and red onion.

BROILED FIELD MUSHROOMS

Clean **8–12 large flat mushrooms** of any dirt. Remove the stems and discard (or use in stock). Put the mushrooms in a marinade of **6 tablespoons olive oil**, **1 stem of rosemary leaves**, **1 tablespoon balsamic vinegar**, **2 tablespoons red wine**, **1 small chopped onion** and **salt** and **freshly ground black pepper** and leave for 30–45 minutes, turning them occasionally. Preheat the broiler, and broil for 5 minutes on each side, brushing with the marinade juices. Serves 4

SPRING VEGETABLE STEW

SERVES 4

If you've got a vegetable patch or have just raided the local farmer's market, this is an excellent way to use up some of Spring's bounty. If eating a stew at this time of year seems a bit odd to you, think of it as a thick, nutritious soup.

1 tablespoon olive oil
2 tablespoons unsalted butter
2 shallots, chopped
1 fat garlic clove, crushed
3 cups vegetable stock
1 pound baby new potatoes, scrubbed
*   and halved if large*
12 baby carrots, halved lengthwise
8 baby zucchini, topped and tailed and
*   chopped into large chunks*

1 bunch asparagus, trimmed and sliced
*   into 2 inch lengths on the diagonal*
1 bunch scallions, trimmed and sliced into
*   2 inch lengths on the diagonal*
1 cup freshly shelled peas
1 cup freshly shelled and skinned
*   fava beans or edamame*
1 tablespoon freshly chopped tarragon
salt and freshly ground black pepper
extra virgin olive oil, for drizzling
a handful of chopped flat-leaf parsley

Heat the olive oil and butter in a large sauté pan. Add the chopped shallots and cook over medium heat until tender but not browned. Add the crushed garlic and cook for a further 30 seconds. Add the vegetable stock to the pan and bring to a boil. Boil for 5 minutes to reduce slightly. Add the new potatoes. Cook the potatoes for about 10 minutes until just tender.

Meanwhile prepare the other vegetables. Add the carrots to the pan and cook until al dente. Add the zucchini, asparagus, scallions, peas, fava beans (or edamame), and tarragon, and cook for a further couple of minutes until tender but still vibrant.

Season to taste with salt and freshly ground black pepper. Ladle the stew into bowls, drizzle with extra virgin olive oil, scatter with parsley, and serve immediately.

BEST EVER BANANA BREAD

Preheat the oven to 350°F. Grease and line a 1 pound loaf pan. Cream **9 tablespoons butter** and **1/2 cup superfine sugar** until light and fluffy. Beat in **2 organic eggs**, one at a time. Gently stir in **3 mashed bananas**. Sift **1 cup ground rice flour**, **1/2 cup cornflour**, **1 teaspoon pumpkin pie spice**, **2 teaspoons baking powder** and **1/4 teaspoon salt** into the mixture and fold until incorporated. Pour into the loaf pan and bake for 1–1½ hours until a skewer inserted into the center of the loaf comes out clean. Cool on a wire rack. Makes 12 slices

WEEK 03

BREAKFAST

STRAWBERRY AND BANANA SMOOTHIE

Put **8 ounces of strawberries** (leaves removed), **1 roughly chopped medium banana, 1¼ cups 1% organic milk, 5 ounces plain yogurt,** and **1 tablespoon honey** into a food processor, blender, or smoothie maker. Blend until smooth. Adjust the sweetness, adding a little more honey if you prefer, and pour into serving glasses. Serves 3–4

PACKED LUNCH

HUMMUS AND FLATBREAD

SERVES 4

Homemade hummus puts the store-bought equivalent in the shade. It's fresher and creamier and you can tailor it exactly to your taste. If you've got a blender, it's also remarkably easy to make.

14 ounce can chickpeas, drained
4 tablespoons tahini
juice of 2 lemons, to taste
4 garlic cloves, crushed
salt

2 tablespoons olive oil
1 teaspoon ground cumin
1 teaspoon ground paprika
1 tablespoon freshly chopped
flat-leaf parsley

Put the chickpeas in a blender and process to make a thick paste. Tasting as you go, add the tahini, lemon juice, garlic, and salt, and blend very thoroughly to a light cream (you may need to add a little water). Drizzle with olive oil and sprinkle with cumin, paprika, and parsley. Serve with flatbread.

LUNCH

VEGETARIAN CROQUE MADAME

Preheat the oven to 350°F. Spread **4 slices of bread of your choice** with **2 teaspoons Dijon mustard.** Top two of the slices with **1 cup grated Gruyère,** then place the other slices on top to make two sandwiches. Heat **2 tablespoons butter** in a large frying pan until foaming, and cook the sandwiches for 2 minutes on each side until golden. Transfer the sandwiches to a baking sheet and place in the oven for 5 minutes until the cheese has melted. Meanwhile, fry **2 organic eggs** in the hot pan. Remove the sandwiches from the oven and top each with a fried egg. Serve immediately. Serves 2

SIDE

SWEET AND SOUR CHINESE CABBAGE

Heat **2 tablespoons olive oil** in a heavy-bottomed pan and cook **1 sliced onion** until soft. Stir in **2 tablespoons white wine vinegar, 2 teaspoons sugar, 1 tablespoon sambal oelek** (Indonesian chile sauce) and **6 tablespoons chopped tomatoes** and mix well. Add **one small head of shredded Chinese cabbage** and **salt** and **freshly ground black pepper**. Cook for 10 minutes with the lid on, stirring occasionally, until the cabbage is tender. Serve hot with **2–3 scallions** and **1 finely sliced red chile** sprinkled over the top. Serves 4

DINNER

CRISPY SPRING ROLLS

SERVES 4

These light, crunchy spring rolls are a million miles from the greasy, tired offerings served up by many take-outs. Making them is a lot of fun—you'll have a real sense of achievement.

8 ounces fresh bean sprouts
8 ounces Napa cabbage
4 ounces bamboo shoots
4 ounces button mushrooms
2–3 carrots
vegetable oil for stir-frying and deep frying
1 teaspoon sugar

1 tablespoon light soy sauce
1 tablespoon rice wine
salt and freshly ground black pepper
20 frozen spring roll wrappers, defrosted
1 tablespoon all-purpose flour mixed with 1 tablespoon water

Wash the bean sprouts and roughly chop all the other vegetables to the same size. Heat a little oil in a wok until smoking and stir-fry the vegetables for 1 minute, then add the sugar, soy sauce, rice wine, and seasoning, and cook for an additional 1–2 minutes. Place in a bowl and let cool.

Place a teaspoon of the vegetable mixture in the center of each spring roll skin and roll up neatly, folding in all the corners. Place on a lightly floured plate and brush the upper edges with a little flour/water paste to seal.

Heat enough oil to deep-fry until steaming and drop in the spring rolls for 3–4 minutes, until crispy, cooking in batches. Drain and serve with chile sauce.

DESSERT

LIMONCELLO AND RICOTTA CHEESECAKE

GINO D'ACAMPO

To make the base put **1 cup crushed graham crackers**, **1/2 teaspoon ground cinnamon**, and **6 ounces melted butter** in a large bowl and use your fingertips to create a mixture with the texture of wet breadcrumbs. Grease a 8-inch springform cake pan with **1 tablespoon butter**. Press the graham cracker mixture firmly over the base of the pan and let set in the fridge for 30 minutes. In a large clean bowl, whisk **2 organic egg whites** until stiff, then set aside. Squeeze **the juice of 2 lemons** into a measuring cup, add **4 tablespoons limoncello,** and top up with enough cold water to make **1/2 cup**. Sprinkle with **1 1/2 tablespoons agar-agar powder** and leave to soak for 3 minutes. Place the bowl over a pan of simmering water and stir until the agar-agar powder is dissolved. Leave to cool slightly. In another bowl, whisk together **1 cup ricotta cheese,** **2/3 cup low-fat plain yogurt,** and **5 tablespoons honey**. Stir in the **zest of 2 lemons** and the limoncello mixture. Gently fold the egg whites into the mixture, pour into the pan, and level the surface. Chill for at least 5 hours until set. Remove from the pan and serve. Serves 8

WEEK 04

BREAKFAST

FABULOUS FIBER MUFFINS

Preheat the oven to 375°F. Line a 12-hole muffin pan with paper cups. In a bowl mix together **2¹/2 cups bran flakes, 1¹/4 cups all-purpose flour, ¹/4 cup raisins, a pinch of salt,** and **2 teaspoons baking powder.** In a separate bowl, beat together **4 tablespoons butter** and **¹/3 cup soft brown sugar.** Add **1 lightly beaten organic egg** and **1 ripe mashed banana,** beating well after each addition. Add **²/3 cup organic milk,** and continue to beat until you have smooth batter. Stir in the bran flakes and flour mixture. Divide the batter among the muffin cups and bake for 30 minutes or until a wooden toothpick inserted in the center comes out clean. Makes 12

PACKED LUNCH

WALDORF SALAD

Quarter **1 apple,** core, slice thinly and place in a bowl. Add **1 thinly sliced celery rib** and **1 tablespoon chopped toasted walnuts.** Peel and thinly slice **¹/2 red onion,** add to the bowl and combine. Whisk together **3 teaspoons olive oil, 1 teaspoon cider vinegar,** season with **sea salt** and **freshly ground black pepper,** pour over the salad and mix well. Serves 1

LUNCH

BRUSCHETTA BROCCOLI DI RAPE

SERVES 2

Bruschetta—it's pronounced "broos-keta," in case you're wondering—is an Italian recipe consisting of toasted bread rubbed with garlic and drizzled with olive oil. It's usually topped with something else, typically chopped tomatoes and basil. This version shows the versatility of the dish. As ever, it's as good as the basic ingredients—you wouldn't want to make this with supermarket sliced white bread.

2 bunches broccoli rabe
4 slices good white Italian-style bread
2 garlic cloves, crushed
olive oil
salt and freshly ground black pepper
1 garlic clove, roughly chopped

Steam the broccoli rabe for roughly 10 minutes until just tender in a pan of boiling water with a steamer rack. Cut the broccoli in half lengthwise and keep it warm. Then toast the bread slices and rub them with the crushed garlic cloves. Drizzle with a little olive oil and arrange the broccoli pieces on top. Season with a good sprinkling of salt and freshly ground black pepper and the chopped garlic clove. Drizzle with a little more olive oil and serve.

SNACK

MARINATED OLIVES

Heat **1 tablespoon olive oil** in a small pan, add **1 minced garlic clove**, **½ tablespoon coriander seeds**, **¼ teaspoon red pepper flakes**, and the **zest of half a lemon**. Warm through until fragrant, then add **1 cup black and green olives**. Serve at room temperature. Serves 2

DINNER

SPRING RAGOUT OF ARTICHOKE HEARTS, LIMA BEANS, PEAS, AND TURNIPS

STEPHANIE ALEXANDER

SERVES 3–4

A ragout is basically a well-seasoned stew. This one takes its flavor from the tarragon, which brings out the best in the array of seasonal vegetables.

8 garlic cloves, whole and unpeeled
2 pounds fresh fava beans in pods, shelled
ice cubes
4 tablespoons unsalted butter, chopped
4 trimmed and cooked artichoke hearts,
    halved or quartered, depending on size
12 baby turnips, peeled

1 cup vegetable stock
1 pound peas in pods, shelled
2 teaspoons coarsely chopped
    French tarragon
1 tablespoon finely chopped flat-leaf parsley
freshly ground black pepper

Put the garlic in a saucepan and cover with water. Bring slowly to a boil over low-medium heat, then drain. Repeat this process and then slip the skins off each clove and set aside in a bowl.

Refill the saucepan with water and return to a boil over high heat, and drop the fava beans into the boiling water for 1 minute only. Immediately drain in a colander and tip into a bowl of ice-cold water. Then peel the beans. Reserve until needed.

Melt half of the butter in a sauté pan over a medium heat. Once it starts to froth, add the artichoke pieces, turnips, and peeled garlic, and sauté until the artichoke pieces become golden flecked with brown. Add the vegetable stock and peas, then cook, covered, for 5 minutes. Uncover, scatter with the beans and herbs, and shake gently to mix; there should be very little liquid remaining in the pan. If it still looks sloppy, increase the heat to high and continue to shake the pan. Add the remaining butter to form a small amount of sauce. Taste for seasoning; there probably won't be any need to add salt. Grind over some black pepper and serve at once.

DESSERT

BANOFFEE PIE

Preheat the oven to 350°F. Melt **6 tablespoons butter** in a pan, add **2 cups graham cracker crumbs,** and stir to combine. Press the crumb mixture in an even layer over the base of an 8-inch springform pan, then chill in a refrigerator until set, about 1 hour. Spread the crumb base with **1¾ cups dulche de leche** or caramel and chill for an hour. Slice **4 bananas** and, reserving 1 banana for decoration, arrange in a layer over the caramel. Whip **1½ cups heavy cream** until soft peaks form, and spoon over the bananas. Decorate with the remaining banana slices and **¼ cup grated chocolate**. Serves 4–6

WEEK 05

BREAKFAST

OATMEAL WITH BLUEBERRIES

Pour a **cup of organic milk** and the same of **water** into a saucepan and bring to a boil. Add **1/2 cup of oats**, with **a pinch of salt**, and stir briskly. Simmer for 10–15 minutes or until thickened (the coarser your oats the longer they will take to cook), stirring occasionally. Serve with blueberry compote made from **1 heaping cup frozen blueberries**, **2 tablespoons superfine sugar,** and a **squeeze of lemon** simmered for 10 minutes. Serves 2

PACKED LUNCH

WHITE BEAN AND ARUGULA SALAD

Cook **1 small red onion** in **2 tablespoons olive oil**, together with **1 tablespoon fresh thyme leaves**, for about 5 minutes. Drain and rinse **14-ounce can white beans**, and stir into the onion until warmed through. Remove from the heat and stir in **2 1/2 cups arugula**. Whisk together an additional **2 tablespoons olive oil** and the **juice of 1 lemon**. Pour over the beans, season with **salt** and **freshly ground black pepper**. Serves 2

LUNCH

CAESAR SALAD

SERVES 2

The world's most famous salad was developed in Tijuana, Mexico, during the 1920s by Italian restaurateur Caesar Cardini. It proved a big hit among the thirsty Californians who flocked over the border to escape the rigors of Prohibition. Who can blame them? It still boggles the mind that something so delicious can be concocted from such simple ingredients. Cardini's original masterpiece didn't contain anchovies and neither does this excellent vegetarian recipe.

1/2 small ciabatta, cut into large cubes
4 tablespoons olive oil
salt and freshly ground black pepper
1 Romaine lettuce, washed, torn, or
   chopped into large pieces
1 large organic egg

1 large garlic clove, minced
1 tablespoon lime juice
1 teaspoon vegetarian Worcestershire sauce
1 teaspoon Dijon mustard
1/4 cup coarsely grated vegetarian Parmesan

Preheat the oven to 375°F. To make the croûtons, toss the ciabatta in 1 1/2 tablespoons oil and season well. Spread on a baking sheet and cook until crisp and golden, about 10 minutes.

Place the lettuce in a salad bowl. Place the egg in a pan of cold water and bring to a boil. Boil for 1 minute then plunge the egg into cold water to stop it cooking. Once it is cool enough to handle, crack the egg into a food processor and add the garlic, lime juice, Worcestershire sauce, mustard, and remaining oil. Process well, then add salt and freshly ground black pepper to taste. To serve, pour the dressing over the leaves and add the croûtons and Parmesan. Toss well and serve at once.

SIDE

GLOBE ARTICHOKES WITH FAVA BEANS AND OREGANO

In a large pan add **1 cup marinated and grilled artichoke hearts**, the **juice of 2 lemons**, **3 tablespoons olive oil**, **1 tablespoon chopped oregano**, **2 minced garlic cloves**, and some **salt** and **freshly ground black pepper**. Cover with cold water and bring to a boil, simmering for just 10 minutes. Add **2 pounds fava beans** (or edamame) and cook until the beans are tender. Sprinkle with **freshly chopped flat-leaf parsley** and **a drizzle of olive oil** and serve with **good bread**. Serves 4-6

DINNER

SPINACH TART

SERVES 4

A lot of people are put off spinach as kids, partly because it is a bit strong for some children's palates, partly because it is often murdered in the kitchen, and partly because the adults go on about how healthy it is. If this applies to you, think again. Popeye was right—spinach is good for you, being rich in iron, Vitamin A, and antioxidants—but it is also one of the tastiest vegetables around. It goes particularly well with cheese, as in this scrumptious tart.

8-inch deep tart pan, lined with flaky pie dough
9 ounces spinach
4 tablespoons butter
1 onion, finely chopped
2 heaping cups grated Cheddar cheese
2 whole organic eggs, plus 2 yolks
2/3 cup heavy cream
1 teaspoon Dijon mustard
salt and freshly ground black pepper

Preheat the oven to 400°F. Place the lined tart pan in the oven and bake for 10-15 minutes.

Gently cook the spinach with half the butter, until wilted. Remove from the heat and chop finely. Heat the remaining butter and cook the onions until soft. Spread the spinach and onion over the bottom of the pie crust.

Pulse together the cheese, eggs, yolks, cream, mustard, and seasoning. Pour over the spinach and onion and return to the oven for 20–30 minutes, until the top is golden. Turn off the heat and leave on the bottom shelf for 5 minutes. Serve with a green salad.

DESSERT

CHERRY SHORTBREAD

Preheat the oven to 350°F and line a baking sheet with parchment paper. Put **1 cup all-purpose flour**, **2/3 cup ground almonds**, **10 tablespoons diced unsalted butter**, **3/4 cup superfine sugar** and **a pinch of salt** into the bowl of a food processor and pulse until it forms a smooth dough. Pulse in **1/2 cup dried cherries** and the **finely grated zest of 1 orange** to combine evenly. Place the dough onto a lightly floured work surface and press into an even layer, about 1/2 inch thick. Using a 3-inch cookie cutter, cut out as many circles as possible, then lightly knead the remaining dough, flatten, and cut out more. Repeat until you have used all the dough. Bake for 20 minutes until lightly colored or the edges have turned golden. Let cool on the baking sheet for 5 minutes before removing to cool completely on a wire rack. Makes about 15 slices

WEEK 06

BREAKFAST

ALCOHOL-FREE PINA COLADA

Place **2 tablespoons coconut milk**, **1/4 cup pineapple chunks**, **1 1/2 cups organic milk**, and **1 teaspoon sugar** in a blender and purée. Pour into a glass and drink. Serves 1–2

PACKED LUNCH

SPICY TOMATO AND BEAN SALAD

Drain and rinse **14-ounce can white beans** and place in a mixing bowl. Make a small cross in the base of **1 pound tomatoes** and tip them into a bowl. Pour hot water over them and leave for 10 seconds. Remove, then when cool enough to handle, slip off the skins. Chop the tomatoes and add to the beans. Place **1 tablespoon sun-dried tomatoes**, **1 red chile**, **a small bunch of basil** (reserving a few small leaves), **1 garlic clove**, **1 tablespoon olive oil**, and **1 tablespoon red wine vinegar** in a food processor then pulse until smooth. Add to the tomatoes and beans, season with **salt** and **freshly ground black pepper**, and mix. Serve scattered with **a few small basil leaves**. Serves 2–3

LUNCH

SPAGHETTI OMELETTE

SERVES 2

An unusual way of serving spaghetti that will become a firm favorite. If you like, you can add 1/4 cup chopped Fontina to the tomato filling, or if you prefer you can leave out the filling altogether.

2 organic eggs
3 ounces spaghetti
2 tablespoons butter
2 tablespoons freshly grated vegetarian Parmesan

2 tablespoons freshly chopped parsley
4 ripe tomatoes, skinned and seeded, and roughly choppped
salt and freshly ground black pepper

Lightly beat the eggs in a large bowl, and season with salt and freshly ground black pepper. Cook the spaghetti in boiling salted water. Drain, return to the pan, and quickly stir in half of the butter, the Parmesan, and chopped parsley, then add to the bowl with the eggs and stir so that the spaghetti is well coated.

Melt the remaining butter in a frying pan. When the butter is foaming, add half the egg and spaghetti mixture and spread level. Top with the chopped tomato and then cover with the remaining egg and spaghetti mixture. Cook on a medium heat for 4–5 minutes, or until almost set. Transfer to a hot broiler for an additional 3–4 minutes, until golden. Leave to cool slightly then cut into wedges and serve.

SNACK

SPICED PEA DIP

Purée **1¹/₂ cups cooked frozen peas** with **2 tablespoons Greek yogurt**, **1 chopped green chile**, **1 large garlic clove**, **2 teaspoons olive oil**, **a squeeze of lemon juice**, and **1 tablespoon freshly chopped mint** to form a chunky paste. Season to taste with **salt** and **freshly ground black pepper**. Serve with **vegetable crudités** and **toasted pita**. Serves 4

DINNER

SUPER VEGETABLE SALAD

PAUL McCARTNEY

SERVES 4

This is a fantastic salad that can accompany whatever you like—here it's served with tofu, but you could just as easily serve it with veggie burgers or vegetarian sausages, as well as fries and new or mashed potatoes. You can also vary the steamed vegetables according to what's in season.

28 cherry tomatoes
3 florets of broccoli
12 green beans, cut into 1 inch lengths
2 carrots, peeled and siced into 1 inch pieces
1 lettuce—I like Romaine
3 scallions, finely chopped
²/₃ cup cornmeal
a handful of chopped herbs of your choice
9 ounces tofu, cut into slices
olive oil for frying

FOR THE DRESSING
2 tablespoons olive oil
1 tablespoon red wine vinegar
1 teaspoon Dijon mustard (optional)
1 teaspoon maple syrup (if you like a bit of sweetness)

Preheat the oven to 400°F and roast the cherry tomatoes for 10 minutes.

Cover the bottom of a pan with cold water and place a steamer above it. Put the broccoli, green beans, and carrots in the steamer, turn the heat on quite high, and steam for about 15 minutes, occasionally prodding the carrots with a fork to see if they are done. Some people like them slightly crunchy, others prefer them a little softer.

While the vegetables are steaming, make a salad with the leaves and scallions.

Combine the cornmeal and herbs in a bowl. Heat some olive oil in a frying pan. Dip the tofu in the cornmeal mixture, then fry until golden.

Whisk together the ingredients for the dressing, but only pour over at the last minute.

Assemble your meal by first putting the salad on the plate, then the warm vegetables, and finally the tofu. Pour over the dressing then add a little seasoning sauce such as Braggs or a sauce of your choice.

DESSERT

ALMOND CAKE

Preheat an oven to 350°F and line a 6-inch round cake pan with parchment paper. Cream **8 tablespoons butter** with **³/₄ cup superfine sugar**, then beat in **2 organic egg yolks** and **1 teaspoon vanilla extract**. Fold in **1¹/₂ cups sifted self-rising flour** and **1 teaspoon baking powder**, then add **1/₂ cup organic milk** and **1/₂ cup ground almonds**. In a separate bowl, beat **2 organic egg whites** until stiff, then gently fold into the cake batter. Pour into the prepared pan and bake for 40 minutes or until a toothpick inserted in the middle comes out clean. Cool, then cut into three horizontally. Sandwich with butter icing made by combining **2 tablespoons butter** with **1 cup confectioner's sugar**, **1 tablespoon organic milk** and **1 teaspoon vanilla extract**. Makes 6–8 slices

WEEK 07

BREAKFAST

CARAMELIZED GRAPEFRUIT

Take **1 pink grapefruit** and cut it in half horizontally. Gently remove the segments from the peel, discarding all pith and membranes, and put into a small bowl. Stir in **1/2 cup plain yogurt** and then replace the mixture equally into the 2 grapefruit shells (use ramekins if damaged). Sprinkle with **1 tablespoon brown sugar** and pop the grapefruit under a preheated, hot broiler for 2–3 minutes until the sugar starts to bubble. Serve immediately. Serves 2

PACKED LUNCH

VIETNAMESE STYLE ROLLS

Soak **2 ounces rice paper wrappers** according to the package instructions. Remove and let cool on some paper towels. Soak **2 ounces rice noodles** according to the package instructions, then drain and cut them into 1-inch strips. Grate **2 carrots** and finely chop **1/2 cucumber, 1 seeded red pepper,** and **1/2 iceberg lettuce** into strips. Place a rice pancake on a board and arrange some of the rice noodles, grated carrot, and strips of red pepper, cucumber, and iceberg lettuce plus **a few cilantro leaves** about a third of the way up, leaving a 1/2-inch edge at the side. Fold the sides over the vegetables and then roll up lengthwise to make a cigar shape. Repeat with the remaining pancakes. You can store in the fridge, covered with moist paper towels, for up to a day. To eat, dip each roll in **hoisin, sweet chile,** or **soy sauce** according to your taste. Serves 1–2

LUNCH

HOT MOZZARELLA SANDWICH

SERVES 1

The simple things are often the best and this sandwich is a case in point. The fresher the ingredients you use, the better it will be. The dipping sauce elevates it into something special.

1 ciabatta roll
2 tablespoons pesto sauce
1 ripe tomato, sliced
1 ounce mozzarella, sliced
3 teaspoons olive oil
1 teaspoon balsamic vinegar
a pinch of red pepper flakes

Preheat the broiler. Cut the ciabatta roll in half and lightly grill on all sides. Spread one half of the roll with the pesto sauce. Layer the other first with the tomato and then the mozzarella slices. Place this half back under the broiler until the mozzarella has melted, then sandwich the two halves together. Whisk together the olive oil with the balsamic vinegar and add the red pepper flakes and use as a dipping sauce.

SIDE

ARUGULA WITH CREAMY MUSTARD SAUCE

In a bowl mix together **1 teaspoon Dijon mustard, 1 teaspoon coarse-grain mustard,** and **1 tablespoon crème fraîche.** Mix in **7 ounces arugula** and season to taste with **salt** and **freshly ground black pepper.** Serves 2

DINNER

PORCINI AND CELERY RISOTTO

THEO RANDALL

SERVES 4

Good-quality porcini mushrooms, celery, thyme, and a touch of garlic are pretty much all it takes to create this delicious, delicately flavored risotto.

2 ounces dried porcini mushrooms
1/2 head celery, finely chopped
1 small onion, finely chopped
2 tablepoons olive oil
1 garlic clove, finely chopped
2 cups risotto rice
2 1/2 quarts vegetable stock
2 tablespoons butter
handful of freshly grated vegetarian Parmesan
1 teaspoon freshly chopped thyme leaves

Soak the porcini in warm water for 20 minutes. In a pan, sweat the celery and onion in the olive oil until soft but not colored. Add the garlic and cook for 1 minute, then add the risotto rice, porcini, and some stock. Stir until the mixture thickens, then add more stock. Continue the process until the rice is cooked. Stir in the butter, and serve scattered with the Parmesan and thyme leaves.

DESSERT

DOUBLE CHOCOLATE CRACKLE COOKIES

Preheat the oven to 350°F and cover two solid baking sheets with parchment paper. Tip **8 ounces chopped dark chocolate (70% cocoa solids)** into a heatproof bowl and place over a pan of barely simmering water; do not allow the bottom of the bowl to touch the water. Melt the chocolate, stirring from time to time. Remove from the heat and cool slightly. Cream **8 tablespoons softened unsalted butter** and **1 1/4 cups soft light brown sugar** until pale and light—this will take about 3 minutes. Gradually add **2 beaten large organic eggs,** mixing well between each addition, and then add **1 teaspoon vanilla extract** and the melted chocolate. Sift **1 1/4 cups all-purpose flour, 1/2 cup cocoa powder, 2 teaspoons baking powder,** and **a pinch of salt** into the bowl. Add **2–3 tablespoons organic milk** and **1/2 cup white chocolate chips,** and mix until thoroughly combined. Cover the bowl and chill the dough for at least 2 hours or until firm. Tip **6 tablespoons confectioner's sugar** into a bowl. Scoop a spoonful of the cookie dough into the palm of your hand and roll into a smooth ball roughly the size of a walnut. Roll the cookie in the sugar to coat completely and place on the baking sheet. Repeat with the remaining cookie dough, arranging the cookies spaced well apart on the baking sheets. You will need to bake the cookies in batches. Bake the cookies on the middle shelf of the preheated oven for about 12 minutes until the top is firm but not crisp. Cool the cookies on the baking sheets. Makes 30

WEEK 08

BREAKFAST

HUEVOS RANCHEROS

Soften **1/2 onion** in **1 tablespoon olive oil** in a pan. Add **a half can of tomatoes, 2 teaspoons white wine vinegar, a pinch of dried red pepper flakes,** and season with **salt**. Cook, stirring occasionally, over medium heat until thickened, about 20 minutes. Heat **2 soft flour tortillas** in the oven and place on warmed plates. Heat **14 ounces refried beans** in a pan, then spoon onto each of the tortillas and sprinkle with **1/2 cup freshly grated Cheddar**. Fry **2 organic eggs** in **1 tablespoon oil** and top each tortilla with 1 egg. Spoon the tomato sauce over the eggs and serve. Serves 2

PACKED LUNCH

CARROT AND HUMMUS CRUNCH ON SOURDOUGH

NICK SANDLER

Fry **2 coarsely grated large carrots** in a pan with **1 tablespoon olive oil, 2 chopped garlic cloves, 1/2 chopped red chile,** and **1 teaspoon caraway seeds** over moderate heat for 5–8 minutes, stirring frequently. Cool before using in the sandwich. Cut **4 slices of sourdough bread** or slice **2 sourdough baguettes** with a serrated knife along the middle so they are still connected at the back. Spread some **hummus** onto the baguettes, followed by the grated carrots. Remember to scrape in the caraway seeds and chile. Add **2 tablespoons Greek yogurt** to the baguette in dollops, followed by **a generous handful roughly chopped cilantro**. Season with **freshly ground black pepper**. Serves 2

LUNCH

GOOD OLD FASHIONED MACARONI AND CHEESE

SERVES 6

There's nothing more comforting than a good macaroni and cheese. This one doesn't have any superfluous flourishes—it's just an excellent, tried-and-true version of a classic dish.

1 pound elbow macaroni
1 tablespoon olive oil
4 slices stale white bread

FOR THE CHEESE SAUCE
6 tablespoons butter
6 tablespoons all-purpose flour
1 teaspoon Dijon mustard
2 3/4 cups organic milk

3/4 cup freshly grated strong Cheddar
3/4 cup freshly grated Monterey Jack
3/4 cup freshly grated vegetarian Parmesan
salt and freshly ground black pepper

Preheat the oven to 350°F.

First make the cheese sauce. In a heavy-bottomed saucepan, melt the butter then stir in the flour and cook for 2 minutes. Beat in the mustard, then stir in the milk, whisking as the mixture thickens. Add the three cheeses. Season with salt and freshly ground black pepper, and mix well.

Bring a large pan of cold water to a boil, add plenty of salt, and cook the pasta for about 10 minutes until al dente, then drain. Spread the pasta out in a shallow baking dish and pour over the cheese sauce.

To make the breadcrumbs pulse the bread in a food processor for 10 seconds or grate by hand.

Sprinkle the breadcrumbs over the macaroni and bake in the oven for 30–40 minutes or until the top is golden. Serve with a mixed salad.

SNACK
LABAN BIL BAYD

Mince **3 garlic cloves** with **2 teaspoons dried mint** and some **sea salt**. In a small pan, melt **4 tablespoons unsalted butter**, then add the garlic and, stirring often, cook over gentle heat for a couple of minutes. Beat together **2 cups Greek yogurt** and **1 organic egg**, then distribute the yogurt into 6 ramekin dishes. Crack **6 organic eggs** into the ramekins and top with the garlic mixture and a seasoning of **freshly ground black pepper**. Bake in a preheated oven at 425°F, for about 7 minutes until the egg whites are just cooked. Serves 6

DINNER
ASPARAGUS TART

ANNIE BELL

SERVES 4

Locally grown asparagus is one of the great treats of Spring. It's only in season for a couple of months, but when it comes, it comes thick and fast. Great on its own with melted butter, it adds a real touch of class to this simple but yummy tart.

1 pound finger-thin asparagus spears
8 ounces puff pastry
2/3 cup crème fraîche
1/2 teaspoon Dijon mustard
2 tablespoons freshly grated vegetarian
    Parmesan
2 medium organic egg yolks
sea salt and freshly ground black pepper

Preheat the oven to 400°F. Bring a large pan of salted water to a boil. Cut the asparagus spears where they begin to become woody. Add to the pan, bring back to a boil and cook for 4 minutes. Drain and refresh in cold water. Remove and dry on a clean towel.

Roll the pastry thinly into a rectangle 16 x 8 inches and trim to neaten the edges—if you don't have a baking sheet large enough, adjust the dimensions accordingly. Lay the pastry on the baking sheet. Blend the crème fraîche, mustard, Parmesan, 1 beaten egg yolk, and seasoning together in a bowl. Spoon this cream over the pastry, leaving 1 inch of pastry clean around the borders. Place the asparagus on top in a single layer. Beat the remaining egg yolk and paint the pastry borders. Bake the tart for 30 minutes.

Serve 5 minutes out of the oven, although it is excellent cold.

DESSERT
LEMON AND PISTACHIO BISCOTTI

Preheat the oven to 350°F. In a mixing bowl, place **2 1/4 cups all-purpose flour**, **1 teaspoon baking powder**, **3/4 cup superfine sugar**, **a pinch of salt**, **2 organic eggs**, grated zest of **3 lemons**, **1 tablespoon lemon juice**, **2/3 cup blanched almonds, toasted and chopped**, and **2/3 cup chopped pistachios**. Mix to form a firm dough. Roll into a ball, cut in half, and roll each portion into a sausage shape before placing on a lightly floured baking sheet. Place in the preheated oven for 10 minutes until golden. Remove from the oven, cool for 10 minutes, then use a serrated knife to cut into diagonal slices 1/2 inch thick. Arrange the slices on the baking sheet and return to the oven for an additional 15 minutes until slightly golden. Transfer to a wire rack to cool and crisp up. Makes 16

WEEK 09

BREAKFAST

CREPES WITH LEMON AND SUGAR

Sift **1 cup all-purpose flour** and **a pinch of salt** into a bowl. Add **1 organic egg** and gradually beat in **1/2 cup organic milk**. Add another **1/2 cup milk** and beat until smooth. Lightly oil a frying pan and place over medium heat. Pour in just enough batter to cover the base of the pan. Cook until the underside is golden, then turn and cook the other side. Repeat with the remaining batter. To serve sprinkle with **lemon juice**, roll up, and top with a sprinkling of **sugar**. Makes 8–10

PACKED LUNCH

VEGETABLE PILAU

In a large saucepan, soften **1 finely chopped medium onion** and **1 minced garlic clove** in **1 tablespoon corn oil**, then add **2 teaspoons ground cardamom**, **1 teaspoon ground turmeric**, and **1 teaspoon ground cinnamon**, and fry for 1 minute. Break up **1 cup cauliflower florets** into tiny pieces, and add to the pan with **2/3 cup frozen peas** and **1/3 cup raisins**. Stir for half a minute, then add **3/4 cup rinsed basmati rice** and **1 1/4 cups water**. Bring to a boil, stirring occasionally. Cover with a tight-fitting lid and simmer for 15 minutes. Stir occasionally, adding a little more warm water during cooking if necessary. Serves 4

LUNCH

CREAMY BROCCOLI SOUP

LAURA AND WOODY HARRELSON

SERVES 8

It'd be hard not to love any recipe devised by Woody Harrelson, star of Cheers and numerous Hollywood movies. This soup comes highly recommended. It's creamy but it doesn't have any cream in it and it's incredibly easy to make.

1 1/2 *pounds red potatoes, diced into cubes*
2 *pounds broccoli, chopped into small florets*
2–3 *leeks, trimmed and roughly chopped*
1 *garlic clove*
8 *cups water*
4 *tablespoons olive oil*
3 *vegetable stock cubes*
2 *teaspoons Himalayan salt (or table salt*
   if you can't find this)
freshly ground black pepper, to taste

Prepare the vegetables and steam the potatoes and broccoli until tender (approximately 15–20 minutes). Cook the leeks in a small amount of water until tender. Place half the vegetable mixture, 4 cups of the water, and the rest of the ingredients (except the olive oil) in a high-powered blender. Build power up to the highest level. At that point, slowly pour 2 tablespoons of the olive oil into the mixture. Blend until smooth. Pour the mixture into a large pot and start warming it over low heat. Blend the remaining vegetable mixture and water and repeat the slow addition of the oil while blending at the highest speed. Add to the pot, and stir every few minutes while warming the soup to the desired temperature. Serve hot.

SIDE
GARLIC BREAD

Preheat the oven to 350°F. Make diagonal cuts along **1 long French bread** at about 1-inch intervals—cut deeply into the bread but don't slice all the way through. Soften **6 tablespoons butter** in a small pan and stir in **2 minced garlic cloves** and **1 teaspoon freshly chopped parsley**. Brush the garlic butter on each side of each cut in the bread until it is all used up. Wrap the whole French bread in aluminum foil and heat it through for 10 minutes. Unwrap and serve immediately. Serves 3–4

DINNER
LINGUINE WITH ALMONDS AND CACIOCAVALLO

MARIO BATALI

SERVES 8

Mozzarella and Parmesan are rightly famous but it's sometimes good to cook with one of Italy's other excellent cheeses. Caciocavallo is a speciality of the south, made by repeatedly stretching and pulling raw cow's milk curd. It comes in a distinctive gourd shape and is hung up to dry by a string tied around the neck. The almonds and red pepper flakes are also typical of southern Italy and give this recipe its nuttiness and bite.

⅓ cup extra virgin olive oil
6 garlic cloves, thinly sliced
1 tablespoon dried red red pepper flakes
1 cup sliced blanched almonds, chopped
salt
2 pounds linguine fini
3 tablespoons finely chopped fresh parsley
1 cup (4 ounces) freshly grated Caciocavallo

Bring 8 quarts of water to a boil in a large pasta pot. While the water is heating, heat the oil in a large sauté pan over medium heat. Add the garlic and cook until it is light brown. Add the dried chile and the almonds, and cook until the almonds are light golden brown, 2–3 minutes. Remove from the heat.

Add 2 tablespoons salt to a boiling water. Drop the linguine into the water and cook for 1 minute less than the package instructions indicate. Just before the pasta is done, carefully ladle ¼ cup of the cooking water into the pan containing the almonds.

Drain the pasta, and add it to the almond sauce. Add the parsley and toss over medium heat for about 30 seconds, until the pasta is nicely coated. Then remove from the heat, add half the cheese, and toss like a salad for 15 seconds. Pour into a warm serving bowl and serve immediately with the remaining cheese on the side.

DESSERT
CASSATA

Put **2½ cups vanilla ice cream** in a mixing bowl. Allow to soften slightly. Crumble **3 ounces amaretti biscuits** into the ice cream and add **½ cup mixed dried fruit** and **¼ cup toasted slivered almonds**. Gently mix to incorporate all the ingredients. Transfer to a small freezerproof bowl or ice cream container and place in the coldest part of the freezer for 1 hour. Melt **2 ounces semisweet chocolate** in a heatproof bowl over a pan of gently simmering water. Remove from the heat. When ready to serve, scoop the ice cream onto chilled serving plates and drizzle with the melted chocolate. Serve immediately. Serves 4

WEEK 10

BREAKFAST

FRUIT AND NUT BREAKFAST BARS

Preheat the oven to 350°F. Grease and line with parchment paper a baking dish measuring 8 x 12 inches. Melt **4 tablespoons butter** and **1 cup honey** in a saucepan. Add **2¼ cups rolled oats**, **⅓ cup sunflower seeds**, **⅓ cup pumpkin seeds**, **½ cup chopped almonds**, **½ cup chopped hazelnuts**, and **½ cup chopped dates** and **½ cup dried apricots**, and mix together really well. Spoon into the prepared baking dish and bake for 20 minutes or until golden brown. Remove from the oven and cool completely before lifting it from the dish. Cut into rectangles or squares. The bars will keep for a week in an airtight container. Makes 16 bars

PACKED LUNCH

PASTA WITH FRESH SPRING HERBS

Cook **12 ounces spaghetti or macaroni** until tender, rinse under cold water and drain. Mix **3 tablespoons freshly chopped parsley**, **3 tablespoons freshly chopped basil**, **1 tablespoon freshly chopped oregano**, **1 minced garlic clove**, **⅓ cup olive oil**, and **1 cup (8 ounces) cottage cheese** in a blender. Puree to make a sauce. Add the sauce to the cooked pasta and gently heat, while stirring. Serves 4

LUNCH

CRUNCHY CAULIFLOWER AND MACARONI

SERVES 4

Nothing beats a good cauliflower and cheese, except possibly a good macaroni and cheese. This dish combines the best of both. It's also a cinch to make.

1 cauliflower, chopped into small florets
4 ounces macaroni
4 tablespoons butter
4 ounces mushrooms, sliced
¼ cup all-purpose flour
1 cup organic milk, heated just to boiling point
salt and freshly ground black pepper
½ cup mild Cheddar, grated
2 tablespoons dry breadcrumbs

Cook the cauliflower florets in boiling water for 5–10 minutes until just tender. Drain. While the cauliflower is cooking, cook the macaroni according to the package instructions. Drain.

Melt the butter in a large saucepan and cook the mushrooms until they are soft. Stir in the flour until you have a glossy paste. Cook for 1 minute. Pour in the hot milk, a little at a time, and whisk vigorously until the milk has been incorporated. Keep adding the milk, continuing to whisk, until it has all been added and you have a smooth, glossy, creamy, mushroom sauce.

Stir in the cauliflower, macaroni, and salt and pepper to taste. Preheat the broiler to hot. Spoon the mixture into a shallow, ovenproof dish.

Sprinkle with the cheese and breadcrumbs and brown lightly under the broiler. Carefully remove the dish using oven mitts and serve at once.

SIDE
GREEN BEANS WITH FENUGREEK BUTTER

Cook **8 ounces thin green beans** in boiling salted water for 5–10 minutes until tender but still crunchy. Drain and set aside. Melt **2 tablespoons butter** in the saucepan and stir in the **juice of 1 lime**, **1/3 cup finely chopped fresh cilantro**, and **1 teaspoon ground fenugreek**. Pour in the beans and shake the pan to coat them in butter. Season to taste and serve immediately. Serves 2–4

DINNER
STIR-FRY WITH SPRING VEGETABLES AND NOODLES

SERVES 4

Stir-fries always seem to go down well and they are quick and easy to make. The broccoli and bok choy in this one provide freshness and bite, while the fava beans add a note of pungency. Feel free to incorporate other spring vegetables if you like.

8 ounces noodles of your choice
1 tablespoon vegetable oil
8 ounces broccoli, cut into small florets
4 garlic cloves, finely chopped
1/2 inch piece fresh ginger, finely chopped
1 red chile, seeded and finely sliced
1 bunch scallions, sliced

5 ounces fava beans or edamame (1 pound, 4 ounces unshelled weight), cooked and peeled of outer skins if large
2 heads bok choy, cut into eighths
1 1/2 tablespoons hoisin sauce
1 tablespoon soy sauce (add extra to suit your own taste)

Bring a large saucepan of water to a boil and cook the noodles according to the package instructions, or until just tender. Drain well and rinse with cold water.

Heat the oil in a nonstick wok. Add the broccoli, then stir-fry over high heat for 5 minutes or until just tender, adding a little water if it begins to stick. Add the garlic, ginger, and chile, stir-fry for an additional minute, then toss through the scallions, fava beans or edamame, and bok choy. Stir-fry for 2–3 minutes. Add the hoisin and soy sauces and warm through. Toss the noodles in with the vegetables and serve.

DESSERT
LEMON AND LIME TART

Prepare the pastry by adding **1 3/4 cups all-purpose flour**, **8 tablespoons diced butter**, **1/2 cup confectioner's sugar**, and a pinch of **salt** into the bowl of a food processor. Use the pulse button to rub the butter into the flour until the mixture resembles fine breadcrumbs. Mix **2 large organic egg yolks** with **1 tablespoon cold water**, add to the flour mixture, and pulse again until a dough starts to form. Lightly shape the dough into a smooth ball, flatten into a disk, cover with plastic wrap, and chill for an hour until firm. Lightly dust a work surface with flour, roll out the dough into a disk, and use to line a 9-inch springform tart pan. Prick the base with a fork and chill the pastry again for 20 minutes. Preheat the oven to 375°F and place a solid baking sheet on the middle shelf of the oven. Line the pastry shell with parchment paper and fill with baking beans or rice. Cook on the hot baking sheet for 15–20 minutes until pale golden. Remove from the oven and cool slightly while you prepare the filling. Turn the oven down to 300°F. Finely grate the zest from **1 lemon** and **1 lime** into a bowl and squeeze the juice from **2 lemons** and **3 limes**. Set aside. Whisk **6 large organic eggs** and **1 heaping cup superfine sugar** together in a large bowl, add **1/2 cup heavy cream**, mix to combine, and add the lemon and lime juice. Strain into a large measuring jug, add the grated zests, and stir to combine. Pour the mixture into the baked pastry case and carefully slide the baking sheet back into the oven. Bake for 30–40 minutes until the center is only just set. Remove from the oven and leave to cool to room temperature. Dust the top with **confectioner's sugar** and, if desired, caramelize to a light amber color using a blow torch. Serve at room temperature. Makes 10–12 slices

WEEK 11

BREAKFAST

BREAKFAST BRIOCHE

Cut **4 slices of brioche**, spread with **3 tablespoons apricot jam** and sandwich together. Whisk together **2 organic eggs**, **2 tablespoons sugar**, and **5 tablespoons organic milk**. Melt **1 tablespoon butter** in a frying pan. Dip the brioche sandwiches in the egg mixture and fry for 2 minutes on each side until golden brown. Serves 2

PACKED LUNCH

MELON, LIME, AND MINT SOUP

STEFAN GATES

Cut **3 chilled ripe melons** in half, scoop out the seeds and discard. Scoop the flesh out of the melons and put in a food processor with **3/4 cup orange juice**, the **juice of 1 lime**, **a pinch of salt**, **1 teaspoon sugar**, and **a few fresh mint leaves**. Pulse until smooth—if the mixture is too stiff, add a little more orange juice. If you kept the melons in the fridge, you can serve the soup right away. If not, refrigerate for about 30 minutes. Scatter the **zest of 1 lime** and **some fresh mint leaves** on top just before serving. Serves 6

LUNCH

PAD THAI NOODLES

SERVES 2

This is the classic dish of Thailand, sometimes served as accompaniment to other food but more than good enough to eat on its own. It is a riot of textures and flavors, from the crunch of the peanuts to the tartness of the tamarind and the smoothness of the noodles.

4 ounces medium rice noodles
1 teaspoon tamarind paste
1½ tablespoons vegetarian oyster sauce
1 teaspoon sugar
1 garlic clove, finely chopped
2 scallions, cut into thin slices about ½ inch

1 red chile, seeded and finely chopped
1 organic egg
a handful of bean sprouts
a handful of peanuts, chopped
a handful of cilantro leaves
wedges of lime

Tip the noodles into a large bowl and cover with boiling water. Leave to stand for 5–10 minutes until the noodles are soft, then drain well. (You can do this part ahead of time—then just run the noodles under cold water until cool, and toss through a little oil to stop them from sticking.)

Next, mix together the tamarind paste, vegetarian oyster sauce, and sugar in a small bowl.

Heat a wok or large frying pan over high heat. Add the garlic, scallions, and chile. Toss the ingredients around the wok so they are constantly moving. Cook for 30 seconds, until they begin to soften. Push the vegetables to the sides of the wok, then crack the egg into the center. Keep stirring the egg for 30 seconds until it begins to set and resembles a broken-up omelette. Add the bean sprouts, followed by the noodles, then pour over the sauce mixture. Toss everything together and heat through. Spoon out onto plates. Serve with the chopped peanuts and cilantro leaves sprinkled over the top and wedges of lime on the side.

SIDE

CANNELLINI BEAN AND ASPARAGUS GRATIN

Preheat the oven to 350°F. Sauté **1/2 chopped onion** and **2 minced garlic cloves** in olive oil until tender. Add **1 bunch asparagus cut into 1-inch pieces** and season with **salt** and **freshly ground black pepper**. Stir in around **a cup of cooked cannellini beans** and set aside. Sauté the other **1/2 chopped onion** in **1 tablespoon butter**, then add **3/4 cup breadcrumbs**. Place the bean and asparagus mixture in a buttered baking dish, dot a few tablespoons of **ricotta** over the mixture, and top with the breadcrumb mixture. Bake for 15 minutes, or until the breadcrumb topping is golden brown and crusty. Serves 4

DINNER

SPINACH, RICOTTA, AND PARMESAN GNOCCHI WITH TOMATO SAUCE

Here's another mouthwatering variation on the gnocchi theme (see Spring, Week 1, Lunch). This time, the base vegetable is spinach, which gives these mini-dumplings their pleasing green color. The tomato sauce recipe is a classic—you may find it comes in useful in other contexts.

FOR THE GNOCCHI
1 pound fresh spinach, discard any tough stalks
2 tablespoons butter
1 onion, finely chopped
freshly grated nutmeg
2/3 cup ricotta
1 cup freshly grated vegetarian Parmesan
1/3 cup all-purpose flour, plus extra for dusting
2 large organic egg yolks
salt and freshly ground black pepper

FOR THE TOMATO SAUCE
1 tablespoon olive oil
1 fat clove of garlic, minced
14-ounce can tomatoes
1 teaspoon superfine sugar
1 tablespoon freshly chopped basil leaves
salt and freshly ground black pepper

TO SERVE
freshly grated vegetarian Parmesan
extra virgin olive oil

SERVES 4

Cook the spinach in a large pan over medium heat until the leaves are wilted and tender. Drain and let cool, then squeeze the spinach between your hands to remove as much water as possible, and roughly chop.

Melt the butter in a sauté pan, add a quarter of the chopped onion, and cook over a medium heat until tender but not colored. Add the chopped spinach and cook for an additional 2 minutes. Tip into a bowl, season with freshly grated nutmeg, salt and black pepper, and let cool. Add the ricotta, Parmesan, all-purpose flour, and egg yolks to the mixture and mix until smooth. Cover and chill the mixture for a couple of hours to firm up.

Meanwhile prepare the tomato sauce. Heat the olive oil in a saucepan over a medium heat, add the remaining onion, and cook until soft but not colored. Add the minced garlic and cook for an additional minute. Add the canned tomatoes and sugar, and season well with salt and freshly ground black pepper. Bring to a boil and simmer over medium heat for about 7 minutes until slightly thickened. Add the chopped basil.

Lightly dust the work surface with a little flour, and roll the spinach mixture into a log about an inch in diameter. Cut the log into inch-long pillows, or gnocchi, and place on a baking sheet that has been lightly dusted with flour. Bring a large pan of salted water to a boil. Add the gnocchi and cook for about 3 minutes until tender and the gnocchi float to the surface of the water. Drain the gnocchi and serve in bowls with the tomato sauce, scattered with grated Parmesan and drizzled with extra virgin olive oil.

DESSERT

GOOSEBERRY FOOL

Put **10 ounces topped and tailed gooseberries** in a pan with **2 tablespoons superfine sugar** and **2 tablespoons water**. Gently stew until the gooseberries are soft and pulpy. Set aside and let cool. Once cooled, add half the gooseberry mixture to **1 cup Greek yogurt** and mix together. Take 6 glasses and fill with the gooseberry yogurt mixture and top with the remaining stewed gooseberries. Decorate with **whole poached gooseberries**, if you wish. Serves 6

WEEK 12

BREAKFAST

FRIED BANANAS WITH PECANS AND MAPLE SYRUP

Halve **2 bananas** lengthwise and sprinkle with the juice of **¹/₂ lemon**. Melt **2 tablespoons butter** in a frying pan, add the bananas, cook until browned on both sides, then transfer to warm plates. Add **¹/₄ cup chopped pecans** to the pan and cook until lightly toasted. Stir in **2 tablespoons maple syrup** and heat through. Pour over the bananas and serve at once on their own or with yogurt. Serves 2

PACKED LUNCH

TANGY CAULIFLOWER RELISH AND CHEESE SANDWICH

This relish is incredibly quick and easy to make and is an unusual and tasty way to eat an often maligned vegetable. Heat **2 tablespoons sunflower oil** in a large frying pan set over medium heat. Add **1 teaspoon yellow mustard seeds** and fry until they begin to pop. Add **1 pound small cauliflower florets** and cook for 3–4 minutes, stirring occasionally. Add **¹/₂ teaspoon red pepper flakes** and **¹/₂ teaspoon ground turmeric**, and cook for an additional 2–3 minutes or until the cauliflower is tender and can be easily pierced with a fork. Remove the pan from the heat and stir in **¹/₂ teaspoon toasted fenugreek seeds**, **1 teaspoon sea salt**, and **1 tablespoon lemon juice**. Spoon into sterilized jars and seal. To make your sandwich, take **2 slices of whole-wheat bread** and spread with butter. Layer **several Cheddar slices** over one of the slice of bread, spread with 1 tablespoon of the relish, and top with the remaining slice of bread. Serves 1

LUNCH

FATOUSH SALAD WITH GRILLED HALLOUMI

This lunch hails from the eastern Mediterranean. Fatoush is made with the Lebanese/Syrian equivalent of croutons—small pieces of toasted pita bread—which soak up the juices of this hyper-fresh salad and provide its body. Squeaky grilled halloumi is the perfect accompaniment.

3 pita breads
4–5 tablespoons olive oil
2 round leaf lettuces, roughly shredded
1 medium size cucumber, peeled,
*   seeded, and diced*
6 scallions, trimmed and sliced
8 ounces baby plum or cherry tomatoes,
*   halved*

6 radishes, sliced
1 red pepper, seeded and roughly chopped
1 green pepper, seeded and roughly chopped
3 tablespoons freshly chopped flat-leaf parsley
2 tablespoons freshly chopped cilantro
juice of 1 lemon
1–2 teaspoons sumac
salt and freshly ground black pepper

SERVES 4

Preheat the broiler. Toast the pita breads on both sides until puffed up and starting to crisp. Split in half, brush with a little olive oil, and toast the insides until lightly golden. Break into bite-size pieces and cool.

Tip all of the prepared vegetables into a bowl and gently mix with the chopped herbs.

In a small bowl mix together the lemon juice and remaining olive oil, and season well with salt and freshly ground black pepper. Pour over the salad, sprinkle with the sumac, and mix to combine. Leave to one side for 30 minutes to let all of the flavors mingle, and then serve with hummus (see page 23) and pan-fried halloumi.

SIDE

BAKED ZUCCHINI, FETA, AND TOMATOES

Preheat the oven to 400°F. Heat a grill pan. Take **4 zucchini** and cut each in half lengthwise. Brush with **olive oil** and cook them quickly for 2 minutes on the flesh side until lightly charred. Repeat the process with **3 halved tomatoe**s. Put the zucchini and tomatoes into a shallow ovenproof dish and season. Drizzle over **1 tablespoon balsamic vinegar**, a little **olive oil**, **4 ounces diced feta**, a few sprigs of **lemon thyme**, and **salt** and **freshly ground black pepper**. Cook in the oven for 20–30 minutes or until the zucchini are tender. Serve with some **fresh basil leaves**. Serves 4

DINNER

ASPARAGUS RISOTTO

SERVES 4

Morels are wild mushrooms with strange, pitted surfaces that make them look like little brains on stalks. They appear in the Spring and have a wonderful nutty flavor that infuses this delicate risotto. We wouldn't advise you to eat wild morels you've foraged unless you really know what you are doing, but fortunately they are readily available in dried form.

6 morels, fresh or dried
8 ounces thin asparagus, cut into 1-inch pieces
2 tablespoons unsalted butter
1¹/2 tablespoons olive oil
1 red onion, finely chopped
1¹/2 cups Arborio rice
3 cups vegetable stock, boiling

1 tablespoon fresh marjoram or oregano
(or 1 teaspoon dried)
2 tablespoons mascarpone
salt and freshly ground black pepper
freshly grated vegetarian Parmesan
(optional)

Soak fresh morels in salted water for 10 minutes and wash thoroughly. Pat dry and cut each into several pieces. If using dried morels, soak in hot water for 30 minutes before draining, drying, and cutting up. Blanch the asparagus in boiling water for 1 minute, drain, and set aside. Heat the butter and oil in a heavy-bottomed pan and sauté the onion and morels until soft. Stir in the rice and coat it well with the oil and butter. Pour in a cup of the stock and the marjoram and cook over low heat, stirring frequently, until the liquid is absorbed. Add more cupfuls of stock one at a time and continue cooking until the rice is just tender and the consistency is creamy. Stir in the asparagus and the mascarpone and season well. Serve with Parmesan, if you wish.

DESSERT

RASPBERRY AND ALMOND BARS

Preheat the oven to 350°F. Grease a rectangular cake pan (about 12 x 8 x 2 inches). Put **2 cups self-rising flour**, **2/3 cup ground almonds**, **14 tablespoons diced butter**, and **1¹/4 cups superfine sugar** into a food processor, and pulse until the butter is evenly distributed—or rub together by hand in a large mixing bowl. Add **2 medium organic eggs** and the **finely grated zest of 2 oranges** and pulse quickly in the food processor or mix with a wooden spoon. The mixture does not need to be very smooth. Spread the mixture on the base of the cake pan, then scatter **2 cups frozen raspberries** over the top. Bake in the oven for 45 minutes. Remove from the oven and scatter another **2 cups frozen raspberries** over the surface. Cook for an additional 15 minutes, until firm to the touch. Cool in the pan and cut into squares. They will keep for up to two days in the fridge. Makes 16–24 slices

WEEK 13

BREAKFAST

SCONES

Preheat the oven to 400°F. Grease a baking sheet with oil or butter. Sift **1 cup whole-wheat stoneground flour, 1 cup self-rising flour, 1 teaspoon baking powder,** and **a good pinch of salt** into a bowl, and tip in any bran caught in the sifter. Add **6 tablespoons of butter** (cut into small pieces) and rub it into the flour using your fingertips until the mixture looks like breadcrumbs. Mix in **about ¼ cup organic milk** to form a soft dough; don't make it too firm because the flour will continue to absorb moisture and firm up while you work. Place the dough onto a floured surface and knead it lightly. Roll out the dough to a thickness of around half-inch. Using a 2-inch cutter, cut out 12 scones, and place on the baking sheet. Bake for 15–20 minutes until golden and risen. Cool on a wire rack. Makes 12

PACKED LUNCH

BLUE CHEESE PATE

Hardboil **2 organic eggs** and separate the cooked egg yolks from the whites. Blend **2 cups vegetarian blue cheese of your choice** with the egg yolks and **4 tablespoons unsalted butter.** Chop the egg whites finely and stir them and **2 tablespoons lightly toasted pine nuts** into the mixture. Transfer to a small dish and chill thoroughly. Serve with **bread**. Serves 2

LUNCH

WATERCRESS SOUP WITH TOASTED ALMONDS

Watercress makes you feel alive. It is packed with freshness and iron and has more than enough flavor to carry a dish. Linda used to make a version of this soup, which is incredibly easy to make. Eating it will make you feel both virtuous and satisfied. The cream and garlic toasts add a touch of luxury, as do the sliced almonds, which are Stella's addition.

4 tablespoons unsalted butter
2 medium onions, chopped
1 garlic clove, minced
2 medium potatoes, peeled and diced
3 cups vegetable stock
3 bunches watercress, roughly chopped
½ cup heavy cream
salt and freshly ground black pepper
2–3 tablespoons crème fraîche, to serve
2 tablespoons toasted sliced almonds, to serve

FOR THE GARLIC TOASTS
6 thin slices of baguette, cut on the diagonal
2 tablespoons olive oil
*1 heaped tablespoon freshly grated
     vegetarian Parmesan*
1 fat garlic clove
1 tablespoon finely chopped parsley

SERVES 3

Heat the butter in a large saucepan and lightly cook the onions and garlic for 2–3 minutes until tender but not colored. Add the potatoes and sauté gently for an additional 3 minutes. Add the vegetable stock, cover, and simmer gently for 15 minutes or until the potatoes are tender.

Meanwhile, make the garlic toasts. Preheat the broiler and toast the baguette slices on one side. Mix the olive oil, Parmesan, garlic, and parsley together and spread over the untoasted side. Place back under the broiler until golden and toasted.

Add the watercress to the pan, cook for 2–3 minutes, then pour the mixture into a blender and blend until velvety smooth. Return to the pan, add the cream, season well, and reheat gently. Serve in bowls with a swirl of crème fraîche, the garlicky toasts, and a scattering of toasted sliced almonds.

SNACK

CHEESE AND ASPARAGUS CROQUETTES

Boil **1 pound of potatoes**, drain, mash, and place in a bowl. Steam **a few spears of asparagus** until just tender, cut into thin slices, and add to the potato. Beat in **2 organic egg yolks**, and season with **salt** and **freshly ground black pepper**. Cut **4 ounces mozzarella** into cubes. Take a large spoonful of the potato mixture and mold around a teaspoonful of the cheese to form a sausage shape. Repeat until both mixtures have been used up. Lightly coat the croquettes in **all-purpose flour**, then dip them first in **1 lightly beaten organic egg** and then **1 cup toasted breadcrumbs**. Half-fill a deep saucepan with **vegetable oil**, heat to 325°F and deep-fry the croquettes in small batches for 2–3 minutes until golden and crisp. Remove and drain on paper towels. Serves 4

DINNER

SICILIAN CAULIFLOWER PASTA

Sicily was ruled by Arabs in the tenth and eleventh centuries, and their culinary legacy lives on in the use of ingredients like saffron, raisins, and pine nuts in the island's cooking. Here all three are combined with the humble cauliflower to create a memorable pasta dish.

a pinch of saffron threads
1 small-medium cauliflower, chopped into small florets
3 tablespoons olive oil
1 onion, finely chopped
2 fat garlic cloves, minced
a pinch of red pepper flakes
1/3 cup raisins
1/2 cup pine nuts

2 tablespoons sun-dried tomato paste
1 bay leaf
14 ounces whole-wheat mafalda corta pasta
1 tablespoon lemon juice
2 heaping tablespoons freshly chopped flat-leaf parsley
freshly grated vegetarian Parmesan to serve
salt and freshly ground black pepper

SERVES 4

Soak the saffron threads in 2 tablespoons boiling water and set aside.

Cook the cauliflower florets in a large pan of boiling salted water for about 4 minutes until tender. Scoop the cauliflower out of the pan, drain, and set aside, and reserve the water.

Heat the olive oil in a large sauté pan, add the onion, and cook over medium heat until tender but not colored. Add the garlic and chile and cook for an additional minute. Add the raisins and pine nuts to the pan and continue to cook until the pine nuts are toasted and lightly golden.

Add the cauliflower, steeped saffron, sun-dried tomato paste, and bay leaf to the pan along with 1/2 cup of the cauliflower cooking water. Season and cook over low to medium heat for about 5 minutes, lightly mashing the cauliflower with the back of a wooden spoon to make a sauce and adding more water if necessary if it starts to look dry.

Meanwhile cook the mafalda corta in the cauliflower water according to the package instructions. Drain, reserving 1 cup of the water, and put the pasta into the sauté pan with the cauliflower sauce. Add the lemon juice and chopped parsley and stir to combine. Add some of the reserved water if needed. Serve with lots of freshly grated Parmesan.

DESSERT

PEANUT BUTTER AND BANANA CUPCAKES

Preheat the oven to 350°F. Line a 12-hole muffin pan with paper cases. In a large bowl, cream together **4 tablespoons unsalted butter, 1 cup smooth peanut butter**, and **1/2 packed cup soft brown sugar** for 3–5 minutes until pale and fluffy. Beat in **2 organic eggs** one at a time, whisking between each addition. Fold in **1 1/4 cups sifted all-purpose flour** and **1 tablespoon baking powder** until you have a thick batter. Stir in **1/3 cup sour cream**, then gently fold in **2 mashed ripe bananas**. Spoon the mixture into the muffin cases until two-thirds full. Bake for 20–25 minutes until risen and the top bounces back when touched. Remove from the oven and let cool on a wire rack. For the icing, place **1/3 cup cream cheese** and **1/3 cup smooth peanut butter** in a large mixing bowl, and using a handheld electric mixer, whisk until light and fluffy. Slowly add **2 cups confectioner's sugar** one tablespoon at a time, whisking between each addition. The icing will be stiff to begin with, but don't be tempted to loosen it with any liquid—just continue whisking and it will soften. Spoon the icing into a piping bag fitted with a star nozzle. Pipe swirls of frosting over the cupcakes, and sprinkle with **chopped peanuts** to decorate. Makes 12

MSUM

R

E

WEEK 01

BREAKFAST

FRUIT, SEED, AND NUT MUESLI

Mix together **1 pound oat flakes**, **8 ounces barley flakes**, and **¼ cup each of yellow raisins**, **raisins**, **chopped dried apricots**, **sunflower seeds**, **chopped pecans**, and **chopped brazil nuts**. To serve, add **organic milk** and drizzle with **honey**, or moisten with a splash of milk and stir in some **plain yogurt**. Keep in a sealed container. Makes 12 servings

---

PACKED LUNCH

MEXICAN BEAN SALAD

Warm **½ cup cooked black-eyed beans** in a pan and mix them with **3 tablespoons olive oil** and **1 tablespoon red wine vinegar**. Allow to cool then stir through **half a diced red pepper**, **1 diced plum tomato**, **1 minced garlic clove**, **½ finely sliced red onion**, and **2 tablespoons freshly chopped flat-leaf parsley**. Season to taste with **salt** and **freshly ground black pepper**. Serves 2

LUNCH

ZUCCHINI, POTATO, AND DILL FRITATTA

A frittata is an Italian-style omelet, thicker than the standard kind. As with its famous Spanish cousin, it isn't folded but is cooked in two stages: first bottom up on the stove, then top down under the broiler. The second process creates a delectable savory crust, as in the recipe below.

6 medium new potatoes, scrubbed
2 tablespoons olive oil
1 large zucchini, cut into ½-inch slices
1 garlic clove, minced
6 large organic eggs

1 rounded tablespoon freshly chopped dill
2 tablespoons freshly grated vegetarian Parmesan
salt and freshly ground pepper
1 teaspoon butter

SERVES 4

Cook the potatoes in boiling salted water for 20 minutes or until tender. Drain, allow to cool, and then cut into slices.

Heat 1 tablespoon of the olive oil in a large frying pan and cook the zucchini slices over high heat until golden on both sides. Remove from the pan and cool. Add the remaining oil to the pan as well as the sliced potatoes, and sauté until golden, then add the garlic and cook for an additional 30 seconds. Remove from the pan and cool.

Whisk the eggs together with the chopped dill and half of the Parmesan, and season with salt and freshly ground black pepper.

Preheat the broiler. Melt the butter in a large 8-inch frying pan and add the sautéed veggies in an even layer. Pour the cheesy egg mixture around the vegetables, scatter with the remaining Parmesan, and cook over low to medium heat for 3–4 minutes until the egg starts to set. Slide the pan under the broiler and continue to cook until the top is set, golden, and bubbling. Cool briefly and then cut into wedges to serve.

SNACK

SPINACH FILOS

Preheat the oven to 350°F and grease a baking sheet. Wash **1 pound spinach leaves**, discard the stems, and cook the leaves in their own juice in a pan with the lid on until they wilt, then drain well and roughly chop. Mix with **1/3 cup mashed feta** (or cottage cheese), **a good pinch of nutmeg**, and **1 organic egg**, and season with **salt** and **freshly ground black pepper**. If using feta, you may not need to add salt. Cut **4 ounces filo pastry sheets** into rectangular strips about 3 inches wide. Put the strips in a pile and cover with plastic wrap to prevent them from drying out. Brush a strip of filo with **melted butter**, put 1 heaping teaspoon of filling at one end about 1 inch from the edge, and fold one corner up over it. Then fold again and again until the whole strip is folded into a small triangle (ensure you close any holes, as liquid from the filling can ooze out). Place close to each other on the baking sheet and brush lightly with melted butter. Bake the filo parcels for 30 minutes or until crisp and golden. Serve hot. Makes about 15

DINNER

EGGPLANT PARMIGIANA

SERVES 4

With its tender eggplant and gooey mozzarella, this is deservedly a classic. Cooking with eggplant can seem daunting—they seem to absorb an impossible amount of olive oil if you fry them, for instance—but the Italians have it down to a tee. The secret is to make sure you cook them all the way through.

5 tablespoons olive oil
2 garlic cloves, thinly sliced
2 x 14 ounce canned tomatoes
1 small bunch basil leaves, torn
salt and freshly ground black pepper
1 teaspoon superfine sugar

1 cinnamon stick
3 medium eggplants, cut lengthwise into 1/4-inch slices
2 balls mozzarella, sliced
freshly grated vegetarian Parmesan

Preheat the oven to 350°F. Heat 2 tablespoons olive oil in a pan, add the garlic, and cook gently for 2 minutes. Add the tomatoes and cinnamon stick, and simmer for 15 minutes until thickened. Stir in the basil, and season with salt and freshly ground black pepper and the sugar.

Preheat a ridged grill pan. Brush both sides of the eggplant slices with the remaining oil, season, and grill, turning a few times until completely tender (you could also do this in a nonstick frying pan). It's important to get the eggplant as tender as possible.

Put a few spoonfuls of the tomato and basil sauce in the bottom of a 8 x 10 inch ovenproof dish, cover with the eggplant and mozzarella, then repeat, ending with a thin layer of sauce (you'll have roughly 3-4 layers). Sprinkle with Parmesan, and bake for 30-40 minutes until bubbling and golden.

DESSERT

STRAWBERRIES WITH MASCARPONE AND CREAM

PINK

Hull **8 ounces of strawberries**. Mix together **1 tablespoon mascarpone**, **1/2 cup heavy cream**, **1/4 teaspoon vanilla extract**, and **sugar to taste**. Scoop some over the strawberries and throw **a couple of blueberries** on top. Serves 2

WEEK 02

BREAKFAST

NECTARINE SMOOTHIE

Roughly chop **1 banana** and place in a blender. Add **1 cup nectarine flesh**, **1/2 cup rolled oats**, **1/3 cup Greek yogurt**, **1/2 cup organic whole milk**, **6 ice cubes** and **honey** to taste. Blend until smooth. Any ripe fruit, such as strawberries, raspberries, peaches, or blueberries can be substituted for the nectarines, if you prefer. Serves 2

LUNCH

FRESH TOMATO AND BASIL SOUP

Heat **1 tablespoon olive oil** in a saucepan, add **1 large diced onion** and cook for 8–10 minutes until softened. Halve **3/4 pound ripe tomatoes** and add to the pan with the onion, and cook for another 5 minutes, breaking down with a spoon. Take another **3/4 pound tomatoes**, pierce each one, and place in a bowl of boiling water for 20 seconds to remove the skins. Cut into chunks, removing the seeds, and set to one side. Place the onion mixture in a blender with **1/2 cup vegetable stock** and blend until smooth. Pass through a sieve to remove the skin and seeds and return to the pan with **4 cups of tomato juice**, **salt** and **freshly ground black pepper**, **a few shredded basil leaves,** and the diced tomatoes. Heat through and serve sprinkled with **shredded basil leaves** and a swirl of **cream**, if desired. Serves 4

PACKED LUNCH

FAVA BEAN SALAD WITH CHEESE CHIPS

GIORGIO LOCATELLI

SERVES 4

This salad proves the rule that the simplest recipes are often the best. Aside from the vinaigrette, it only has four ingredients, but they complement each other so well that the whole is greater than the sum of the parts. Peeling the leathery skin of the broad beans may seem like hard work but releasing the delicate green nuggets within is worth the effort.

4 big handfuls of fava beans (or edamame)
3 tablespoons olive oil
1 tablespoon white wine vinegar
salt and freshly ground black pepper
1 cup pecorino, finely grated
4 handfuls of mixed salad leaves

FOR THE CHIPS
1/2 cup flour
1/2 cup vegetarian Parmesan, finely grated
1 cup pecorino, finely grated

Bring a large pan of salted water to a boil, put in the fava beans, and blanch them for 2–3 minutes, then drain and refresh in iced water. Peel off the outer skins of the beans if needed. If the beans differ strongly in size, cook them separately according to size.

To make the chips, mix the flour with the Parmesan and the pecorino. Heat a couple of small nonstick pans and sprinkle a thin layer of the mixture all over the pan. Let it cook until it starts to turn golden. Turn the chips over and let them color on the other side. Keep separate.

Whisk together the olive oil and white wine vinegar. Season the beans with salt and freshly ground black pepper, pour over the vinaigrette, and add the pecorino. Place the beans flat in the center of the plate. Dress the salad leaves and put on top of the beans. Serve with the pecorino chips.

SIDE
MEXICAN CORNBREAD

Preheat the oven to 350°F. Lightly grease an 8-inch round baking dish and dust with a little flour. Seed **1 green chile** and **1 red chile** and chop finely. Trim and slice **6 scallions**. Heat **a little olive oil** in a frying pan over medium heat, add the scallions and chiles, and cook for a couple of minutes until soft but not colored. Remove from the heat, tip into a bowl, and add **a 14-ounce can drained corn** and **2 tablespoons finely chopped cilantro**. Beat **2 large organic eggs** together with **1/2 cup of sour cream** and add to the corn mixture. Sift **a heaping cup polenta** and **2 1/2 teaspoons baking powder** into the bowl, add **1 1/2 cups grated Cheddar**, and season with **salt** and **freshly ground black pepper**. Pour into the prepared pan, spread level, and scatter with another **1/2 cup grated Cheddar**. Bake on the middle shelf of the preheated oven for 35–40 minutes or until golden and well risen, and a skewer inserted into the middle of the cornbread comes out clean. Serves 4–6

DINNER
QUESADILLAS WITH AVOCADO, SOUR CREAM, AND SALSA

SERVES 4

Quesadillas are the Mexican equivalent of grilled cheese sandwiches. They can be made with corn tortillas, which need to be softened before they are folded, but this recipe uses the soft flour kind, which are more pliable.

4 teaspoons olive oil
4 large flour tortillas
1 cup Cheddar, grated
1/2 cup chestnut mushrooms, thinly sliced
1 bunch scallions, thinly sliced
4 tomatoes, peeled and chopped
2 ripe avocados, peeled and sliced
1/2 cup sour cream

FOR THE SALSA
4 large tomatoes, seeded and roughly chopped
2 scallions, finely chopped
1 red chile, seeded and chopped
1 tablespoon white wine vinegar
3 tablespoons extra virgin olive oil
1 teaspoon sugar
1 tablespoon freshly chopped basil leaves

First make the salsa. Mix the tomatoes with the scallions, chile, white wine vinegar, extra virgin olive oil, sugar and basil. Chill until required.

Pour 1 teaspoon of the olive oil into a large heavy-bottomed frying pan set over medium-high heat, tipping the pan so the base becomes covered in oil. Take one of the tortillas and place in the pan. After 10 seconds, flip the tortilla over. Continue to flip the tortilla at 10-second intervals until air pockets begin to form within it.

Take a quarter of the cheese and sprinkle it over the tortilla, then add a quarter of the mushrooms, scallions, and tomatoes, taking care not to layer the ingredients too thickly.

Reduce the heat to medium-low and cover the pan with a lid. If the quesadilla begins to smoke, remove from the heat. After a minute, check to see if the cheese is melted. If not, replace the cover and check again after 15 seconds. When the cheese is melted, carefully lift up one side of the quesadilla and fold it over. Remove from the pan and keep warm. Repeat with the remaining tortillas. Serve with the avocado and sour cream.

DESSERT
MANGO LASSI

In a food processor, pulse **4 cups plain yogurt**, **2 peeled and diced mangoes**, **3 tablespoons pomegranate seeds**, and **1 tablespoon honey** until smooth. Pour into 4 glasses and serve immediately. Serves 4

WEEK 03

BREAKFAST

MELON AND STRAWBERRIES

Heat **1 cup water** and add **2 teaspoons sugar** and simmer for 10 minutes. Strain and leave the syrup to cool. Add the chopped leaves from a **small bunch of mint**. Prepare **2 honeydew melons** by dicing into small pieces, mix together with **6 ounces strawberries**, hulled and halved. Pour over the syrup mixture to coat the fruit. Serves 6

PACKED LUNCH

ASPARAGUS, EGG, AND CRESS SANDWICH

TRISTAN WELCH

Cook **20 asparagus spears** in boiling salted water for 3½ minutes. Cut **8 thin croûtons** into large rectangles and dice **2 soft-boiled organic eggs**. Take 2 croûtons and arrange pieces of the egg, asparagus, some **mayonnaise** and a bit of **watercress** in the croûtons. Season with salt and **freshly ground black pepper**. Serves 4

LUNCH

YELLOW SQUASH AND GARLIC BRUSCHETTA

SERVES 2

Bruschetta (see Spring, Week 4, Lunch) is a classic Italian appetizer, but it is also great as a light lunch. It is incredibly quick to prepare and very versatile—add or take away ingredients according to your preferences. A delicious way to eat summer squash when they are at their most plentiful.

2 yellow summer squash, cut into
  ¼-inch thick slices
3 tablespoons extra virgin olive oil
1 tablespoon balsamic vinegar
a pinch of sugar
4–6 slices stone-baked baguette
1 garlic clove
freshly grated vegetarian Parmesan, optional

Place the slices of summer squash in a bowl. Whisk together the extra virgin olive oil, balsamic vinegar, and sugar. Pour the dressing over the squash, season with salt and freshly ground pepper, stir, and set aside for 30 minutes.

Preheat a grill pan to hot, and grill the squash slices for 3–4 minutes each side until nicely charred. Set aside.

Preheat the broiler and toast the baguette slices until golden on both sides. Crush the garlic clove with a little salt to form a paste. While still hot, spread each slice with some of the garlic paste and drizzle with a little more olive oil. Top each slice with a spoonful of the squash, and, if you wish, grate over a little Parmesan.

SNACK
CASSAVA CHIPS

Slice **1 cassava** very thinly and leave to dry. Heat some **peanut or vegetable oil** (do not allow it to smoke) in a wok or a deep pan. Deep fry 1–3 slices at a time by immediately submerging each below the surface of the oil. Remove quickly from the heat and drain well on layers of paper towels. Season with **salt** and **freshly ground black pepper** and serve right away. Serves 2

DINNER
PAPAYA SALAD

SERVES 2

Papayas, or pawpaws as they are known in some parts of the world, are sweet, perfumed tropical fruits with deliciously soft flesh. This is an ideal dish for communal eating on a hot summer evening, with everyone tucking in using lettuce leaves as scoops.

2 garlic cloves, peeled
3–4 small fresh red or green chiles, chopped
2 yard-long beans or 20 French beans, chopped into 2-inch lengths
1¹/2 cups fresh papaya, peeled, seeded, and finely chopped
1 tomato, cut into wedges
1 tablespoon sugar
2 tablespoons lime juice

TO SERVE
Boston lettuce leaves

Pound the garlic in a large mortar, then add the chiles and pound again. Add the beans, breaking them up slightly, then tip into a bowl. Add the papaya to the bowl and lightly mash together, then stir in the tomato and lightly mash again.

Add the sugar and lime juice, stirring well, then transfer to a serving dish. Serve with lettuce leaves, which can be used as a scoop for the mixture.

DESSERT
PINEAPPLE FRITTERS

Peel, core, and thickly slice **1 large pineapple**. Coat the pineapple slices in **superfine sugar** and set aside for 30–40 minutes. Sift **2¹/2 cups self-rising flour** into a bowl, make a well in the center, and add **2 beaten organic eggs** and **1¹/2 cups cold club soda (or sparkling) water**. Stir until smooth and free from any lumps. Heat some oil to 350°F for deep-frying in a deep heavy-bottomed pan (or when a cube of bread sizzles and turns golden when dropped into it). Dip the pineapple slices into the batter, drain off the excess, and lower into the hot oil using a slotted spoon. Cook until golden and crisp. Carefully remove the fritters from the oil with a slotted spoon and drain on paper towels. Sprinkle with a little sugar and serve hot. Serves 4

WEEK 04

BREAKFAST
PEACH AND MELON SALAD

A deliciously refreshing salad that will keep a day or so in the refrigerator. Peel and slice **3 ripe peaches** and place in a bowl. Halve **1 small cantelope or honeydew melon** and scoop out the seeds. Cut the flesh into bite-size pieces and add to the bowl. Whisk together **2 tablespoons lemon juice, 2 tablespoons orange juice,** and **2 tablespoons superfine sugar.** Pour over the fruit and gently toss. Chill before serving. Serves 4

PACKED LUNCH
CARROT SOUP

ANTHONY DEMETRE

We don't appreciate cold soups enough. This one is deliciously refreshing, with the sharpness of the grapefruit contrasting nicely with the sweetness of the carrots. The olives and hazelnuts give it a definite Spanish feel.

4 tablespoons butter
1 pound carrots, peeled and sliced
1 garlic clove, peeled and minced
2¹/2 cups water
1 stem fresh thyme leaves, freshly chopped
1 stem rosemary leaves, freshly chopped
salt and freshly ground black pepper

¹/2 cup organic milk
2 pink grapefruits, peeled and segmented, segments halved
1 handful green olives, pits removed, halved
1 handful hazelnuts, crushed and toasted
1 container fresh baby cilantro or cress
2 tablespoons hazelnut oil

SERVES 4

Heat a large pan until hot, then add the butter, carrots, and garlic, and gently cook over medium heat for 2–3 minutes. Add the water, thyme, and rosemary, and season with salt and freshly ground black pepper. Bring to a simmer, then cover and cook for 5–6 minutes, or until the carrots are tender.

Remove the pan from the heat and stir in the milk. Allow to cool slightly, then transfer the mixture to a blender and blend until smooth. Place in the fridge to chill for at least 30 minutes.

To serve, divide the soup among four serving bowls. Arrange the grapefruit segments, olives, nuts, and cress on top of the soup, then drizzle with the hazelnut oil.

LUNCH
EGGPLANT WITH TOMATOES AND CREME FRAICHE

Preheat the oven to 350°F. Cut **3 pounds of eggplant** into slices ¹/2 inch wide. Lay on paper towels, sprinkle with salt, and let rest for 30 minutes. Pat them dry and heat **6–8 tablespoons olive oil** in a shallow frying pan and cook on both sides until nicely browned. Drain on paper towels. Melt **1 tablespoon unsalted butter** in a pan and add **1¹/2 pounds roughly chopped tomatoes, 2 seeded, roughly sliced red peppers,** and **4 roughly chopped garlic cloves.** Cook over low heat for 15 minutes to soften. Boil **1 cup good-quality crème fraîche,** stirring over high heat, and then reduce the heat to medium. Add some chopped fresh herbs—**lemon thyme, parsley,** and **tarragon** are particularly good. Throw in **2 tablespoons finely grated Parmesan.** Assemble in a shallow baking dish, starting with a layer of eggplant followed by one of the tomato/pepper sauce, and continue, finishing with a layer of tomato/pepper sauce. Then pour over the reduced crème fraîche/herb mixture and finally sprinkle with another **2 tablespoons grated Parmesan.** Bake for 25–30 minutes. Remove from the oven and let cool a little before serving. Good brown bread is a lovely accompaniment. Serves 4

SIDE

SUMMER COLESLAW

STELLA McCARTNEY

Peel and coarsely grate **2 medium-large carrots** into a large mixing bowl. Finely shred **1/2 small white cabbage** and **a handful of trimmed snow peas** and add to the bowl. Finely slice **6 scallions** and **a handful of trimmed radishes**, and add along with **1 tablespoon poppy seeds**, **2 tablespoons roughly chopped toasted hazelnuts**, and **2 tablespoons freshly chopped flat-leaf parsley**. In a separate small bowl, whisk together the **juice of 1/2 lemon** and **3 tablespoons hazelnut oil** and season well with **salt** and **freshly ground black pepper**. Pour over the coleslaw and gently mix together. Spoon the salad into a serving bowl and scatter with baby mustard sprouts and cress to serve. Serves 4

DINNER

REFRIED BEAN TACOS

PAUL McCARTNEY

SERVES 4

Refried beans are essential to a good taco. You don't have to fry them twice—the name comes about because of a mistranslation of the Spanish name frijoles refritos. The re bit doesn't mean again, it just means very. Half the fun of eating tacos is making them—filling the corn shells with garnishes to your taste.

1 medium onion, chopped
1 tablespoon olive oil
8-ounce can refried beans
2 medium tomatoes, chopped
salt
4 taco shells
1/2 cup Cheddar, grated
1 Boston lettuce, shredded
1–2 teaspoons hot chile sauce (optional)

TO SERVE
avocado, sliced
sour cream
a squeeze of lime and lemon juice

Gently cook the onion in the olive oil in a large frying pan for 4–5 minutes, stirring frequently until soft but not colored. Stir in the refried beans. Add the chopped tomato and cook until heated through. Season with salt.

Warm the taco shells according to the instructions on the package and half-fill with the refried bean mixture. Top with grated cheese and shredded lettuce, then garnish with sliced avocado, sour cream, and a squeeze of lime and lemon juice. If you like your tacos spicy (which I don't!) add 1–2 teaspoons hot sauce to the tomato mixture.

DESSERT

ZUCCHINI CUPCAKES

FEARNE COTTON

Preheat the oven to 350°F. Line a 12-hole muffin pan with paper cases. Coarsely grate **2 medium zucchini** into a bowl. If they seem watery, place in a clean cloth and wring out as much of the liquid as you can. Combine **2 large organic eggs**, **1/2 cup vegetable oil** and **1/2 cup superfine sugar** in a bowl. Sift in **2 cups self-rising flour** and **1/2 teaspoon baking soda** and beat until well combined. Stir in the zucchini and **1 cup chopped toasted walnuts**. Pour into the paper cases and bake for 30 minutes until risen, golden, and firm to the touch. Allow to cool. Make the frosting by beating together **1 cup cream cheese**, **2 cups confectioner's sugar**, and the **vanilla extract**. Spread the frosting on top of the cooled cupcakes and serve. Makes 12

WEEK 05

BREAKFAST

GRANOLA AND BERRIES

In summer, liven up your usual granola with a delicious combination of fresh and dried berries. Place **3 tablespoons granola** (storebought is fine, or see page 193) in a bowl. Add **1 tablespoon mixed dried cranberries and cherries**. Moisten with **2 tablespoons organic milk** and stir in **2 tablespoons plain yogurt**. Top with a handful of fresh berries of your choice—**strawberries, blueberries**, or **raspberries** all taste wonderful. Serves 1

PACKED LUNCH

CANNELLINI BEAN AND ROSEMARY HUMMUS

Put **14 ounces cannellini beans** into a food processor with the **juice of 1 lemon, 1 crushed garlic clove, 1/3 cup plain yogurt**, and **a handful of rosemary leaves** and pulse until smooth. Season with **salt** and **freshly ground black pepper** and serve with **sticks of carrot, celery, and cucumber** for dipping. Serves 2

LUNCH

MOZZARELLA AND TOMATO SALAD

This classic, Italian-inspired salad is the perfect al fresco lunch and showcases summer's sun-ripened tomato harvest. It can be put together in a matter of minutes.

1/2 pound buffalo mozzarella, thinly sliced
6 ripe tomatoes, finely chopped
1/3 cup black olives
3 tablespoons extra virgin olive oil
3 tablespoons white wine vinegar
1 teaspoon coarse-grain mustard
2 tablespoons freshly chopped oregano
*   or basil*
freshly ground black pepper

SERVES 4

Put the mozzarella and tomatoes on a serving dish with the olives. Make a dressing by combining the extra virgin olive oil, white wine vinegar, coarse-grain mustard, oregano or basil, and freshly ground black pepper. Shake the dressing well, pour over the salad, and serve immediately.

SNACK

GREEN PEA CURRY

Put **4 finely chopped and seeded fresh green chiles** and **a grated ¹/₂-inch piece of ginger** in a mortar or strong bowl and crush to a paste with a pestle or the end of a rolling pin. Put **2 tablespoons vegetable oil**, **1¹/₂ cups water**, **a pinch of baking soda,** and the ginger and chile paste in a saucepan. Add **salt** and **asafetida powder** to taste, stir well, and heat. When hot, add **1¹/₄ pounds fresh or frozen peas** and cook for 10 minutes until warmed through. The peas should not change color. Remove from the heat and serve with **naan bread** and garnish with **cilantro** and **coconut shavings**, if you wish. Serves 6

DINNER

BOSTON, SOFT-BOILED EGG, ROAST TOMATOES, CAPERS, AND PARMESAN DRESSING

With its croutons, lettuce, and Parmesan, this flavor-packed dish is a relative of the Caesar salad (see Spring, Week 5, Lunch). The salty, savory capers do a similar job to the anchovies in nonvegetarian versions, while the peppery arugula, roast tomatoes, and tangy dressing provide a symphony of complementary flavors. We defy anyone to eat this and say that vegetarian food is bland.

8–10 medium size tomatoes, halved
5 tablespoons olive oil
salt and freshly ground black pepper
1 bunch thyme leaves
8 baby leeks, trimmed and finely sliced
4 slices sourdough or country bread
2 garlic cloves, minced
2 tablespoons chopped flat-leaf parsley
4 organic eggs

3 tablespoons extra virgin olive oil
1 tablespoon white wine vinegar
1 teaspoon Dijon mustard
2 teaspoons roughly chopped capers
4 Boston lettuces, leaves separated
1 bunch wild arugula
1 tablespoon finely chopped chives
vegetarian Parmesan shavings, to serve

Preheat the oven to 325°F. Arrange the tomatoes on a small baking sheet, cut-side up, drizzle with 2–3 tablespoons of olive oil, and season with salt and freshly ground black pepper. Scatter with the thyme leaves and cook on the middle shelf of the oven for around 20 minutes. Add the leeks to the baking sheet and cook for another 15 minutes until soft and starting to caramelize at the edges. Remove from the oven and let cool to room temperature.

SERVES 4

Meanwhile, prepare the herby croutons. Slice the bread into rough chunks and toss with 2 tablespoons of olive oil, the garlic, and the chopped parsley, and season well. Tip onto a baking sheet and cook on the top shelf of the oven until golden and crisp. Soft-boil the eggs in salted water, drain, and refresh under cold running water.

To make the dressing, combine the extra virgin olive oil, vinegar, mustard, and capers in a small jar, season, screw on the lid, and give a good shake. Taste and adjust the seasoning if necessary.

To serve, arrange a pile of the lettuce and arugula on individual plates and tuck in the tomatoes and leeks. Quarter the soft-boiled eggs and divide between the plates, scatter with the chives and herby croutons, and drizzle with the dressing. Using a vegetable peeler, shave some Parmesan over the top of each salad and serve immediately.

DESSERT

SUPER SMOOTH RASPBERRY SORBET

Put **1 cup superfine sugar** in a saucepan with **³/₄ cup water**, bring to a simmer, and cook for 2 minutes. Allow to cool completely. Pulse **1 pound raspberries** in a food processor then push through a fine nylon sieve. Stir in the cooled sugar syrup and **2 teaspoons balsamic vinegar.** Lightly whisk **1 organic egg white**, add it to the raspberry mixture, then churn in an ice cream maker according to the manufacturer's instructions. Spoon into a container and freeze until ready to serve. Serves 4

WEEK 06

BREAKFAST

YOGURT, BANANA, AND RYE TOAST

A more substantial version of Greek yogurt and honey. Toast **1 slice of rye bread** and spread with **2 tablespoons Greek yogurt**. Layer with **1 sliced banana**, and drizzle with **2 teaspoons honey**. Serves 1

PACKED LUNCH

RATATOUILLE

Preheat the oven to 350°F. Slice **1/2 eggplant, 1 zucchini,** and **1/2 red** and **1/2 yellow pepper** into wedges. Put the vegetables, **1 minced garlic clove** and **4 quartered tomatoes** in a roasting dish. Drizzle with **olive oil**, season with **salt** and **freshly ground black pepper,** and mix well. Bake in the oven for 30 minutes or until the vegetables are tender. Stir in some **fresh basil leaves**. Serves 2–3

LUNCH

FRENCH BEAN, ROQUEFORT, AND WALNUT SALAD

SERVES 4

Roquefort is a blue cheese matured in the caves of Mont Combalou in Southern France. Made from sheep's rather than cow's milk, it is similar to Stilton but creamier and sharper. Like its English cousin, it goes extremely well with walnuts.

12 ounces French beans, topped and tailed
8 ounces Roquefort
1 cup walnuts, toasted
1 small radicchio
1–2 red and white chicory

FOR THE DRESSING
3 tablespoons of extra virgin olive oil
1 tablespoon balsamic vinegar
1 garlic clove, minced
salt and freshly ground black pepper

Wash the beans and steam them over a pan of boiling water until just crunchy. Keep warm. Crumble the Roquefort and lightly crush the walnuts. Wash the radicchio and chicory thoroughly and shake dry. Whisk together the remaining ingredients to make a dressing.

Arrange the leaves in a bowl, top with the beans, walnuts and cheese. Pour over the dressing.

MELON GAZPACHO

Finely chop **1 small red onion** and deseed and dice **1 green pepper**, **1 small round melon**, and **2 big beefsteak tomatoes**. Put the prepared fruit and vegetables in a large bowl, along with **1 tablespoon superfine sugar**, **5 tablespoons extra virgin olive oil**, **3 tablespoons sherry vinegar** and **2 slices good crusty white bread**, cut into chunks. Give a good seasoning with **salt** and **freshly ground black pepper**. Add **1 quart water** and gently mix all together. Chill in the fridge for at least 3 hours and garnish with **a bunch of flat-leaf parsley** just before serving. So refreshing! Serves 4

DINNER

EGGPLANT AND DRIED APRICOT PASTILLA

BRUNO LOUBET

SERVES 4

Reading the ingredients for this recipe, you might think you were about to make a dessert rather than a main course. That's because in Morocco, where this dish originates, the distinction is less clear than in most other places. A pastilla is a sweet-savory pie, often containing pigeon. You'll find this vegetarian version a revelation.

4 medium eggplants, diced
salt and freshly ground black pepper
1 cup dried apricots, diced
1 tiny drop almond extract
⅓ cup olive oil
2 medium onions, finely chopped
6 garlic cloves, finely chopped
1 tablespoon chopped ginger
1 tablespoon ground cumin
4 tablespoons honey

5 tablespoons red wine vinegar
1 handful fresh cilantro
1 handful fresh mint
zest of ½ lemon
36 squares filo pastry
8 tablespoons melted butter
½ cup sliced almonds, toasted
¼ cup confectioner's sugar
1 tablespoon ground cinnamon

Preheat the oven to 350°F. Sprinkle the eggplant with salt and leave for 20 minutes before rinsing with cold water, making sure to squeeze the water out. Place the dried apricots in a pan, cover with water, and add the almond extract. Bring to a boil then let rest for 5 minutes. Heat a frying pan on low heat, add a film of olive oil, then add the onion. Stir occasionally until soft and golden brown, then add the garlic, ginger, and cumin. Stir well then set aside in a bowl.

In the same pan, add some more olive oil and start to pan-fry the eggplant in batches, until golden brown and soft. When all of the eggplant is cooked, add the onion, honey, vinegar, and drained apricots. Cook slowly to stew for about 10 minutes (covered with a lid), then remove from the heat and add the herbs and lemon zest.

Brush the sheets of pastry with butter, then layer six sheets on top of each other. You should now have six pieces of pastry. Place one on a 4-inch tartlet mold, push in, and fill two-thirds with the eggplant mixture. Finish with toasted almonds. Close by folding over the pastry, then turn upside down and place on a baking sheet. Brush the top with butter, then bake for around 12 minutes, until golden and crisp. To serve, dust the top of the pastry lightly with confectioner's sugar and a sprinkle of cinnamon.

DESSERT

RED CURRANT CHEESECAKE

Melt **6 tablespoons butter** in a pan, add **35 crushed gingersnaps**, and stir to combine. Press the cookie mixture in an even layer over the base of a 8-inch springform pan, then chill until set, about 1 hour. Beat together **1¼ cups cream cheese**, **1 cup mascarpone**, **1 cup superfine sugar**, and the **grated zest and juice of 1 lemon** until smooth. Add **1 cup heavy cream** and continue to beat until the mixture is well combined. Spoon over the cookie base, smooth the top, and chill for at least 2 hours or overnight. Place **½ pound red currants** and **1–2 tablespoons superfine sugar** in a pan and heat gently. Simmer until soft, about 15 minutes. Strain into a bowl through a nylon sieve, taste for sweetness, adding more sugar if necessary, and chill. Top the cheesecake with another **½ pound red currants**, and serve the purée on the side. Serves 6–8

WEEK 07

BREAKFAST

SUMMER BERRY MUFFINS

Preheat the oven to 350°F. Line a muffin pan with 8 paper cases. Mix together **1/2 pound mixed summer berries**, such as strawberries, raspberries, and blueberries. Hull the strawberries and roughly chop if using. Sift **2 1/2 cups all-purpose flour, 2 teaspoons baking powder, 1/2 teaspoon baking soda, 1/2 cup superfine sugar,** and **a pinch of salt** into a large mixing bowl. In a separate bowl mix together **8 tablespoons melted unsalted butter** with **1 beaten organic egg, 3/4 cup buttermilk,** and **1 teaspoon vanilla extract**. Make a well in the middle of the dry ingredients, pour in the buttermilk mixture, and add the mixed berries. Stir until just combined and divide among the muffin cases. Sprinkle the tops with **1 teaspoon soft light brown sugar** and bake on the middle shelf of the oven for 15–20 minutes until golden brown and well risen. Best served warm or at room temperature on the day of baking. Makes 8

PACKED LUNCH

CHICKPEAS WITH RED CHARD AND ASPARAGUS

In a large frying pan or wok, heat **2 tablespoons olive oil** and cook **1 chopped red onion** and **1 seeded and finely chopped red chile** gently for 2–3 minutes until softened. Add **3/4 cup white wine** and **1 tablespoon tomato purée** and cook until reduced by half. Add **5–6 cups finely shredded red Swiss chard**, a **14-ounce can of drained chickpeas, 35 halved asparagus tips**, blanched and refreshed and cook for a further 2–3 minutes. Transfer to a serving bowl and sprinkle with **a handful of freshly chopped parsley leaves**. Serves 2

LUNCH

MOZZARELLA PASTA

TWIGGY

SERVES 2

This quick and easy recipe is like the greatest hits of Italian cooking rolled into one dish.

6 ounces penne rigate
14-ounce can plum tomatoes
2 tablespoons olive oil
1 cup freshly grated vegetarian Parmesan
2 tablespoons freshly chopped basil leaves
salt and freshly ground black pepper
6 ounces mozzarella, diced

Preheat the oven to 400°F.

Cook the pasta in boiling water for 10 minutes until just tender. Meanwhile heat the tomatoes and oil in a pan, breaking down the tomatoes gently with a wooden spoon. Add half the Parmesan and basil, and season to taste. Bring to a boil and remove from the heat.

Drain the pasta and place in an ovenproof dish. Pour the sauce over the pasta and stir through the diced mozzarella. Sprinkle with the remaining Parmesan and place in the preheated oven for 10 minutes until the cheese is golden. Serve immediately.

SNACK

BAYD MAHSMI

Hard-boil **6 organic eggs** and, when cool enough to handle, shell the eggs and cut them in half. Place the yolks in a small bowl, and mash them with **2 tablespoons Greek yogurt**, **1 small grated onion**, and **1 finely diced pickle**, and season with **salt** and **freshly ground black pepper**. Gently fill the whites with the mixture and top each egg with **a pitted black olive**. Serves 4

DINNER

ROASTED VEGETABLE PIZZA

SERVES 4

Everyone loves pizza but they don't always have to be topped with mozzarella. This one is made with Gruyère, which has a stronger taste that brings out the flavor of the roasted vegetables. Making it is easy—you don't have to swirl the dough around your knuckles like a theatrical Italian chef unless you can't resist it.

1¼ cups all-purpose flour
½ teaspoon salt
1 envelope instant yeast
1 organic egg
1 small eggplant, cut into ¾-inch wedges
1 red, green, and yellow pepper, each seeded and cut into eighths
1 zucchini, cut into ½-inch pieces
3 medium mushrooms, halved
3 garlic cloves, halved lengthwise

1 tablespoon fresh rosemary leaves, roughly chopped
3 tablespoons olive oil
salt and freshly ground black pepper
flour, for dusting
3 tablespoons sun-dried tomato paste
1 tablespoon freshly chopped basil leaves
2 tablespoons sun-dried tomatoes, roughly chopped
¾ cup Gruyère, grated

Preheat the oven to 400°F. You will need a 11-inch pizza pan or baking sheet.

Sift the flour and salt into a bowl and add the yeast. Beat the egg with a 3 tablespoons water. Add to the flour mixture to make a stiff dough, adding a little more water if necessary. Knead for 5 minutes for the dough to become smooth. Leave the dough in a warm place to rise for 1 hour or until doubled in size. Meanwhile, roast the vegetables and garlic cloves on a baking sheet, sprinkled with the rosemary, olive oil, and salt and freshly ground black pepper, for 25–30 minutes until softened.

Roll out the dough, place in the pan or baking sheet, lightly dusted with flour, and spread with the sun-dried tomato paste. Arrange the roasted vegetables on top. Sprinkle wth the basil leaves and sun-dried tomatoes, cover with the Gruyère, and bake for 25 minutes until the base is crispy and the cheese melted.

DESSERT

WATERMELON GRANITA

Place **4 cups watermelon chunks** in a food processor or blender and blend to a smooth purée. Add **½ cup superfine sugar**, **2 cups water**, and **3 tablespoons lemon juice**, and process again. Press the mixture though a fine sieve to remove the seeds. Pour into a suitable freezer container, cover with a lid, and place in the freezer for 2 hours. Remove and stir so that the ice that has formed around the sides and base of the container is mixed into the unfrozen center, then cover and return to the freezer for another hour until firm. Remove, mix thoroughly again and then refreeze for another hour. Serves 4

WEEK 08

BREAKFAST

MANGO AND LIME

Cut in half **3–4 ripe mangoes**. Peel them and cut the flesh into chunks of about 3 inches. Sprinkle with the **juice and zest of 2 limes**. Very refreshing. Serves 4

PACKED LUNCH

TRICOLOR CIABATTA

Cut a **small ciabatta** in half and toast under the broiler. Drizzle some **olive oil** over the toasted ciabatta and layer some **slices of tomato and avocado** over one half of the bread. Tear **half a mozzarella ball** over the top and season with some **salt** and **freshly ground black pepper** and then sprinkle with some **fresh basil leaves**. Place the other half of the ciabatta on top. Serves 1

LUNCH

STUFFED TOMATOES WITH GRUYERE

SERVES 4

Shirley Conran once famously said that "life's too short to stuff a mushroom." Well it isn't too short to stuff a tomato with this light savory filling. When you eat the result, you'll consider it time well spent.

8 large ripe tomatoes or 4 beef tomatoes
salt and freshly ground black pepper
3 cups white breadcrumbs (made from day-old bread)
½ cup organic milk
2 organic eggs, lightly beaten
2 garlic cloves, minced

2 tablespoons freshly chopped basil leaves
2 tablespoons finely chopped fresh parsley
1 onion, finely chopped
2 tablespoons toasted breadcrumbs
5–6 tablespoons grated Gruyère
olive oil

Preheat the oven to 350°F.

Remove a slice from the top of each tomato and scoop out the pulp. Season the insides of the tomatoes with salt and freshly ground black pepper and arrange in a greased baking dish.

To make the stuffing, combine the white breadcrumbs with the milk and eggs in a bowl, and add the garlic, herbs, and onion. Season with salt and freshly ground black pepper. Fill the insides of the tomatoes. Sprinkle with the toasted breadcrumbs and Gruyère, and drizzle with a little olive oil to prevent burning. Bake until the tomatoes are tender, about 30 minutes.

SIDE

BASIL-SCENTED BRAISED FENNEL

Heat **4 tablespoons of olive oil** in a large flameproof casserole dish. Add **3 large fennel bulbs**, trimmed and cut into ¹/₂ inch thick wedges, and cook for 5–8 minutes until golden brown, turning carefully with the aid of a fork. Pour in **¹/₂ cup vegetable stock**, cover, and simmer gently for 20 minutes until the fennel is tender. Add a **handful of basil leaves** and seasoning 1 minute before the end of the cooking time. Serves 4

DINNER

RISOTTO WITH ARTICHOKES

Who'd have thought something so good could be made from the buds of a giant thistle? You need to use young artichokes for this recipe—older ones are delicious if you just nibble the tender bases of the leaves but the rest of them (apart from the soft hearts) can be unpalatably tough.

8 small artichokes, prepared and trimmed (chokes removed if at all prickly)
2 garlic cloves, finely chopped
2 tablespoons olive oil
sea salt and freshly ground black pepper
1 quart vegetable stock

6 tablespoons butter
1 medium red onion, very finely chopped
1¹/₂ cups risotto rice
3–4 tablespoons extra dry white vermouth
³/₄ cup freshly grated vegetarian Parmesan

SERVES 4

Cut the artichokes in half and slice as thinly as possible. Cook gently with the garlic in 1 tablespoon of the olive oil for 5 minutes, stirring continuously, then add ¹/₂ cup water and salt and freshly ground black pepper, and simmer until the water has evaporated. Set aside.

Heat the vegetable stock and check for seasoning. Melt half the butter in the remaining oil in a large heavy-bottomed saucepan and gently cook the onion until soft, about 10 minutes. Add the rice and, off the heat, stir for a minute until the rice becomes totally coated. Return to the heat, add 2 or so ladlefuls of hot stock or just enough to cover the rice, and simmer, stirring, until the rice has absorbed nearly all the liquid. Add more stock as the previous addition is absorbed. After about 15–20 minutes, nearly all the stock will have been absorbed by the rice; each grain will have a creamy coating, but will remain al dente. You may not need to add all of the stock.

Add the remaining butter in small pieces, then gently mix in the vermouth, Parmesan, and artichokes, being careful not to overstir.

DESSERT

FRUITY AMARETTI

Lightly crush **28 Amaretti cookies** and place in the base of a serving dish or 4 individual dishes. Place **1 cup ricotta cheese**, **2 tablespoons fresh orange juice**, and **2 teaspoons clear honey** in a food processor or blender and blend until softened. Alternatively place the ingredients in a bowl and beat together well. Scatter **1³/₄ cups halved strawberries** over the Amaretti cookies, then add a layer of **peach slices** and top with the cheese mixture. Place in the refrigerator to chill. The cookies will remain crisp for a couple of hours. Serves 4

WEEK 09

BREAKFAST

BROILED FIGS WITH RICOTTA

Preheat a broiler. Cut **2 fresh figs** in half lengthwise. Lightly grease a small baking pan. Place the figs, cut side up, in the pan and broil for 3–4 minutes until they begin to soften. Meanwhile, combine **2 tablespoons ricotta** with **1 teaspoon honey** and stir until smooth. Place the figs on a plate and spoon the ricotta mixture over the top. Serves 1

PACKED LUNCH

PEPPER POCKETS

JAMES TANNER

SERVES 4

You ate tortillas back in week 2, in the form of quesadillas. Now we're going to show you how to make them yourself. It's easy and very satisfying but if you don't have the time, you can always use ready-made tortillas for the recipe below. You will end up with neat savory packages that are equally good hot or cold.

FOR THE TORTILLAS
1³/4 cups self-rising flour, sifted
a pinch of crushed sea salt
³/4 cup boiling water
1 teaspoon olive oil, plus extra for brushing
sunflower oil

FOR THE FILLING
2 red peppers
1 tablespoon olive oil
7 cups fresh spinach, chopped
2 cups Emmental, cut into 1/2-inch cubes
1/2 cup black Niçoise olives, pitted and
chopped

Preheat the oven to 425°F. Place the whole peppers on a baking sheet and roast for 25–30 minutes until the skins start to blacken. Remove from the oven, place in a plastic bag, seal and set aside for 5 minutes (to help loosen their skins). Reduce the oven to 350°F.

For the tortillas, sift the flour into a mixing bowl with the crushed sea salt. Add the water and 1 teaspoon olive oil and mix with your hands to form a soft dough. Knead for 2 minutes on a lightly floured surface until smooth and elastic. Brush the top of the dough with olive oil, return to the bowl, cover with a clean kitchen towel, and let rest for 10 minutes.

For the filling, heat the tablespoon of olive oil in a wok or large nonstick frying pan. Add the spinach and stir-fry over medium heat for 4 minutes until wilted. Remove from the heat and drain, squeezing out any excess moisture. Remove the peppers from the plastic bag. Skin, deseed and slice, then set aside.

Divide the dough into 8 pieces and roll into small balls in your hand. On a lightly floured surface roll each dough ball into a circle roughly 8–9 inches in diameter. Repeat with the remaining dough to make 8 flour tortillas. Place the spinach in a large bowl. Add the sliced red pepper, Emmental, and olives. Mix together and season with freshly ground black pepper. Divide the spinach mixture into 8 and spoon into the center of the tortillas. Brush the edge of each tortilla with water and fold the edges up around the spinach filling to make a package.

Heat sunflower oil in a deep fryer. Add the tortilla pockets and deep fry for 2 minutes on each side. Transfer to a baking sheet and bake for 12–15 minutes until golden.

Remove from the oven and leave to stand for 2 minutes before serving or leave to cool completely.

SNACK

GUACAMOLE

Halve, stone, and peel **2 ripe avocados**. Put the avocado into a food processor with **1 cup drained and chopped sun-dried tomatoes**, **1 garlic clove**, and **1/2 teaspoon ground coriander**. Pulse the ingredients together until the avocados are well chopped but not smooth. Add **1–2 tablespoons of lime or lemon juice** to taste and stir in **1 tablespoon freshly chopped cilantro**. Season with **salt** and **freshly ground pepper**. Serve with tortilla chips and salsa. Serves 2

SIDE

SALSA

Skin and seed **4 large tomatoes**, and cut into rough dice. Slice **2 scallions** very finely and mix with the tomatoes, **1 tablespoon white wine vinegar**, **3 tablespoons extra virgin olive oil**, **1 teaspoon sugar** and **1 tablepoon shredded basil**. Chill well. Serve with tortilla chips. Serves 2

DINNER

LENTIL STEW WITH PAN-FRIED HALLOUMI AND POMEGRANATE

KEVIN SPACEY

SERVES 4

The pomegranate seeds in this dish not only provide jewel-like color but also offer a contrasting burst of flavor and texture to the halloumi and lentils.

1½ cups Puy lentils, washed
3 tablespoons olive oil
8 baby zucchini, sliced into ½-inch pieces
1 large onion, chopped
2 garlic cloves, minced
½ teaspoon ground cumin
pinch dried red pepper flakes
1 tablespoon tomato paste
½ cup dry white wine
1 cup vegetable stock
8-ounce can chopped tomatoes
1 bay leaf
3 cups sliced chard (or cavalo nero or spinach)
8 cherry tomatoes

1 tablespoon pomegranate molasses

FOR THE MINT SALSA
3 tablespoons fresh mint, roughly chopped
2 tablespoons flat-leaf parsley, roughly
   chopped
1 heaping teaspoon capers
3–4 tablespoons extra virgin olive oil
1 garlic clove, minced
juice of ½ lemon
salt and freshly ground black pepper

TO SERVE
8–9 ounce block halloumi, sliced

Cook the lentils in a pan of boiling water until only just tender and then drain.

Meanwhile, heat the olive oil in a large pan set over medium heat. Add the zucchini and cook until golden, remove from the pan, and set aside. Add another tablespoon of olive oil to the pan, add the onion, and cook until tender but not colored. Add the minced garlic, ground cumin, and red pepper flakes, and cook for another 30 seconds. Add the tomato purée, stir to combine, and pour in the wine, vegetable stock, and canned tomatoes. Pop in the bay leaf and bring to a boil. Reduce to a gentle simmer and cook for 20 minutes. Add the lentils and cover and cook for another 10 minutes until softened. Add the zucchini, chard, cherry tomatoes, and pomegranate molasses, cover, and cook for another 5 minutes.

Prepare the mint salsa. Combine all of the ingredients in a food processor and pulse until combined. Taste, and add salt and freshly ground black pepper.

Heat a nonstick frying pan over medium heat, add the sliced halloumi cheese, and cook until golden brown on both sides. Spoon the lentils into bowls, top with hot halloumi and a good spoonful of mint salsa, and serve.

DESSERT

BLACK CURRANT ICE CREAM

Wash **1 pound black currants** then tip into a heavy-bottomed saucepan with **3/4 cup granulated sugar** and **3 tablespoons water**. Warm the pan over low heat, and stir until the black currants are soft and the sugar has dissolved. Purée in a food processor, sieve out the seeds, and let cool. When ready to make the ice cream, stir in **2 cups heavy cream** and **3 tablespoons Crème de Cassis**. Put into an ice cream machine and churn for 20–30 minutes. Makes around 3 cups ice cream

WEEK 10

BREAKFAST

BANANA AND HONEY MUFFINS

Preheat the oven to 350°F. Line a 12-hole muffin pan with paper cases. Place **2¼ cups self-rising flour**, **2 tablespoons dark brown sugar**, **4 tablespoons melted butter**, and **2 small mashed bananas** in a large bowl and mix them together. In a second bowl, whisk together **2 medium organic eggs**, **2 tablespoons honey**, and **5 tablespoons organic milk** and beat into the other ingredients to form a mixture of soft dropping consistency. Divide the mixture among the cases, filling almost to the top. Bake for 15 minutes until risen and firm to the touch. Remove from the oven and transfer to a wire rack. To make the frosting, mix together some **honey**, **confectioner's sugar**, and **lemon juice** and place a little on top of each muffin. Makes 12

PACKED LUNCH

FREGOLA SARDA PASTA WITH TOMATOES

Sardinian food is very trendy at the moment and a taste of this rustic dish should show you why. One of the island's signature cooking ingredients is fregola sarda, a kind of pasta consisting of tiny beads. It's like couscous but nuttier, as the grains are lightly toasted after they are formed.

10 ounces cherry tomatoes, halved
3 garlic cloves, whole and unpeeled
1 teaspoon sugar
½ teaspoon dried oregano
salt and freshly ground black pepper
5 tablespoons olive oil
7 ounces fregola sarda pasta

2 tablespoons pine nuts, toasted
¾ cup roughly chopped basil leaves
2 tablespoons freshly grated Parmesan
¾ cup pitted black olives, halved or roughly chopped
½ cup soft goat cheese

SERVES 4

Preheat the oven to 375°F.

Put the tomatoes and garlic into a small roasting pan. Sprinkle the tomatoes with a little sugar and the oregano, season with salt and freshly ground black pepper, and drizzle with 2 tablespoons olive oil. Roast for about 25 minutes until soft and starting to caramelize.

Cook the fregola sarda in boiling salted water according to the package instructions.

Make a pesto using a pestle and mortar or in a small food processor. Take the garlic from the roasting pan and squeeze the flesh from the skin and pound it together with the pine nuts. Add the basil and the remaining olive oil and pound again until finely chopped. Add the Parmesan, season with salt and freshly ground black pepper, and mix again until amalgamated.

Tip the warm fregola sarda into a bowl, and add the roasted tomatoes and black olives. Crumble the goat cheese over the top, and gently fold the pesto into the pasta. Serve warm or cold.

LUNCH

FRESH PEA AND FAVA BEAN OMELET

Heat the broiler to medium. Boil **1 cup peas** and **1 cup fava beans** (or edamame) for 4 minutes until just tender, then drain well. Beat **8 large organic eggs** with **a splash of organic milk** and some **salt** and **freshly ground black pepper**. Stir the vegetables into the egg mixture along with **1–2 tablespoons lemon zest** and **1 minced garlic clove**. Lightly **oil** an ovenproof shallow pan and place on medium heat. Pour in the egg mix and gently cook for 8–10 minutes until there is just a little unset mix on the surface. Place under the broiler and cook until set. Serves 4

SNACK

JACKET FRIES WITH TARTARE-STYLE SAUCE

Cut **3 pounds potatoes** into ¹/₂-inch thick slices, then cut again to give long fries about ¹/₂ inch thick and 3 inches long. Blanch in boiling water for 3–4 minutes. Drain well on paper towels until dry to the touch. Heat enough **vegetable oil** for deep-frying at 375°F and cook the fries until golden brown and crispy. Drain well and sprinkle with **salt**. Keep hot. Make the sauce by mixing together **1 cup mayonnaise, 5 tablespoons chopped capers** and **5 tablespoons chopped pickles**. Season to taste with **salt** and **freshly ground black pepper** and serve with the fries. Serves 4–6

DINNER

SALAD OF WILD RICE, CHARRED CORN, SPICED PECANS, AVOCADO, AND FETA

ANNA HANSEN

SERVES 8

Wild rice has an earthy, nutty taste that domesticated strains lack. It makes the perfect base for this inventive, flavor-packed dish. It's probably been quite a while since you last used confectioner's sugar in a salad!

2 ears of corn
2 tablespoons olive oil
³/₄ cup wild rice
1 small cinnamon stick
1 red chile, split lengthways
1 red onion, finely chopped
3 tablespoons good-quality red wine vinegar
¹/₄ teaspoon sweet smoked paprika

¹/₂ cup pecan nuts
1 tablespoon confectioner's sugar
1 teaspoon cumin seeds
pinch of salt
¹/₂ tablespoon freshly chopped cilantro
1 avocado, cut into pieces
small bunch of watercress, washed
4 ounces marinated feta

Preheat the oven to 300°F.

Cut the kernels off both ears of corn. Put 1 tablespoon of the oil in a big pan, add the corn, and cook over high heat until charred in places. Simmer the wild rice, cinnamon, and chile in plenty of water until tender but still al dente, and drain (check your package of wild rice for timings, and taste for tenderness). Let cool.

Caramelize the red onion in a pan in the remaining oil until soft. Add the vinegar and paprika and continue to cook until the vinegar has evaporated, remove from the heat, let cool, and add the corn. Toss the pecans with the sugar, cumin seeds, salt, and 1 tablespoon water. Bake for 10 minutes or until golden (keep checking to make sure they don't burn).

Mix together the rice, corn, and onion, cilantro, avocado, and watercress. Crumble the feta over the top and sprinkle with the pecans. Serve.

DESSERT

PISTACHIO MERINGUES

Preheat the oven to 225°F. Line 2 large solid baking sheets with parchment paper. Combine **4–5 large organic egg whites, 1¹/₄ cups superfine sugar,** and **a pinch of salt** in a medium heatproof mixing bowl, and whisk to combine. Set the bowl over a pan of simmering water, but do not allow the bottom of the bowl to touch the water. Whisk constantly until the sugar has dissolved and the mixture has turned from opaque to white and is warm. Tip the mixture into the bowl of a freestanding electric mixer and whisk on high speed for about 5 minutes until very stiff, glossy, white, and cold. Add **¹/₄ cup finely chopped pistachios** and fold in using a large metal spoon. Divide the meringue into 8 evenly sized portions. Scatter another **¹/₄ cup pistachios** on top. Bake for 1–1³/₄ hours, swapping the trays around halfway through. Remove from the oven and let cool on the baking trays. Place **1 pound halved strawberries** in a large bowl with **10 ounces raspberries**, the **juice of ¹/₂ lemon**, and **3 tablespoons sugar**, and set aside for an hour or so to allow the juices to start to run. Whip **2 cups heavy cream** and fold in **¹/₂ cup of Greek yogurt**. Serve the meringues with a good spoonful of the cream mixture, the macerated berries, and **a drizzle of passion fruit**. Serves 4

WEEK 11

BREAKFAST

OEUF EN COCOTTE

Preheat the oven to 350°F. Lightly grease a ramekin dish or teacup with **butter**. Crack in **1 organic egg** and pour **1 tablespoon heavy cream** over the top. Place in the oven and bake for 10 minutes or until the white of the egg is cooked through but not hard. Serve with **toast** cut into strips to dip into the soft yolk. You can also add a **some fresh thyme** or grate some **Gruyère** on top before baking. Serves 1

PACKED LUNCH

GREEK SALAD

In a shallow bowl, arrange **2 sliced beefsteak tomatoes** and **1 finely sliced shallot**. Pour over some **extra virgin olive oil**. Scatter with **1/2 cucumber, peeled and diced, 1/2 cup black olives, 1 cup cubed feta**, a handful of freshly chopped flat-leaf parsley, and leaves from 2 stems of oregano. Season generously with **salt** and **freshly ground black pepper** and serve with **warmed pita bread**. Serves 4

LUNCH

STILTON PATE WITH MELBA TOAST AND CHERRY TOMATOES

ANDREW MAXWELL

SERVES 4

This is a very adult recipe. The pungency of the Stilton is diluted by the sweetness of the cream cheese, and the splash of brandy adds a touch of luxury. Roasting the accompanying cherry tomatoes in the way described concentrates the flavor and slightly caramelizes them.

4 ounces Stilton
10 ounces cream cheese
1/2 tablespoon brandy
2–3 tablespoons heavy cream
freshly ground black pepper

9 ounces vine ripened cherry tomatoes
olive oil
balsamic vinegar
8 wafer-thin slices white bread

Preheat the oven to 425°F.

Remove the rind from the Stilton. Place the Stilton in a food processor and blend until smooth. With the motor running, add half the cream cheese, then the brandy very slowly. Do not overmix. Add the remaining cream cheese and sufficient heavy cream to give the desired consistency. Season with black pepper. Place in a serving dish and smooth the surface.

Drizzle the cherry tomatoes with olive oil and balsamic vinegar and roast in the oven for 4 minutes, until the skin is just peeling off.

For the melba toast, turn the oven down to 300°F. Remove the crusts of the bread and cut each slice diagonally. Place on a baking sheet and bake in the oven until crisp and golden brown.

SIDE

WATERCRESS AND LETTUCE SALAD

Wash, trim, and dry **1 bunch watercress** and **1 large leaf lettuce**. Make a dressing by mixing together **4 tablespoons olive oil, 2 tablespoons vinegar or lemon juice, salt** and **freshly ground black pepper, 1 tablespoon chopped onion, 1 minced garlic clove** and **1 teaspoon mild mustard**. Coarsely chop the drained watercress and lettuce, place in a salad bowl, and add the dressing. Serves 4

DINNER

PAELLA VERDURAS

JOSÉ PIZARRO

SERVES 6

This recipe showcases summer vegetables like zucchini and fresh peas. Sweet pimentón (ground red pepper) and saffron are essential to any authentic paella. The latter is made from the stamens of crocuses—there are only three per plant, which explains why it's so expensive. Fortunately, you only need to use a tiny quantity.

1/2 teaspoon saffron strands
1 quart vegetable stock
1 1/2 cups shelled fava beans
4 ounces fine green beans, topped and tailed and halved
4 ounces fine asparagus, in 2-inch lengths
3 tablespoons extra virgin olive oil
3 small zucchini, cut into thick slices
1 medium onion, finely chopped
1 large red pepper, seeded and chopped into 1/2-inch pieces
1 large green pepper, seeded and chopped into 1/2-inch pieces

3 garlic cloves, finely chopped
1 teaspoon sweet pimentón
2 medium tomatoes, fresh, peeled and chopped
fine sea salt and freshly ground black pepper
2 cups short grain paella rice, such as Calasparra or Bomba
2 tablespoons freshly chopped flat-leaf parsley
2/3 cup shelled peas
10-ounce jar chargrilled artichokes in olive oil, drained

Shake the saffron strands around in a slightly hot frying pan for a few seconds until dry but not colored, then tip into a small mortar or coffee cup and grind to a powder with the pestle or a wooden spoon. Add a splash of the stock and set aside.

Bring a pan of salted water to a boil. Drop in the fava beans, bring back to a boil, and cook for 2 minutes. Lift out with a slotted spoon into a colander, drain, then tip into a bowl. Bring the pan of water back to a boil, add the green beans, and cook for 3 minutes. Lift out with the slotted spoon into the colander and refresh under cold water. Tip onto a plate. Bring the water back to a boil once more, add the asparagus, bring back to a boil, drain and refresh under cold water. Pop the fava beans out of their skins and add to the plate of green beans with the asparagus.

Heat 2 tablespoons of the olive oil in a large nonstick frying pan or shallow flameproof casserole dish over medium-high heat. Add the zucchini and cook them for 2–3 minutes until a light golden brown. Lift out onto a plate.

Add the remaining tablespoon of oil and the onion to the pan and cook gently for 5 minutes. Add the red and green pepper and continue cooking until the onion is soft and lightly golden. Stir in the garlic and pimentón and cook for 1 minute more. Add the tomatoes and cook for 2–3 minutes until softened, then stir in the rest of the stock, the saffron mixture, and some seasoning to taste, and bring to a boil. Sprinkle in the rice and the parsley, stir lightly to evenly distribute the rice around the pan, then scatter the cooked beans, asparagus, zucchini, peas, and artichokes, and shake the pan gently so that they all bed down slightly into the rice. Lower the heat and simmer vigorously for 6 minutes, then lower the heat again and simmer gently for another 14 minutes, until all the liquid has been absorbed and the rice is tender, but still with a little bit of a bite to it. Remove the pan from the heat, cover with a large lid or clean towel, and let rest for 5 minutes before serving.

DESSERT

GRILLED PEACHES WITH GREEK YOGURT

Preheat the oven to 400°F. Spray **oil** on the bottom of a grill pan or frying pan, heat, then add **4 halved and pitted peaches** cut-side down and cook for 5 minutes. Set the peach halves cut-side up in a roasting pan, pour **1/2 cup orange juice** around them, and drizzle with **1–2 tablespoons honey**. Roast for 10–15 minutes, depending on their ripeness. Place the peach halves into individual warmed bowls cut-side up, spoon on a **dollop of Greek yogurt** and scatter with **pistachio nuts**. Serves 4

WEEK 12

BREAKFAST

APRICOT AND OAT BARS

Preheat the oven to 375°F. Grease and line a baking pan. Place **finely chopped dried apricots** and **3 tablespoons apple juice** in the small saucepan and simmer over low heat for 5 minutes until soft. Place **²/3 cup sunflower oil** and **4 tablespoons honey** in a medium saucepan and stir over low heat until evenly blended. Add **2 cups rolled oats, 1¹/2 cups all-purpose flour,** and **¹/2 cup walnuts,** and mix together thoroughly. Put half the mixture into the 9 x 13 inch baking pan and press down firmly with the back of the wooden spoon. Cover with the apricot mixture, then sprinkle with the remaining oat mixture and press down firmly. Bake for 35 minutes until golden brown. Remove from the oven and leave to cool for 5 minutes, then cut into 14 bars. Allow to cool completely before removing from the pan. Makes 14 pieces

PACKED LUNCH

GREEN CLUB SANDWICH

Toast **3 slices wholegrain or rye bread** and slice **1 small avocado.** Spread **3 tablespoons hummus** (store-bought or see Spring, Week 3, Lunch) evenly over one side of each slice of toast. Lay half the avocado, some **arugula leaves,** and **alfafa sprouts** over the hummus. Season with **freshly ground black pepper,** then cover with another slice of toast. Pile on the rest of the avocado, some more arugula and alfafa sprouts, season again and top with the third slice of toast. Serves 1

LUNCH

ORANGE MARINATED TOFU SKEWERS

PAMELA ANDERSON

SERVES 4

Tofu is great at absorbing flavors, in this case of a zesty citrus marinade. The only thing that's remotely difficult about this recipe is remembering to start marinating the skewers four hours before cooking them. Here, they're broiled but you could easily barbecue them.

FOR THE SKEWERS
24 ounces firm tofu, drained and cut into 1-inch cubes
2 large onions, cut into 1-inch pieces
1 red pepper, seeded and cut into 1-inch pieces
1 green pepper, seeded and cut into 1-inch pieces
1 yellow pepper, seeded and cut into 1-inch pieces
1 pound whole cherry tomatoes
fresh orange pieces, to garnish

FOR THE MARINADE
1 cup orange juice
2 tablespoons lemon juice
1 teaspoon chopped garlic
1¹/2 teaspoons whole black peppercorns
2 teaspoons fresh thyme leaves
zest of 1 orange
1¹/2 cups olive oil

10 bamboo skewers

Combine all the ingredients for the marinade, except the oil, in a food processor and blend for 15 seconds. While the machine is running, slowly add the oil until blended.

Thread the tofu, onions, peppers, and tomatoes onto the skewers. Place in a shallow dish and pour the marinade over the tofu and vegetables. Leave to marinate for 4 hours. Remove the skewers from the marinade and either grill over a medium flame for about 4 minutes on each side or place under a broiler, until the veggies are lightly cooked and have grill marks. Serve with the orange pieces.

SIDE

POTATO AND GRUYERE FOCACCIA

NICK MALGIERI

Make the dough by mixing **5¼ cups unbleached all-purpose flour or bread flour** and **2 teaspoons salt**. Set aside. In a large mixing bowl, stir an **envelope of instant yeast** into lukewarm **1½ cups tap water**. Wait 2 minutes and stir again to make sure the yeast is completely dissolved. Whisk in **4 tablespoons olive oil**. Use a large rubber spatula to smoothly stir half the flour mixture into the liquid. Stir this into the dough mixture, using the spatula to dig up any unmoistened flour from the bottom of the bowl. Use the spatula to beat the dough vigorously for about 15 seconds. Cover the bowl with plastic wrap and let the dough rise until it has doubled in size, about 1 hour. Move the dough into an oiled 9 x 13 inch pan, being careful not to fold the dough over on itself. Reach under it and flip it over—now the top is coated with oil. Use the palms of your hands to press the dough into the pan. If it resists, cover, and let rest for 10 minutes, then press again to cover the entire base of the pan. Cover with plastic wrap and let rise until puffy, about 30 minutes. Set a rack on the lowest level of the oven and preheat to 450°F. Peel and thinly slice **2 medium potatoes** and place in a saucepan, cover with water, and bring to a boil over a medium heat. Drain, rinse, and set aside in a colander. Once the focaccia is risen, use your index finger to dimple the top all over at 1-inch intervals. Cover with the potato slices. Season with a little **salt and freshly ground black pepper** and evenly scatter with **½ cup coarsely grated Gruyère**. Drizzle with **2 tablespoons olive oil**. Place the focaccia in the oven and reduce the temperature to 425°F. Bake until the dough is firm and the topping is golden, about 30 minutes. About halfway through, use an offset spatula to lift the corner of the focaccia to check that the base is starting to color. If it is coloring too quickly, slide a baking sheet under the pan the focaccia is in to insulate it. Cool the focaccia on a rack so that the base doesn't become damp. Makes approximately 12 squares

DINNER

WARM HALLOUMI, APPLE, AND RADISH SALAD

SERVES 4

The first word that comes to mind to describe this salad is crisp. The crunchiness of the apple and lettuce contrasts beautifully with the fried halloumi, which is so dense it's almost meaty. The red chile adds a bit of heat.

3 eating apples, cored and finely sliced
2 tablespoons lemon juice
3 Boston lettuces, leaves separated
8 ounces radishes, trimmed and sliced
1 cup walnuts, toasted and roughly chopped
4 tablespoons olive oil

1 tablespoon wholegrain mustard
2 tablespoons honey
1 red chile, seeded and finely chopped
2 x 9-ounce packages halloumi, each block cut into 4 slices

Place the apple slices in a bowl and toss in a tablespoon of the lemon juice to prevent them browning. Arrange the lettuce leaves on a platter. Scatter the apples, radishes, and walnuts.

Whisk together 3 tablespoons of the olive oil with the remaining lemon juice, mustard, and honey, and drizzle over the lettuce, apple, and radishes.

Add the remaining tablespoon of olive oil to a large nonstick frying pan set over medium heat and stir in the chile. Add the halloumi slices and cook for 2–3 minutes on each side until golden. You will need to do this in batches. Place the hot halloumi over the salad and serve.

DESSERT

PAVLOVA WITH RASPBERRIES

Preheat the oven to 350°F. Mark out an 8-inch diameter circle on a sheet of parchment paper and place on a baking sheet. Beat **3 organic egg whites** with **¾ cup superfine sugar**, adding the sugar a tablespoon at a time, until the egg whites are glossy and form stiff peaks. Beat in **1 level teaspoon cornstarch** and **1 teaspoon white wine vinegar**. Spoon the mixture onto the parchment paper and shape to the circle, making a slight well in the center so the edges are raised. Place in the oven and immediately reduce the heat to 250°F. Bake for 1½ hours, then turn off the oven and leave the pavlova inside to cool completely. When ready to serve, whip **1 cup heavy cream** and spoon onto the pavlova. Top with **1 pound sliced raspberries** and dust with **a little confectioner's sugar**. Serves 4

WEEK 13

BREAKFAST
BANANA YOGURT POT

Dollop about **1 tablespoon thick Greek yogurt** into the bottom of a small glass or bowl. Chop **1 banana** and add a layer of banana slices over the yogurt, then top with another layer of yogurt. Repeat the layers until the glass or bowl is full. Drizzle with some **honey** and scatter with some **granola** (see Winter, Week 5, Breakfast), if you wish. Serves 1

PACKED LUNCH
GRILLED VEGETABLE BLOOMER

Preheat the broiler. Cut **3 red peppers** in half, seed, and place, cut-side down, on a baking sheet. Place under the broiler and char until the skins are blackened. Put the peppers in a plastic bag, seal, and let cool. When cool enough to handle, remove the skins, cut into strips, drizzle with **1 tablespoon olive oil,** and set aside. Slice **1 eggplant** into rounds about 2 inches thick, and place on another baking sheet. Add **2 thinly sliced red onions**. Drizzle with **2 tablespoons olive oil**, season with **salt** and **freshly ground black pepper**, and broil, turning occasionally, until nicely charred at the edges. Cut **a small round loaf** almost in half lengthwise (leaving a hinge) and carefully hollow out most of the bread, so you are left with a shell that has edges about 1/2 inch thick. Spread the insides with a thin layer of **pesto sauce**, and add the peppers in a layer, followed by the eggplant and onion mixture. Close, cut into thick slices, and wrap tightly with plastic wrap until ready to eat. Serves 2

LUNCH
PANZANELLA

SERVES 4

This classic Florentine salad of bread and tomatoes is ideal for a summer lunch. Until the twentieth century, the salad was based on onions rather than tomatoes, but its evolution takes advantage of tomatoes when they're at their best.

1/2 loaf ciabatta
6 tablespoons extra virgin olive oil
2 garlic cloves, 1 peeled, 1 minced
1/2 teaspoon dried oregano
2 tablespoons good-quality red wine vinegar
salt and freshly ground black pepper
2 tablespoons freshly chopped flat-leaf parsley

1 tablespoon baby capers, drained
6 plum tomatoes, roughly chopped
1 small red onion, finely sliced
1/2 cucumber, seeded and cut into chunks
2 celery ribs, finely sliced
12 fresh basil leaves, ripped
1/2 cup pitted black olives, halved

Cut the ciabatta in half and brush the cut sides with a little extra virgin olive oil. Heat a ridged grill pan or broiler and toast the ciabatta until crisp and golden. Rub the peeled garlic clove over the cut sides of the bread, tear the bread into rough chunks, and set aside.

In a small bowl whisk together 5 tablespoons extra virgin olive oil, the crushed garlic clove, and the red wine vinegar. Season well with salt and freshly ground black pepper, and add the freshly chopped flat-leaf parsley.

In a large bowl, mix together the bread and baby capers, plum tomatoes, sliced onion, cucumber, sliced celery, basil leaves, and black olives, and toss with the dressing. Season to taste.

SNACK

MACERATED STRAWBERRIES WITH MASCARPONE ON RYE

Hull and halve **8 ounces strawberries** and place in a bowl. Pour over **2 teaspoons balsamic vinegar** and **1 tablespoon sugar**, season lightly with **freshly ground black pepper**, stir gently, and leave to macerate for 1 hour. Toast **4 slices rye bread** and spread each with **1 teaspoon creamy mascarpone**. Top with a spoonful of macerated strawberries. Serves 4

DINNER

FETA AND COUSCOUS SALAD WITH POMEGRANATE

SERVES 4

Continuing with the hot weather theme, this is a dish you can imagine eating in Iran or Morocco in summer. It is filled with cooling ingredients like couscous, feta, and mint, and the pomegranate seeds pop delightfully when you bite into them.

1¹/2 *cups couscous*
8 ounces feta, roughly crumbled
¹/4 *cup shelled pistachios*
6 ounces pomegranate seeds
2 tablespoons freshly chopped mint

juice 1 orange
2 tablespoons white wine vinegar
2 tablespoons olive oil
salt and freshly ground black pepper

Place the couscous in a shallow bowl, then pour over ³/4 cup boiling water. Cover the bowl with plastic wrap, then leave for 5 minutes until the couscous has swelled up and absorbed all of the water. Ruffle with a fork to separate the grains, then stir through feta, pistachios, pomegranate seeds and mint.

Make a dressing by mixing together the orange juice, white wine vinegar, and olive oil, then stir into the couscous. Season well with salt and freshly ground black pepper and serve.

DESSERT

TIRAMISU

Mix together **2/3 cup strong black coffee**, **3 tablespoons Marsala or sherry**, and **3 tablespoons brandy**. Place **4 ladyfingers** in a serving dish and pour over half the coffee mixture. Mix together **8 ounces mascarpone**, **1 cup heavy cream**, and **4 level tablespoons confectioner's sugar**. Spoon half over the ladyfingers. Place **4 ladyfingers** on top, and pour over the remaining coffee mixture. Smooth the surface. Sieve **¹/4 cup cocoa powder** over the top and chill for at least 2–3 hours before serving. Serves 4–6

U

AU T

N

M

WEEK 01

BREAKFAST

TOASTED RYE BREAD WITH CINNAMON HONEY BUTTER

Beat together **7 tablespoons softened unsalted butter, 2 tablespoons honey** and **¼ teaspoon ground cinnamon** until light and fluffy. Chill in the refrigerator until set. Toast **4 slices of rye bread** in a toaster or under the broiler, then spread with the cinnamon butter. Serves 2

PACKED LUNCH

EASY SPICED DHAL WITH POPPADOMS

Heat **1 tablespoon olive oil** in a saucepan over medium heat. Cook **1 finely chopped small onion, 1 finely chopped garlic clove, 2 peeled and finely chopped 1-inch pieces of ginger** and **1 seeded and finely chopped bird's eye chile** for 2 minutes. Add **1⅓ cups yellow split peas** and **2 cups vegetable stock**. Bring to a boil, reduce the heat, and cook for 40 minutes until the split peas are tender. Stir occasionally, particularly toward the end of the cooking time. Remove from the heat, add **salt** and **freshly ground black pepper** to taste and stir in **½ cup roughly chopped cilantro**. Serve with **mini poppadoms**, if you wish. Serves 4–6

LUNCH

FIG AND GOAT CHEESE SALAD

STELLA McCARTNEY

SERVES 2

Luscious figs are married with the fresh tartness of goat cheese in this recipe. Putting them on the grill pan for a couple of minutes helps bring out their delicate flavor.

3 tablespoons olive oil
1 tablespoon balsamic vinegar
salt and freshly ground black pepper
4 ripe figs, halved
olive oil, for brushing
4 ounces goat cheese, roughly sliced
2 handfuls of watercress, stems removed

Whisk together the olive oil and balsamic vinegar and season with salt and freshly ground black pepper.

Heat a grill pan until very hot. Brush the figs with a little olive oil. Put them cut-side down on the grill pan and cook for 2–3 minutes. Remove carefully.

Arrange the figs, cheese, and watercress on 2 plates. Drizzle with the dressing and serve.

SIDE

STIR-FRIED KALE

Thoroughly wash and dry **1³/4 pounds young kale** in a salad spinner. Chop it roughly. Pour **3 tablespoons peanut or olive oil** in a wok or heavy frying pan over high heat and, when the oil is steaming, toss in the kale and cook for 3 minutes, stirring constantly. Season and add **lemon juice** and shavings of **lemon zest** for decoration, if you wish. Serve piping hot. Serves 4

DINNER

EGGPLANT CASSEROLE WITH POMEGRANATE

MAGGIE BEER

SERVES 3–4

Verjuice, which is made from unripe grapes, was an important cooking ingredient in medieval times. It has recently been repopularized by Australian chef Maggie Beer. Being acidic, it can be used in much the same way as vinegar or lemon juice, for instance in salad dressings or marinades, but it has a mellower, fruitier flavor.

1 cup organic lentils
1/2 cup extra virgin olive oil
3 medium eggplants, sliced
1 large onion, roughly diced
5 garlic cloves, finely chopped
salt and freshly ground black pepper
3 tomatoes, roughly chopped
3/4 cup verjuice

1/2 cup pomegranate molasses
2 tablespoons rinsed and finely chopped preserved lemons
3 tablespoons roughly chopped flat-leaf parsley leaves
3 tablespoons roughly chopped mint leaves
14 ounces quark or mascarpone

Preheat the oven to 300°F.

Place the lentils and 6 cups of water in a saucepan, bring to a simmer, and cook for 15 minutes. Drain and set aside.

Meanwhile, heat 3 tablespoons olive oil in a heavy-bottomed casserole dish, and cook the eggplant in batches until golden. Remove and set aside. Add the onion and cook for 10 minutes or until golden brown, stirring occasionally. Add the garlic and a good pinch of salt, and cook, stirring every now and then to prevent the onion from burning, for 3–4 minutes or until the onions are a golden brown color.

Add the tomatoes with 1 tablespoon olive oil and warm through. Pour in the verjuice and cook, stirring, for 1 minute until the liquid has reduced by two-thirds, then remove from the heat and set aside.

Add half of the eggplant slices, sprinkle with half of the lentils, then add the rest of the eggplant and top with the rest of the lentils. Pour over the remaining olive oil and the pomegranate molasses. Cover, and cook in the oven for 1 hour, then stir through the preserved lemons. Return to the oven for another 45 minutes–1 hour or until the eggplant is cooked through. Check for seasoning and serve warm with the parsley and mint stirred through. Serve on individual plates, top with quark or mascarpone, and drizzle with a last dash of olive oil.

DESSERT

GLUTEN-FREE CRANBERRY POLENTA CAKE

Preheat the oven to 350°F. Grease an 8-inch springform cake pan. Combine **1 cup polenta**, **2¹/4 cups all-purpose gluten-free flour**, **1 heaping teaspoon baking powder**, and **1/2 cup plus 2 tablespoons superfine sugar** in a food processor with the **grated zest of 1 orange**, and process to combine. Add **11 tablespoons diced unsalted butter** and process until the mixture resembles fine breadcrumbs. Combine **1 tablespoon orange juice**, **1 beaten organic egg**, and **1 tablespoon olive oil** in pitcher and, with the motor running, slowly pour into the processor through the feeder. Once combined, stop the machine and press two thirds of the dough into the cake pan. Combine **9 ounces frozen cranberries**, **4 tablespoons soft brown sugar** and **2 teaspoons polenta** and pile onto the base, leaving a border of about 1/2 inch around the edge. Crumble the remaining dough on the top and bake in the oven for 45–50 minutes until golden brown. Serve warm with **crème fraîche**. Serves 6

WEEK 02

BREAKFAST

MARMALADE MUFFINS

Preheat the oven to 350°F. Line a 12-hole muffin pan with paper cases. In a bowl, mix together 1³/4 cups self-rising flour, ½ cup whole-wheat flour, 6 tablespoons superfine sugar, 1 teaspoon baking powder, and a pinch of salt. In a separate large bowl, beat together 1 organic egg, 7 tablespoons melted butter, ½ cup organic milk and the zest and juice of 1 lemon. Gently stir the flour mixture into the egg mixture, followed by ⅓ cup marmalade, taking care not to overmix. If the mixture is too stiff, loosen with another tablespoon of milk. Divide the batter equally among the muffin cases and bake in the oven for 25 minutes or until a wooden skewer inserted in the center comes out clean. Allow to cool slightly and eat warm. Makes 12

PACKED LUNCH

CARIBBEAN RICE AND BEANS

Put ½ cup long grain rice in a roomy saucepan with enough coconut milk to just cover it. Bring to a boil, season with salt, tuck in a stem of fresh thyme leaves, lower the heat, and simmer slowly until all the milk is absorbed. Add water to the rice as it dries to prevent it from sticking. When the rice is perfectly soft, stir in ⅓ cup rinsed and drained red kidney beans and 1 small minced garlic clove. Season to taste with salt and freshly ground black pepper. Serve warm. Serves 1

LUNCH

ROSTI WITH MUSHROOMS

Rösti is a Swiss dish made by forming grated potato into cakes or patties, which are then fried. The outer flakes caramelize delectably during the frying, while the insides remain soft. Mushrooms are an excellent accompaniment to rösti, which soaks up their delicious cooking juices.

5 medium potatoes, peeled
6 tablespoons butter
3 tablespoons olive oil
2 onions, finely chopped
2 tablespoons freshly chopped parsley
1 pound closed cup mushrooms, sliced

2 garlic cloves, minced
2 teaspoons fresh thyme leaves
4 organic eggs
handful of fresh chives, roughly chopped
salt and freshly ground black pepper

SERVES 4

Preheat the oven to 350°F.

Place the potatoes in a large pan of salted water and bring to a boil. Simmer for 15 minutes, drain, and leave until cool enough to handle.

Meanwhile heat 2 tablespoons butter and 1 tablespoon olive oil in a frying pan, add the onions, and cook until soft and starting to turn golden at the edges. Season and tip into a large bowl.

Coarsely grate the potatoes into the bowl with the onions. Add the parsley, and season well with salt and freshly ground black pepper. Mix together using your hands and then shape into 8–12 patties and flatten slightly. Heat 2 tablespoons butter and 1 tablespoon olive oil in a large nonstick frying pan and cook 4 rösti at a time until golden brown on both sides. Keep finished rosti warm in the oven.

Heat the remaining butter and olive oil in a pan and sauté the mushrooms with garlic and thyme on high heat until tender. Season to taste. Bring a shallow pan of salted water to a boil, reduce the heat, and poach the eggs one at a time. Serve each rösti topped with mushrooms and an egg. Sprinkle with chives and salt and freshly ground black pepper. Serve immediately.

SIDE
POTATO SALAD

Cook **1³/4 pounds small potatoes** in salted boiling water until tender, drain and cool slightly, then cut into bite-size pieces and place in a large bowl. Trim and finely slice **1 bunch of scallions**. Cut **6 radishes** into fine matchsticks. Roughly chop **6 cornichons** and **1 tablespoon capers**. In a small bowl whisk together **2 tablespoons wholegrain mustard**, **1 tablespoon white wine vinegar**, and **3 tablespoons olive oil** and season with **salt** and **freshly ground black pepper**. Pour the dressing over the potatoes, add the scallions, radishes, cornichons, capers, **2 tablespoons roughly chopped chives**, and **2 tablespoons freshly chopped flat-leaf parsley**, and gently mix together. Serve at room temperature. Serves 4

DINNER
ROASTED BUTTERNUT SQUASH AND ZUCCHINI

ARTHUR POTTS DAWSON

SERVES 4

This recipe combines two totally different kinds of squash. One (the zucchini) is delicate and watery. The other (butternut squash) is robust and orange. They look—and taste—very good together.

1 butternut squash, sliced lengthwise and seeds scooped out
1 large zucchini, sliced lengthwise and seeds scooped out
2 stems of thyme
6 tablespoons olive oil
9 ounces fresh baby spinach leaves
1 romaine lettuce
1 cup borlotti beans, cooked fresh or canned
1 cup toasted mixed seeds

FOR THE DRESSING
juice of 1/2 lemon
1 teaspoon freshly chopped thyme leaves
2 teaspoons honey
2 teaspoons white wine vinegar
salt and freshly ground black pepper

Preheat the oven to 375°F. Chop the squash and zucchini into thumb-size pieces and arrange in a roasting pan, season with salt and pepper, mix in the thyme stems, and drizzle with 2–3 tablespoons of the olive oil. Roast in the oven for 25 minutes or until the vegetables are soft to the touch and cooked. Remove from the oven, allow to cool, and discard the thyme.

Wash the spinach and romaine lettuce leaves and dry in a salad spinner. Layer the cooked vegetables, borlotti beans, and mixed seeds in a large salad bowl, placing in the salad leaves as you go. To make the dressing, whisk together the remaining olive oil, lemon juice, thyme leaves, honey, and white wine vinegar. Season with salt and freshly ground black pepper and serve drizzled over the salad.

DESSERT
PANNA COTTA

Pour **2 cups heavy cream** into a small saucepan, add the **seeds of 1 vanilla pod**, **zest of 1 lemon**, and **3 tablespoons unrefined superfine sugar**, and heat gently until the sugar dissolves. Place **2 teaspoons powdered agar-agar powder** and **2 tablespoons cold water** in a cup or ramekin, stand in a saucepan holding a small amount of boiling water, and allow the agar-agar powder to dissolve (do not let it get too hot). Take the cream off the heat, remove the lemon zest, and whisk the agar-agar mix into the cream until it dissolves. Pour into 8 individual cups or ramekins. Refrigerate for at least four hours, or overnight, until set. Serves 4

WEEK 03

BREAKFAST

BAKED APPLES WITH YOGURT

Preheat the oven to 350°F. Core **2 large cooking apples**, fill the center with **dried cranberries** and **finely grated zest and juice of 1 orange**, and drizzle **1 teaspoon honey** over the top. Bake in the oven for 30–40 minutes until tender. Serve with **a couple of dollops of Greek yogurt.** Serves 2

PACKED LUNCH

WILD RICE AND APRICOTS

Preheat the oven to 400°F. Cook **1/2 cup long grain rice** and **1/2 cup wild rice** according to the package instructions. Rinse and refresh in cold water. Roughly chop **2/3 cup dried apricots.** Place **1/2 cup blanched almonds** on a baking sheet and roast in the preheated oven for 2–3 minutes until golden brown. When the nuts are cool, mix together with the rice and apricots, along with **2/3 cup plain yogurt**, **1/2 cup raisins**, and **2 tablespoons finely chopped parsley.** Season to taste with salt and freshly ground black pepper. Serves 4–6

LUNCH

CREAMY CELERY SOUP WITH STILTON

SERVES 4

The sharpness of celery combines very well with Stilton, as in this creamy, filling soup. The cheese isn't actually cooked in this recipe—you just crumble it up and pour the hot soup over it.

1 tablespoon olive oil
1 onion, finely chopped
2 large potatoes, peeled and diced
1 head celery, thoroughly washed and
    roughly chopped
1 teaspoon caraway seeds

1 vegetable stock cube dissolved in 2 cups
    boiling water
1 cup 2% organic milk
1/2 cup light cream
3 ounces Stilton, crumbled
1/2 cup fresh chives, roughly chopped

Heat the oil in a large saucepan then add the onion, potatoes, celery, and caraway seeds. Cook gently for approximately 5 minutes until the onion is softened but not colored.

Add the stock and milk and simmer uncovered for 20–30 minutes. Transfer the soup in batches to a food processor and purée until smooth, and pour into a clean saucepan.

Gently reheat the soup, then stir in the cream. Do not allow to boil. Crumble the Stilton into individual soup bowls and pour the soup over the cheese. Sprinkle with chives and serve immediately with hot, crusty bread.

SNACK

CUCUMBER AND YOGURT DIP

Halve, seed, and grate **1 cucumber** on the coarse side of a box grater. Put into a colander and sprinkle with **1–2 teaspoons salt.** Let stand for 15 minutes. Drain and dry the cucumber with paper towels. Mix with **1 cup Greek yogurt** and **2 teaspoons freshly chopped mint,** and season to taste with **cayenne pepper** and **freshly ground black pepper.** Serve with **crudités.** Serves 6

DINNER

SPLIT PEA DHAL AND CAULIFLOWER CURRY

SERVES 4

An estimated 40 percent of Indians are vegetarian, so it's no surprise that the nation has perfected the art of meat-free cooking. This recipe proves the point.

FOR THE CURRY
1 rounded teaspoon cumin seeds
1 rounded teaspoon coriander seeds
2 tablespoons sunflower oil
1 onion or 3 shallots, sliced
2 garlic cloves, minced
1 tablespoon grated fresh ginger
1 green chile, seeded and chopped
1 cinnamon stick
1/2 teaspoon cayenne pepper
1/2 teaspoon ground turmeric
4 medium potatoes, peeled and cut
    into chunks
14-ounce can coconut milk
2 cups vegetable stock
8-ounce can tomatoes
1/2 small cauliflower, cut into florets
handful of green beans, trimmed and cut
    into 2-inch lengths

FOR THE DHAL
1 1/2 cups yellow split peas
1 teaspoon ground turmeric
1 cinnamon stick
3 cardamom pods, lightly crushed
2 slices fresh ginger
3 tablespoons butter
1 onion, finely chopped
1 teaspoon cumin seeds
1 teaspoon coriander seeds
1 red chile, seeded and finely chopped
1/2 tablespoon grated fresh ginger
1 garlic clove, sliced
1/2 teaspoon kalonji (black onion) seeds
1 teaspoon sugar

salt and freshly ground black pepper
cilantro leaves to garnish
brown rice to serve

First make the dhal. Pour the split peas into a large bowl, cover with cold water, and soak overnight. Drain and rinse the split peas, pour into a saucepan, and add the ground turmeric, cinnamon stick, cardamom pods, and ginger. Cover with 2 cups cold water, bring to a boil, reduce the heat to a very gentle simmer, and continue to cook for about 40 minutes until the split peas are very tender and starting to soften at the edges. Season with salt to taste.

Melt the butter in a small frying pan, and add the onions and a pinch of salt. Cook over medium heat until tender but not colored. Meanwhile, lightly crush the cumin and coriander seeds. Add them, along with the chile, ginger, garlic, kalonji seeds, and sugar to the onions, and continue to cook until caramelized and fragrant. Serve scattered over the dahl.

To make the curry, heat a small frying pan over medium heat, add the cumin and coriander seeds, and toast for 1 minute or until fragrant. Lightly grind using a mortar and pestle. Heat the oil in a large sauté pan. Add the onion and cook over medium heat until tender but not colored. Add the garlic, ginger, chile, and the spices and cook for 1 minute until fragrant.

Add the potatoes to the pan and stir to coat. Pour in the coconut milk, stock, and tomatoes, and bring to a boil. Reduce the heat and simmer for 5 minutes before adding the cauliflower. Cover and cook over a low heat for 20 minutes until the potato and cauliflower are tender and the sauce has thickened slightly. Add the beans and cook for 2–3 minutes. Season to taste, garnish with cilantro, and serve with the yellow dahl and brown rice.

DESSERT

LEMON, ALMOND, AND PEAR CAKE

Preheat the oven to 350°F. Line the base of a 8-inch springform cake pan with parchment paper. In a bowl, cream together **18 tablespoons softened unsalted butter** and **1 cup plus 2 tablespoons sugar**. Beat in **4 large organic eggs** one at a time, adding some **all-purpose flour** after each addition (until 1/2 cup flour has been added). Fold in **2 cups plus 2 tablespoons ground almonds**, 1/2 **teaspoon almond extract**, and the **grated zest** and **juice of 2 lemons**. Spoon the mixture into the pan and smooth the surface. Peel, halve, and fan out **4 ripe pears** and place on top of the cake mixture. Bake in the oven for 1 hour or until a skewer inserted into the center of the cake comes out clean. If the cake seems to be browning too quickly, cover with a piece of foil. Glaze with **4 tablespoons apricot jam** while still warm, and allow the cake to cool before removing from the pan. Serves 12

WEEK 04

BREAKFAST

SCRAMBLED EGGS WITH MUSHROOMS

Melt **1 tablespoon butter** in a small saucepan over a low heat. Add **5 button or chestnut mushrooms**, cover with a lid, and cook gently until soft. Meanwhile, beat **2 organic eggs** in a bowl and season with **salt** and **freshly ground black pepper**. Melt another **tablespoon butter** in a nonstick frying pan over medium heat until foaming. Pour in the beaten eggs and let them sit for 10 seconds. Scramble using a wooden spoon until the eggs are cooked but still soft, taking care not to overstir. Spoon onto a plate and add the mushrooms, and serve immediately. Serves 1

PACKED LUNCH

LENTILS WITH TAHINI DIP

Soak **1 cup brown lentils** overnight, drain and rinse thoroughly. Place them in a saucepan with **1 lightly crushed garlic clove** and **1 small peeled onion**. Cover with water and bring to a boil, cooking for 10 minutes, then cover the pan and continue to cook for another 40 minutes until the lentils are tender. Mince **1 garlic clove** and mix it with **2 tablespoons tahini paste**, **1 tablespoon lemon juice**, and some **salt** and **freshly ground black pepper** to make a thick cream. Add a few drops of **cold water** if it is too stiff. Put the lentils, onion, and garlic in a blender, add **1 tablespoon lemon juice** and **1 tablespoon freshly chopped flat-leaf parsley**, and purée. Taste and adjust the seasoning if necessary and spoon into a serving dish. Dust with **paprika** and sprinkle with **1 tablespoon finely chopped flat-leaf parsley**. Make a small well in the middle and add a little more tahini paste. Serve with **hot pita** and **black olives**. Serves 2

LUNCH

FENNEL SAUTEED WITH PEPPERS

SERVES 2

Fennel is one of the stronger-tasting vegetables. Some people find its aniseedy flavor a bit overpowering when it is raw but sautéing it with sweet red peppers, garlic, and peas takes the edge off it. It comes in fat, dense bulbs.

2 tablespoons olive oil
2 red peppers, seeded and cut into
*   thin strips*
1 pound fennel, trimmed and finely chopped
*   (about 3 bulbs)*
2 garlic cloves, crushed
2 cups peas, shelled
salt and freshly ground black pepper
1 tablespoon freshly chopped flat-leaf parsley

In a wok or heavy-bottomed frying pan, heat the oil, add the peppers and fennel, and cook for 10–15 minutes over moderate heat until crunchy, stirring occasionally. Add the garlic and peas and continue cooking for 2 minutes. Season, scatter with the parsley, and serve.

SNACK
BABA GHANOUSH

Preheat the oven to 400°F. Prick **2 medium size eggplants** with a fork several times and place on a lightly greased baking sheet. Bake for 35–40 minutes, until the skins are wrinkled and the flesh is soft. Soak **1 slice brown bread** in **a little water** and squeeze out. Set aside. Cut the eggplants in half lengthwise and use a spoon to scoop out the flesh from the skin. In a food processor, purée the eggplant with **3 minced garlic cloves**, the soaked bread, **juice of 1/2 lemon**, **2 teaspoons cumin**, and **5 tablespoons olive oil** until smooth and creamy. Stir in **3 tablespoons Greek yogurt** and spoon into a large bowl. Scatter with **a handful of freshly chopped flat-leaf parsley** and **2 tablespoons pitted and quartered black olives**. Serve with **vegetable crudités** and **toasted pita**. Serves 4

DINNER
WALNUT AND MUSHROOM RISOTTO

SERVES 4

This is a very autumnal risotto, perfect on a windy evening when the nights are drawing in. It's better to buy your nutmegs whole rather than powdered—they lose their flavor much more slowly and the gratings always taste fresh.

2 cups uncooked long grain rice
2 tablespoons olive oil or butter
1 onion, finely chopped
4 ounces large flat mushrooms, chopped
3/4 cup walnuts, roughly chopped
6 whole cloves

1/4 teaspoon grated nutmeg
salt and freshly ground black pepper
6 tablespoons white wine
1 tablespoon heavy cream
freshly chopped parsley, to garnish

Cook the rice according to the package instructions.

Heat the olive oil or butter in a large saucepan, add the onion, and cook gently for 5–10 minutes until it begins to brown. Add the mushrooms, walnuts, and spices and cook for 5 minutes, or until the mushrooms have begun to soften, adding a little more oil or butter if necessary. Add the wine, season with salt and freshly ground black pepper, and simmer for another 2 minutes until the mushrooms are tender. Stir in the rice and cream and heat through gently, stirring constantly. Remove the cloves and serve hot, garnished with freshly chopped parsley.

DESSERT
APPLE CAKE

Preheat the oven to 350°F. Line an 8-inch springform pan with parchment paper. Purée **8 tablespoons butter** and **3/4 cup superfine sugar** in a mixer until creamy, soft, and pale in color. Add **3 organic eggs**, one at a time, beating gently after each addition. Stir **1 teaspoon baking powder** into **1 1/2 cups all-purpose flour** and add this to the egg mixture. At this stage, add **1 tablespoon organic milk** if desired and stir in **a few drops of vanilla extract**. Peel and core **2 medium apples** and cut them into slices, around 1 inch thick. Put a layer of cake mixture at the base of the pan. Arrange a layer of apples on top, then sprinkle with **1 tablespoon raisins**. Repeat, and finish with a layer of the cake mixture. Bake in the center of the oven for 35–40 minutes, until cooked through. Turn out onto a wire tray, remove the pan, peel off the parchment paper, and allow to cool. Dust with **confectioner's sugar**. Serve at room temperature. Serves 6–8

WEEK 05

BREAKFAST

FRUITY QUINOA

A delicious alternative to oatmeal. In a small saucepan bring **1 cup almond milk** and **½ teaspoon vanilla extract** to a boil. Stir in **⅓ cup quinoa**, reduce the heat to low, and simmer gently for 10 minutes or until most of the liquid has been absorbed. Remove from the heat and stir in **¼ cup blackberries** and **1 tablespoon chopped pecans**. Spoon into 2 bowls and drizzle with **honey**. Serves 2

PACKED LUNCH

BASIL AND MUSHROOM TART

SERVES 4–6

Cèpes are low in fat and high in protein, vitamins, minerals, and dietary fiber, making them a healthful and tasty filling for a tart. Pâte brisée is the French equivalent of flaky pastry.

FOR THE PATE BRISEE
1 cup all-purpose flour
4 tablespoons butter, cubed
1 organic egg yolk
1–2 tablespoons cold water
a pinch of salt

FOR THE MUSHROOM FILLING
6 ounces cèpes, or other small cap wild
    mushrooms or button mushrooms
2 tablespoons unsalted butter
2 small shallots, finely chopped
1 tablespoon all-purpose flour
½ cup light cream
salt and freshly ground black pepper
1 tablespoon freshly chopped basil leaves
2 stems parsley

Preheat the oven to 400°F.

Start by making the pastry. Sift the flour into a bowl and make a well in the center. Add the butter, egg yolk, and water, along with the pinch of salt, and work in the flour and the rest of the ingredients. Form into a ball, using a little extra flour if necessary. Wrap the pastry in plastic wrap and replace in the bowl, chilling in the fridge for 30 minutes.

In the meantime, clean the mushrooms carefully of any dirt and dry them with a cloth; quarter any larger ones. In a heavy-bottomed pan, melt the butter and toss in the mushrooms and shallots, stirring for 3–4 minutes until they are soft. Remove with a slotted spoon and keep warm, reserving the juices.

Roll out the pastry on a lightly floured, cold surface and line a 9-inch tart pan. Prick the base of the pastry, line with parchment paper and baking beans, and bake in the oven for 8–10 minutes.

As the pastry case is cooking, reheat the juices from the mushroom pan, stir in the flour and, over moderate heat, cook gently for 2 minutes. Then add the cream and allow to thicken, stirring all the time. Season with salt and pepper and add the basil.

Assemble the tart by discarding the parchment paper and baking beans. Arrange the mushrooms on the base of the tart, pour the sauce over the top, and put the tart pan back into the oven to heat through, allowing around 10 minutes. Once the filling is lightly set, remove and decorate with the parsley leaves and serve. Delicious with a plain green salad.

LUNCH

EASY EGG FLORENTINE

Preheat the oven to 350°F. Lightly grease a large ramekin dish or teacup with **butter**. Defrost **2 ounces frozen spinach**, squeeze out all excess water, season with **salt** and **freshly ground black pepper**, and spoon into the base of the ramekin dish, making a slight well in the center. Break **2 organic eggs** into the dish, dot with more **butter**, add **1 tablespoon cream**, and sprinkle with **1 tablespoon freshly grated Parmesan**. Bake in the oven for 10 minutes until the edges of the egg whites are just beginning to set and the yolks are firm. Serves 1

SIDE

SHALLOTS GLAZED WITH ORANGE

Take **12 medium size shallots** and trim them but do not peel. Arrange them in a single layer in a shallow baking dish, and drizzle with some **extra virgin olive oil**, along with **2–3 stems lemon thyme**. Roast in a preheated oven, 400°F, for 45 minutes or so. They are cooked when the shallots are tender; remove from the oven and, with a couple of forks, ease the shallots from their skins. Discard the thyme. Put the shallots back in the pan with **the juice and zest of 1 orange**, together with **1–2 teaspoons brown sugar** and put back in the oven and allow to dissolve and brown. This should take 5-10 minutes. Serves 3-4

DINNER

PENNE WITH BROCCOLI, MASCARPONE AND DOLCELATTE

It isn't immediately obvious why the Italians call short tubes of pasta cut at an angle penne (feathers) but if you look at the nib of an old-fashioned quill pen, the name starts to make sense. Brassicas and cheeses often go well together. Here, broccoli is combined with sweet, creamy mascarpone and gorgonzola dolcelatte to make an irresistible sauce, which oozes into the penne and sticks to their ridged sides.

1 pound broccoli, chopped into small florets
¼ cup mascarpone
7 ounces gorgonzola dolcelatte
2 tablespoons crème fraîche
1 tablespoon balsamic vinegar
1 tablespoon dry white wine
14 ounces penne
2 tablespoons capers
4 tablespoons black olives
1 tablespoon hazelnuts, crushed and toasted
salt and freshly ground black pepper

SERVES 4

Steam the broccoli florets over a pan of boiling water for 4–5 minutes. Chill under cold water and set aside.

In a heavy pan, gently heat the mascarpone, dolcelatte, crème fraîche, vinegar, and wine. Add the broccoli florets.

Cook the pasta in boiling salted water until it is just tender, drain well, return to the pan, and add the hot sauce. Sprinkle with capers, olives, and hazelnuts, and toss well. Adjust the seasoning and serve.

DESSERT

PLUM CRUMBLE

Preheat the oven to 375°F. Halve and pit **1 pound plums** and place in an ovenproof dish along with **1 tablespoon water**. Put **1 cup all-purpose whole-wheat flour** in a mixing bowl, add **6 tablespoons butter**, and rub it in with your fingertips until the mixture resembles fine breadcrumbs. Stir in **4 tablespoons sugar**. Sprinkle the crumble mixture over the fruit, and bake in the oven for 25-30 minutes. Serve hot with **yogurt** or **fromage frais**. Serves 4

WEEK 06

BREAKFAST

SPICED PUMPKIN CREPES

Sift **1 cup all-purpose flour** into a bowl. Add **1 teaspoon baking powder, 2 tablespoons sugar, ¹/₂ teaspoon ground allspice,** and **¹/₂ teaspoon cinnamon** and stir to combine. In a separate, large bowl, beat together **4 tablespoons organic milk, ²/₃ cup canned pumpkin or pumpkin purée, 1 organic egg yolk, 2 tablespoons melted butter,** and **1 teaspoon vanilla extract.** Add the dry ingredients, and beat until until you have a smooth, thick batter. In another bowl, whisk **1 organic egg white** until soft peaks form. Fold into the pumpkin mixture. Pour **a little oil** into a nonstick frying pan set over medium heat. Working in batches, ladle 3-4 spoonfuls of the mixture into the frying pan and cook until bubbles form on the surface of the crêpes, and the bottoms are golden, about 1-2 minutes each side. Serves 6

PACKED LUNCH

VEGGIE SAUSAGE SANDWICH

Drizzle **2 slices of sourdough bread** with a little **olive oil** and toast lightly on both sides. Heat a little olive oil in a pan and add **¹/₂ chopped red onion.** Allow the onion to sweat. When it starts to wilt, add **¹/₄ teaspoon sugar, a pinch of salt,** some **freshly ground black pepper,** and **1 teaspoon balsamic vinegar.** Cook for another 3-4 minutes. Now, start to cook **2 vegetarian sausages** in a frying pan with a little olive oil. When they are colored on all sides, turn down the heat and cook for another 6–8 minutes. Halve **2 baby plum tomatoes** and place in the pan with the onions. Add a little water and **¹/₄ teaspoon of sugar** and **1 teaspoon balsamic vinegar,** season again, and reduce a little over medium heat. To assemble, cut the cooked sausages in half lengthwise. Spoon the tomato and onion mix over 1 slice of the bread and place the sausages on top. Top with the remaining slice of bread. Serves 1

LUNCH

CREAMY MUSHROOM SOUP

SERVES 4

Field mushrooms are grown year round in climate-controlled conditions but early autumn is their natural season. This simple recipe brings out their delicate, earthy qualities to the max.

6 tablespoons butter
4 shallots, finely chopped
1 garlic clove, crushed
1 pound field mushrooms, cleaned and sliced
1 quart vegetable stock
1 tablespoon all-purpose flour

TO SERVE
soy sauce
heavy cream
salt and freshly ground black pepper

Heat 4 tablespoons of the butter in a heavy-bottomed pan and sauté the shallots until softened; add the garlic and cook for 1 minute more. Add the mushrooms and stir to coat well. Pour in the stock and bring to a boil. Cover and simmer for 10-15 minutes, until the mushrooms are cooked. Remove from the heat.

In a separate pan, heat the remaining butter and stir in the flour to make a roux. Cook for 2 minutes and remove from the stove. In a blender, combine the roux with the soup (this may need to be done in batches). Return the soup to the pan, bring back to a boil, add the soy sauce to taste, check the seasoning, and stir in a dollop or 2 of cream.

SNACK

CRANBERRY AND APRICOT OAT BARS

Preheat the oven to 350°F. Grease an 8-inch square baking pan. In a saucepan over low heat, gently heat **1 stick butter**, **1/2 cup firmly packed soft brown sugar**, and **2 tablespoons corn syrup** until the sugar has dissolved. Stir in **2 cups rolled oats**, **a pinch of salt**, **2 tablespoons dried cranberries**, and **2 tablespoons dried chopped apricots** and mix well. Spoon into the prepared pan and level. Bake for 30 minutes until golden. Remove from the oven, cut into squares, and leave to cool completely before removing from the pan. Makes 16 squares

DINNER

SAUTEED EGGPLANT AND MOZZARELLA

Eggplants were cultivated by the Chinese as long ago as the 5th century BC, and the Moors introduced them to Europe. Try the many varieties and colors of eggplants now available.

4 small, long, thin eggplants
1 garlic clove, crushed
1 tablespoon freshly chopped parsley
1/2 cup toasted breadcrumbs
3 tablespoons olive oil
salt and freshly ground black pepper
6 ounces buffalo mozzarella, in 2-inch slices
1 tablespoon Greek basil leaves

Preheat the oven to 375°F.

Cut the eggplants in half lengthwise. Score the flesh deeply, but do not cut the skin. Arrange in a shallow pan, skin-side down.

Mix together the garlic, parsley, breadcrumbs, and half the olive oil, season, and press the mixture into the scored eggplants.

Drizzle with the rest of the oil and bake in the oven until golden. Remove from the oven, arrange the mozzarella on top, and return to the oven for another 5 minutes or until the cheese has melted. Scatter with Greek basil to serve.

SERVES 4

DESSERT

GINGERBREAD CAKE

Preheat the oven to 325°F and lightly grease and flour a 6-inch cake pan. Cream **1 stick butter** and **1/2 cup sugar** together in a large mixing bowl. Add **1 organic egg** a little at a time, beating between each addition. Mix together **2 cups self-rising flour**, **1/2 teaspoon ground cinnamon**, **2 teaspoons ground ginger**, and **1/4 teaspoon nutmeg** and add to the butter mixture. Gradually add **1/2 cup organic milk**, stirring to make a smooth batter. Warm **2 tablespoons molasses** slightly and then beat it into the batter. Transfer the batter to the cake pan and bake for 40–45 minutes. Serves 6

WEEK 07

BREAKFAST

AVOCADO ON TOAST

Toast **2 slices of whole-wheat bread** and spread with **butter**. Mash **1/2 avocado** onto the toast with a fork and season with **salt** and **freshly ground black pepper**. Drizzle **a little extra virgin olive oil** over the top if you wish. Serves 1

PACKED LUNCH

TUSCAN BEAN AND VEGETABLE SOUP

SERVES 4

This hearty soup is perfect for a windy autumn day and takes less than half an hour to make. Make sure you serve it with good, crusty bread.

2 tablespoons butter
1 tablespoon olive oil
1 medium onion, finely chopped
1 garlic clove, peeled and finely chopped
1 rib celery, trimmed and finely chopped
1 large carrot, peeled and finely chopped
14-ounce can mixed beans, drained
14-ounce can chopped tomatoes

3 cups vegetable stock
1 teaspoon dried oregano
2 tablespoons pesto sauce, plus extra
    to garnish
salt and freshly ground black pepper
2 medium zucchini, trimmed and finely
    chopped
2 tablespoons sour cream

Melt the butter with the oil in a large saucepan and gently cook the chopped onion, garlic, celery, and carrot for 5 minutes until just tender.

Stir in the beans, tomatoes, and stock. Add the oregano and pesto and season to taste. Bring to a boil and simmer for 10 minutes. Add the zucchini to the soup. Cook for another 5 minutes until all the vegetables are tender. Ladle the soup into warmed bowls and top with the sour cream and pesto sauce.

LUNCH

RED AND YELLOW PEPPER SALAD

Place **1/2 cup couscous** in a wide shallow bowl and cover with **1/2 cup boiling water**. Fork through, then cover tightly with a clean towel. Leave for about 20 minutes. Meanwhile, preheat the broiler. Chop **1/2 red and 1/2 yellow pepper** into large chunks and remove the seeds and membrane. Place on a sheet of foil on a broiler pan and grill for about 5-10 minutes until charred and blistered. Remove from the broiler and wrap tightly in the foil. Leave for about 15 minutes to loosen the skin. Remove the skin, wipe with paper towels, and dice. Fork through the couscous to remove any lumps. Whisk together **11/2 tablespoons olive oil, 1 teaspoon white wine vinegar, 1 minced garlic clove, salt,** and **freshly ground black pepper** and pour over the couscous. Stir well, then allow to cool. Once cool, add the peppers and some **freshly chopped basil leaves** and stir. Check the seasoning and serve at room temperature. Serves 2

SIDE

STIR-FRIED CABBAGE

Cut **1 onion** into thin slices and cook in **1 tablespoon olive oil** until crisp. Set aside. Heat **2 tablespoons butter** and **1 tablespoon olive oil** in a large frying pan or wok, add **1¾ cups chopped cabbage** and stir-fry for 2–3 minutes. Sprinkle with the crispy onion and serve. Serves 2

DINNER

TOMATO, FETA, ALMOND, AND DATE BAKLAVA

MARIA ELIA

SERVES 4

The distinction between main courses and desserts is vaguer in the Near East than elsewhere. Baklava is a flaky filo pastry dish popular from Greece to Central Asia. It's most familiar in its sweet form, filled with chopped pistachio nuts and drenched in honey or syrup, but this savory version is just as good.

7 tablespoons olive oil

5 Spanish onions, halved and finely chopped

2 garlic cloves, finely chopped

2 teaspoons ground cinnamon

a pinch of sugar

a bunch of dill, finely chopped
(or 3 teaspoons dried)

8 plum tomatoes, peeled and roughly chopped (reserve half of the juices)

3 teaspoons tomato paste

9 large sheets filo pastry

11 tablespoons melted butter

7 tablespoons blanched almonds, chopped finely

4 Medjool dates, pitted and finely sliced (any variety of dates can be used)

8 ounces feta

6 tablespoons honey

Preheat the oven to 350°F. Heat the olive oil in a large, wide pan. Gently cook the onions over low heat, add the garlic, cinnamon, and sugar, and increase the heat. Cook for about 6 minutes, until caramelized. Add the dill, tomatoes, and juices, plus the tomato paste, and cook for about 5 minutes longer, until reduced.

Unfold the filo sheets and cut them in half; keep them covered with a damp cloth to prevent them from drying out. Brush a baking sheet (about 8 x 12 inches) with melted butter, line the pan with a sheet of filo, brush with butter, and repeat until you have a 3-layer thickness.

Spread half the onion mixture over the pastry, top with half the almonds, the dates, and half the feta. Sandwich 3 layers of filo together, brushing each with melted butter and place on top of the onion and feta mix. Top with the remaining onions, almonds, and feta, and again top with a 3-layer thickness of filo. Lightly score the top, cutting diamonds or squares, brush with butter, and splash with a little water. Bake for 30–35 minutes until golden. Let cool a little before serving, then drizzle each portion with honey.

DESSERT

PEARS POACHED WITH STAR ANISE

Peel and core **8 firm dessert pears** and cut them in half. Put them into a bowl and sprinkle with the **juice of ½ lemon**, tossing well. Heat **1⅓ cups water** in a large pan and stir in **¾ cup sugar** until it dissolves completely. Add **5 star anise** and just simmer for 5 minutes to infuse. Then add the pears and bring to a boil. Simmer, covered, until the pears are al dente, stirring a couple of times. Remove the pears with a slotted spoon and keep warm. Keep the pan on the stove and turn up the heat to high, boiling to reduce the poaching liquor by about half. Pour in **2 tablespoons Pernod** and leave to cook for a couple of minutes. Pour the liquor through a sieve onto the pears and serve. Serves 4–6

WEEK 08

BREAKFAST

BIRCHER MUESLI WITH APPLE

A healthy breakfast that will keep hunger pangs at bay until lunchtime. In a bowl, mix together **1 cup rolled oats, 1 tablespoon pumpkin seeds, 1 tablespoon sunflower seeds,** and **¼ cup dried apricots.** Mix in **½ cup apple juice** and ideally chill for at least an hour or overnight. When ready to serve, core **1 eating apple** and coarsely grate it into the bowl (there's no need to peel it), and stir it into the oat mixture, together with **1 tablespoon toasted almonds.** Spoon the mixture into two serving bowls, loosening it with a little more apple juice if it is too thick. Top each with **1 tablespoon of Greek yogurt** and drizzle with **honey.** Serves 2

PACKED LUNCH

PEAR, WALNUT, AND STILTON SALAD

Peel and core **1 ripe pear,** slice lengthwise into thin segments, toss in the **juice of ½ lemon,** and place in a bowl. Add **1 cup arugula, 1 tablespoon chopped toasted walnuts, 1 ounce Stilton,** and some **freshly ground black pepper.** Whisk together **3 teaspoons walnut oil, 1 teaspoon white wine vinegar,** and **a pinch of salt** and drizzle over the salad. Serves 1

LUNCH

PASTA WITH BROCCOLI, SUN-DRIED TOMATOES, AND OLIVES

LIVIA FIRTH

|

SERVES 4

↓

Orecchiette means little ears and that's exactly what the pasta scoops used in this recipe resemble. This dish only has 6 ingredients and takes minutes to make, but the broccoli ensures that it is very tasty.

olive oil
2 garlic cloves, finely chopped
1 tablespoon sun-dried tomatoes
3 heads of broccoli, chopped into florets
1 tablespoon black olives, pitted
1 tablespoon pine nuts
1 pound orecchiette pasta
salt
freshly grated vegetarian Parmesan, to serve

Heat the olive oil in a saucepan and add the garlic. Let the garlic brown over low heat, then turn off and add the sun-dried tomatoes.

Fill a large saucepan with water and bring to a boil, add salt, then the broccoli, and cook until very tender. Remove the broccoli from the pan with a slotted spoon and add to the saucepan with the garlic, sun-dried tomatoes, olives, and pine nuts. Put the pan over low heat and crush the broccoli with a fork until it is mashed.

Add the pasta to the water in which the broccoli had been boiled. Cook the pasta until al dente, then drain and mix it with the broccoli sauce. Serve with some grated Parmesan scattered over the top.

SNACK

SWEET AND SOUR TOFU

Preheat the oven to 400°F. Mix **5 tablespoons light soy sauce, 1 tablespoon chopped lemongrass, 1 thinly sliced red chile, 2 tablespoons white wine vinegar, 2 tablespoons sesame oil,** and **2 teaspoons honey** in a bowl to make a sweet and sour sauce. Put **1 carrot, 1 rib of celery, ½ inch piece of peeled ginger** and **1 garlic clove** in a food processor and process at high speed, pulsing until the vegetables are finely chopped but not puréed. Make deep slashes in the narrow sides of **2 x 4-ounces fried tofu slices** to create a pocket, and stuff with the vegetable mixture. Arrange the slices in a baking pan, cover with the sweet and sour sauce, and bake for 15–20 minutes. Serves 2

DINNER

THAI VEGETABLE CURRY

SERVES 4

In just a few decades, Thai food has grown from relative obscurity into one of the most popular cuisines on Earth. This vegetable curry has many of its classic tastes and textures.

FOR THE CURRY PASTE
2 shallots, roughly chopped
2 garlic cloves, finely chopped
1 tablespoon freshly grated ginger
1 stick lemongrass, finely chopped
2 green chiles, seeded and chopped
zest of 1 lime
small bunch fresh cilantro

1 tablespoon sunflower oil
1 small eggplant, cut into chunks
1 red pepper, seeded and diced
8 baby bella mushrooms, halved (or quartered if large)

14-ounce can coconut milk
6 okra, cut on the diagonal into 3 pieces
8 baby corn, cut on the diagonal into 3 pieces
5–6 ounce can bamboo shoots, drained
handful of sugar snap peas, cut in half on the diagonal
2 handfuls of bean sprouts
soy sauce
soft light brown sugar to taste

TO SERVE
fresh cilantro leaves
jasmine rice
lime wedges

Prepare the curry paste first. Place the shallots, garlic, and ginger in a food processor. Add the lemongrass, chiles, lime zest, and cilantro stalks (reserving the leaves) and pulse the mixture until finely chopped. You can also make this paste using a mortar and pestle if you prefer.

Heat the sunflower oil in a large sauté pan. Add the curry paste and cook over medium heat for 1 minute until the mixture smells fragrant. Add the eggplant, red pepper, and mushrooms and cook for 1 minute, stirring frequently until starting to become tender. Add the coconut milk to the pan with ½ cup of water and bring to a boil. Add the okra, baby corn, and bamboo shoots and continue to cook for 5 minutes or so until the veggies are tender. Finally add the sugar snap peas and bean sprouts and cook for another 30 seconds.

Taste and add a dash of soy sauce or teaspoon of sugar if needed. Serve the curry in bowls, garnished with cilantro leaves with jasmine rice and lime wedges.

DESSERT

FLORENTINES

Preheat the oven to 350°F. Line a baking sheet with parchment paper. Mix together **½ cup chopped sliced almonds, ¼ cup chopped hazelnuts, ¼ cup chopped mixed peel, ¼ cup chopped candied cherries,** and **⅓ cup seedless raisins.** Melt **6 tablespoons butter** in a saucepan, stir in **⅓ cup tightly packed soft light brown sugar,** and heat gently, stirring until the sugar has dissolved. Continue to heat until the mixture just starts to bubble. Remove from the heat and stir in the fruit and nuts. Place spoonfuls of the mixture onto the baking sheet, leaving sufficient space between each for spreading. Bake in batches for 10–12 minutes until golden. As soon as the sheet is removed from the oven, use a knife to tidy any uneven edges. Allow to cool a little. When firm, place on a wire rack until cold. Melt **3 ounces semisweet chocolate** and **3 ounces white chocolate** and coat the flat side of the Florentines, using semisweet chocolate on half the Florentines and white chocolate on the others. Using a fork, draw wavy lines on the chocolate. Leave until set. Makes 16

WEEK 09

BREAKFAST

BREAKFAST FRITTATA

Peel and slice **1 large potato**, place in a pan of water, bring to a boil, then drain thoroughly. Pat the potato dry with paper towels. Crack **4 organic eggs** into a bowl, season with **salt** and **freshly ground black pepper**, and beat lightly. Place a small frying pan over medium heat, pour in **2 tablespoons olive oil**, and add **1 finely chopped onion** and the sliced potato. Cook for 10 minutes until golden, then add to the bowl of eggs. Put the frying pan back over low heat, add another **tablespoon of olive oil**, and pour in the egg mixture. Cook for about 10 minutes or until the egg mixture has set. If you like, arrange some **tomato slices** on top, then place under a preheated broiler for 5 minutes until it is golden. Serves 2

PACKED LUNCH

ROAST VEGETABLE TART

Slice **1 large red onion** into chunky pieces. Slice **3 yellow peppers** into thick strips. Cut **1 eggplant** lengthwise into 1-inch thick slices. Peel **4 garlic cloves**. Combine in a roasting pan and drizzle with **olive oil**. Season with **salt** and **freshly ground black pepper** and scatter with some **fresh thyme leaves**. Roast in a preheated 400°F oven for 30 minutes until the vegetables are soft. Remove the garlic, slice thinly, and return to the pan. Roll out **1 sheet puff pastry** into a rectangle roughly 11 x 6 inches and place on a baking tray. Spread with **3 tablespoons sundried tomato paste**, top with the roast vegetables, and **1 tablespoon chopped black olives**. Sprinkle with **1 cup crumbled goat cheese**. Bake in the oven for 20 minutes until the pastry is crisp and the cheese is golden brown. Serve with a green salad. Serves 4

LUNCH

LEEK AND GOAT CHEESE QUICHE

BRYN WILLIAMS

SERVES 4

The sweetness of leeks combines very well with the tartness of goat cheese in this nicely uncomplicated quiche. The real genius of this recipe, though, is the curry power. It isn't the most obvious ingredient for a dish originating in France but it adds a touch of magic.

7 ounces savory pie crust
2 tablespoons butter
2 leeks, trimmed and finely sliced
salt and freshly ground black pepper

1 teaspoon curry powder
6 organic eggs
2 1/3 cups heavy cream
4 ounces goat cheese

Preheat the oven to 325°F.

Roll out the pastry into a 10-inch quiche pan, leave to rest for 1 hour, and then bake blind for 25 minutes.

Melt the butter in a saucepan, then add the leeks, season with salt and freshly ground black pepper, and add the curry powder. Cook the leeks until soft but not colored.

Break the eggs into a large bowl and gently whisk in the cream. Crumble in the goat cheese and season with salt and freshly ground black pepper.

Place the cooked leeks in the quiche pan. Pour in the egg mixture and bake for 35–45 minutes or until cooked.

SIDE
LEMON BROCCOLI

Heat a little **olive oil** in a large pan and cook **1 sliced garlic clove** until softened. Add **3 cups blanched broccoli** and **the zest and juice of ½ lemon** and heat through. Season to taste with **salt** and **freshly ground black pepper**. Serves 2–3

DINNER
CHICKPEA TAGINE WITH HARISSA

SERVES 4

Strictly speaking, a tagine should be cooked in a traditional North African earthenware pot of the same name. One of the beauties of this recipe is that you don't actually need one to make it. Another is that it is extremely Moorish, if you'll pardon the pun. Harissa is a spicy paste made from chile, garlic, and various other seasonings. You can buy it in many stores.

1 teaspoon cumin seeds
1 teaspoon coriander seeds
1 large onion, finely chopped
2 carrots, peeled
1 large sweet potato, peeled and
    cut into chunks
1 red pepper, seeded and diced
1 rib celery, chopped
1 zucchini, chopped
a pinch of saffron
2 tablespoons olive oil
2 garlic cloves, minced

1 tablespoon grated fresh ginger
1 cinnamon stick
8-ounce can chopped tomatoes
14-ounce can chickpeas, drained
2⅓ cups vegetable stock
1 tablespoon honey
salt and freshly ground black pepper

TO SERVE
wholewheat or barley couscous
harissa

Put the cumin and coriander seeds in a small dry frying pan and toast over medium heat for 30 seconds until fragrant. Lightly grind using a mortar and pestle. Soak the saffron in 1 tablespoon of boiling water.

Heat the olive oil in a large sauté pan over medium heat. Add the onion and cook for 3–4 minutes until tender but not colored. Add the ground spices, garlic, grated ginger, and cinnamon stick and continue to cook for a minute. Add the chopped tomatoes and add the vegetables and the drained chickpeas to the pan. Stir to coat the veggies in the spiced mixture and add the stock. Bring to a boil, reduce the heat to a simmer, and continue to cook for 20–25 minutes until the vegetables are tender. Add the honey, and season with salt and freshly ground black pepper.

Serve in bowls with couscous and a good spoonful of harissa.

DESSERT
APPLE SYLLABUB

Peel, core, and chop **3 Golden Delicious apples** and place in a saucepan. Add **2 tablespoons water** and **1 tablespoon superfine sugar** to the saucepan, cover, and cook for 8–10 minutes or until soft. Allow to cool. Place **½ cup sweet white wine**, **zest** and **juice of 1 lemon**, **4 tablespoons superfine sugar**, and **1 cup heavy cream** in a bowl, and whisk until the mixture holds its shape. Carefully fold in the apple purée and spoon into 6 tall glasses. Chill for 1–2 hours, then decorate with **fresh mint leaves** and **apple slices**. Serves 6

WEEK 10

BREAKFAST

POACHED QUINCE WITH VANILLA

Dissolve **1 cup and 2 tablespoons sugar** in 1¹/2 **cups water** slowly and then, when the sugar is melted, bring to a boil and make a syrup, cooking for 2 minutes. Meanwhile, peel, core, and quarter **4 ripe quinces**, and slip them into the hot syrup, together with **6 cloves**. Simmer for about 35-40 minutes and serve, together with some **plain yogurt**, if you like. Serves 4

PACKED LUNCH

PUY LENTILS AND ROASTED RED PEPPERS WITH GOAT CHEESE

People have been cooking with lentils for ten thousand years. Rich in protein and vitamins, they perform a vital dietary role in some of the poorest parts of the world. Many cooks consider Puy lentils to be the best variety. They are a beautiful greeny blue and have a unique, peppery flavor.

3 red peppers
1 cup Puy lentils
1 red onion, whole
stem each of fresh parsley, oregano, and thyme
4 tablespoons sun-dried tomatoes, chopped

4 ounces crumbled goat cheese
salt and freshly ground black pepper
4 tablespoons freshly chopped parsley, oregano, and thyme
4 tablespoons extra virgin olive oil
1 tablespoon lemon juice

Roast the peppers on a baking sheet in an oven preheated to 400°F for 30 minutes. Remove from the oven and put them into a plastic bag. When cooled, seed and peel the peppers, then cut them into strips. Set aside.

SERVES 4

Wash the Puy lentils thoroughly and cook them, covered in 1¹/2 cups water, with the whole onion and herbs. These lentils cook faster than other types, in about 15 minutes. Drain. Roughly chop the onion and add back into the lentils. Discard the herbs. While still warm, add the tomatoes and goat cheese and stir gently. Season.

Make the dressing by combining the rest of the ingredients. Pour dressing over the lentil mixture and mix well. Arrange the lentils with the slices of red pepper on individual plates. Sprinkle with the herbs and serve.

LUNCH

CHEESE AND CHIVE POTATO JACKETS

Preheat the oven to 400°F. Place **4 medium baking potatoes** on a baking sheet and cook for 1¹/2 hours until soft. Remove from the oven, cut in half, and scoop out the potato into a bowl. Combine with **2 tablespoons butter** and ¹/3 **cup warmed organic milk** to achieve a smooth creamy texture. Stir in **1 cup grated Cheddar** and **2 tablespoons chives**. Whisk **4 organic egg whites** in a bowl until they form soft peaks. Fold the egg whites into the mashed potato and spoon back into the potato skins. Return to the oven and cook for 10-15 minutes or until golden brown and well risen. A good green salad goes excellently. Serves 4

SIDE

HERB BREAD

Preheat an oven to 350°F. Slice a stone-baked **baguette** lengthwise, taking care not to cut all the way through. Melt **6 tablespoons butter**, stir in **2 tablespoons freshly chopped parsley, 1 tablespoon freshly chopped basil or oregano, and 1 minced garlic clove,** then spread along the inside of each cut in the bread. Wrap in foil and bake for 10 minutes. Serves 4

DINNER

TAGLIATELLE WITH MUSHROOM SAUCE

SERVES 4

Porcini (little pigs in Italian) are known as cèpes in France and penny buns in some parts of England. They are dense, almost meaty wild mushrooms with pores on their undersides instead of gills. Drying them concentrates the forest-like taste. They give this lovely pasta dish its considerable depth of flavor.

1½ ounces dried porcini mushrooms
2 tablespoons olive oil
1 large onion, finely chopped
8 ounces baby bella mushrooms,
    cut into quarters

salt and freshly ground black pepper
1 pound tagliatelle
6 ounces gorgonzola dolcelatte, crumbled
handful of flat-leaf parsley, finely snipped

Put the porcini into a bowl and cover with 1¾ cups of boiling water. Let them soak and soften for about half an hour. Then drain and gently squeeze out any excess water from the porcini.

In a frying pan, heat the oil and add the onion, cooking for 5 minutes until translucent and soft but not colored. Add the baby bella mushrooms and coat them well in the olive oil, then cover the pan and leave to release their juices, shaking occasionally, for about 15–20 minutes. Chop the porcini finely and stir them into the pan. Continue cooking for about 10 minutes and season with a little salt and freshly ground black pepper.

In the meantime, boil a large pot of salted, cold water then cook the pasta until al dente. Drain well and put into a large serving bowl. Check the seasoning of the mushroom sauce and pour it over the tagliatelle, followed by the gorgonzola dolcelatte. Stir gently to mix the sauce—the heat will melt the dolcelatte. Sprinkle with the parsley and serve.

DESSERT

CARROT CAKE

STELLA McCARTNEY

Grease the insides of two 8-inch cake pans and line the bases with a disk of buttered parchment paper. Preheat the oven to 350°F. Put **1 cup walnuts** into a small roasting pan and toast in the preheated oven for 5 minutes. Reserve a handful to decorate and roughly chop the remainder and let cool slightly. Sift together **3¼ cups all-purpose flour, 2 teaspoons baking powder, 1 teaspoon baking soda, and ½ teaspoon ground cinnamon.** In another bowl beat together **3 large organic eggs, 1⅓ cups peanut or sunflower oil, 2 cups sugar, and 1 teaspoon vanilla extract** until smooth. Add the toasted walnuts, **1 pound coarsely grated carrots, ⅓ cup raisins, 1 cup shredded coconut, and 2 tablespoons of the juice from an orange and its zest,** and mix until thoroughly combined. Stir in the sifted dry ingredients until smooth and divide the batter evenly between the prepared pans. Bake in the preheated oven for about 30–35 minutes or until a toothpick comes out clean when inserted into the middle of the cakes. Remove the cakes from the oven and cool in the tins for 3–4 minutes then invert onto a wire cooling rack and leave until completely cold. Beat together **2 tablespoons unsalted softened butter** and **3 tablespoons honey or maple syrup** until combined. Add **1 cup cream cheese** and mix until smooth. Place 1 of the cake layers on a serving plate and spread with half of the cream cheese frosting. Top with the second cake and cover the top with the remaining cream cheese. Scatter with the reserved toasted walnuts to serve. Serves 8–10

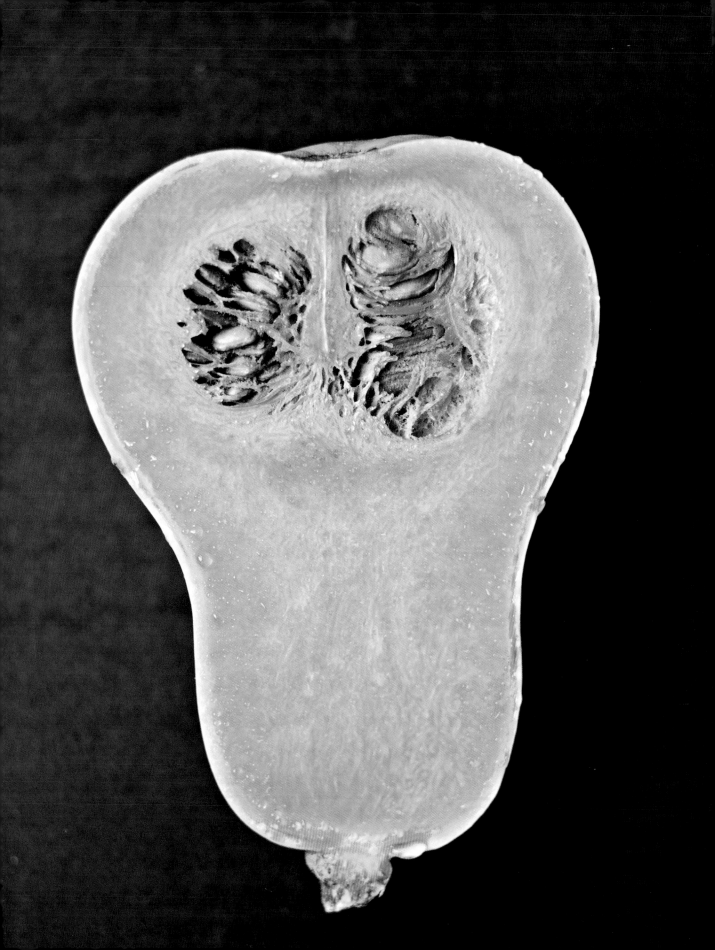

WEEK 11

BREAKFAST

ROASTED MUSHROOMS, TOMATOES, AND PINE NUTS

Preheat the oven to 400°F. Place **4 trimmed portobello mushrooms** on a baking sheet, stalk side up. Season with **sea salt** and **freshly ground black pepper**. Drizzle with **1 tablespoon olive oil** and bake in the oven for 10 minutes. After 5 minutes, add **1 cup cherry tomatoes on the vine** and return to the oven. Meanwhile toast **1 tablespoon pine nuts** in a dry frying pan, taking care not to burn them, and chop **1 tablespoon flat-leaf parsley**. When the mushrooms are tender, remove from the oven, sprinkle with the pine nuts and parsley, and serve with the tomatoes on the side. Serves 2

PACKED LUNCH

SPICY BURRITO WITH SALSA AND GUACAMOLE

In a small bowl, mix **2 chopped scallions** and **1/2 sliced red chile** with some **salt** and **freshly ground black pepper** and set aside. Beat **4 organic eggs** and **1/3 cup organic milk** with a fork and add some salt and freshly ground black pepper. Heat **1 tablespoon olive oil** in a large nonstick pan. Cook the spring onion and chile for 1 minute, then pour in the egg mix. Gently scramble the eggs by dragging the egg mixture as it sets into the middle of the pan. Remove from the heat and mix in **a handful of freshly grated Cheddar**. Divide between **2 tortilla wraps**. Tuck up the top and bottom of each wrap and roll up, then slice in half and serve with **homemade tomato salsa** (see page 102), **sour cream**, and **guacamole** (see page 102), if you wish. Serves 2

LUNCH

ROASTED BUTTERNUT SQUASH WITH PINE NUTS AND GOAT CHEESE

SERVES 2

Butternut squash is extremely tasty and the seeds can be eaten raw, fried, or roasted. Squash is an abbreviation of askuta squash, the Native North American Indian word, and means eaten raw or uncooked.

1 small butternut squash
1 garlic clove, minced
2 tablespoons olive oil
1 red chile, seeded and finely chopped
1 teaspoon fresh thyme leaves
4 ounces goat cheese, crumbled
1/3 cup pine nuts

Preheat the oven to 400°F.

Cut the squash in half, scoop out the seeds, score the flesh with a sharp knife, and place on a baking sheet. In a bowl, mix together the garlic, olive oil, chile, and thyme, and brush over the cut sides of the squash, pouring any excess into the wells left after seeding. Place in the oven and bake for about 40 minutes until the flesh is tender and can be easily pierced with a fork.

Mix together the goat cheese and pine nuts and spoon over the top of each of the squash halves. Return them to the oven and bake for another 10 minutes until the cheese has melted and the pine nuts are lightly toasted.

SNACK

WHOLE ARTICHOKE WITH HAZELNUT DRESSING

OLIVER PEYTON

Bring a large pot of **salted water** to a boil. Cut **a lemon** in half and add it to the water. Break the stalks off **4 whole globe artichokes**. Boil in the salt water for 30 minutes, or until the outer leaves pull off easily. Stick a skewer into the core of the artichoke to check that the heart is tender. Remove from the pot to cool slightly, turned upside down to drain. Discard the center leaves and the choke (fur) in the middle to make room for the vinaigrette. To make the vinaigrette, start by roasting **1 cup hazelnuts** in the oven until golden brown. Put them in a blender along with **2 tablespoons white wine vinegar** and **a tablespoon of English mustard**, then add enough **olive oil** until you have the correct consistency for a vinaigrette, and season to taste. Pour the vinaigrette into the centers of the artichokes. To eat, pull off the remaining leaves, dip the broken end into the vinaigrette and eat. Serves 4

DINNER

EGGPLANT, POTATO, AND PEPPER STEW

SERVES 4

This rich, Mediterranean-inspired stew is full of flavors, which mature if there is any left over for the next day.

3 tablespoons olive oil
1 onion, chopped
1 rib celery, chopped
2 garlic cloves, minced
1 red pepper, seeded and cut into large chunks
1 medium zucchini, cut into large chunks
1 eggplant, cut into large chunks
2 medium potatoes, peeled and cut into large chunks
1 teaspoon dried oregano

2 x 14-ounce cans tomatoes
1 1/3 cups vegetable stock
salt and freshly ground black pepper
1 teaspoon sugar
14-ounce can white beans, drained and rinsed
4 tablespoons kalamata olives
2 tablespoons toasted pine nuts
4 ounces crumbled feta
2 tablespoons freshly chopped flat-leaf parsley

Heat half of the olive oil in a large pot or dutch oven, add the chopped onion and celery, and cook until tender but not colored. Add the garlic and cook for another minute. While the onion is cooking, prepare the other vegetables.

Add the remaining oil, chopped peppers, zucchini, and eggplant to the pan and cook for 3–4 minutes. Add the potatoes, oregano, canned tomatoes, and vegetable stock. Bring to a boil, season with salt and freshly ground black pepper, add the sugar, cover the pan, and reduce the heat to low. Simmer for about 25–30 minutes until all of the veggies are tender. Add the beans and olives and continue to cook for another 5 minutes.

Check the seasoning, adding more salt and freshly ground black pepper if needed. Scatter with toasted pine nuts, crumbled feta, and chopped parsley to serve.

DESSERT

LEMON DRIZZLE SQUARES

Preheat the oven to 350°F. Grease a 9 x 12-inch baking pan. In a large bowl, beat together **14 tablespoons butter** and **1 cup superfine sugar** until light and fluffy. Beat in **3 organic eggs**, one at a time. Gently fold in **1 cup sifted self-rising flour**, then gently stir in **1/2 cup organic milk** and the **grated zest of 2 lemons**. Spoon the mixture into the prepared pan, smooth the surface, and bake for 30 minutes until golden. Using a skewer or toothpick, prick the cake all over. Mix together the **juice of the 2 lemons** with **1/2 cup granulated sugar**, and spoon over the cake. Leave to cool, then cut into squares. Makes 10 squares

WEEK 12

BREAKFAST

ONION AND WALNUT MUFFINS

Preheat the oven to 425°F. Line two 12-hole muffin pans with muffin cases. Peel **1 large onion**, cut it into quarters, and purée. Beat together **18 tablespoons butter**, **2 organic eggs**, and **6 tablespoons sugar**, and add the onion purée. Stir in **1 teaspoon sea salt**, **1 teaspoon baking powder**, **2 cups shelled and coarsely crushed walnuts**, and **3 cups all-purpose flour** one by one and mix thoroughly. Fill the muffin cups almost full. Bake for 20 minutes, or until they are puffed and well browned. Serve warm. Makes 20

PACKED LUNCH

PARSNIP SOUP

Heat **2 tablespoons butter** and **1 tablespoon oil** in a large pan. Add **1 chopped onion**, **1 peeled and chopped carrot**, and **2 cups chopped parsnips** and cook gently for 5–6 minutes until softened but not browned. Add **2½ cups vegetable stock** and bring to a boil. Simmer for 25–30 minutes until the vegetables are soft. Purée the soup in a blender until smooth and return to the pan. You may have to do this in batches. Add **salt** and **freshly ground black pepper** to taste and serve hot with **a swirl of cream**, and **1 tablespoon freshly chopped parsley**. Serves 2–3

LUNCH

BAKED MUSHROOM, MASCARPONE, AND POLENTA

KATIE CALDESI

SERVES 6

Polenta—basically cooked dough made from ground corn—was originally a peasant food. Now it regularly appears on the menus of chic restaurants. It's funny stuff. It can be starchy if it isn't cooked properly, but well handled, as in this cheesy dish, it's delightful.

1 cup uncooked polenta, or 21 ounces cooked polenta
salt and freshly ground black pepper
2 bay leaves
1 onion, sliced in rings
7 tablespoons butter
10 ounces mushrooms (mixed or one type)
2 garlic cloves, finely chopped

2 stems of rosemary leaves
1 cup mascarpone
1 cup organic milk
a good pinch of grated nutmeg
2 cups vegetarian Parmesan

Follow the cooking instructions on the package for the uncooked polenta, using half water, half milk if desired, and adding salt and the bay leaves for extra flavor. Bring the liquid to a boil in a large saucepan, then whisk in the polenta. Keep stirring until all the polenta is incorporated, keeping it over low heat for 40–45 minutes. Pour into a metal pan or glass dish and allow to cool and set. This will take 1–1½ hours.

Preheat the oven to 350°F. Cook the onion rings with a little salt and freshly ground black pepper in half the butter until soft. In another frying pan, cook the mushrooms, garlic, and rosemary in the rest of the butter over high heat, adding salt and freshly ground black pepper to taste. Meanwhile, mix the mascarpone and milk with the nutmeg.

Cut the polenta into quarter-inch slices. Grease a medium ovenproof dish. Place half the polenta slices in the base, scatter with the fried onions followed by the mushrooms, sprinkle with pepper, and add half of the Parmesan. Top with half the mascarpone sauce, and arrange the remaining polenta slices on top. Finish with the remaining sauce and top with the remaining Parmesan. Transfer the dish to the oven and bake for 30 minutes, or until bubbling and browned.

SNACK

HONEY-ROASTED NUTS AND SEEDS

Preheat the oven to 350°F. Combine **1 pound mixed nuts (almonds, brazil nuts, cashews, peanuts, pecans, walnuts)**, **½ cup pumpkin seeds** and **½ cup sunflower seeds** in a bowl. Add **2 tablespoons olive oil** and **2 tablespoons honey** and mix well so the nuts are evenly coated. Transfer to a large baking sheet and spread out. Roast in the oven for 10 minutes, turning the nuts regularly so they brown evenly. When golden, remove from the oven and sprinkle with **1 teaspoon sea salt**. Serves 3-4

DINNER

BAKED PENNE WITH DOLCELATTE AND RADICCHIO

SERVES 4

Radicchio is quite bitter when raw but cooking it mellows the flavor nicely. Some penne are smooth but the rigate kind have little ridges running along them. This allows sauces to cling to them, in this case a creamy mushroom and dolcelatte mixture.

7 ounces penne rigate
4 tablespoons butter
4 ounces button mushrooms, halved
2 garlic cloves, finely chopped
1 tablespoon finely chopped fresh sage
1 small head of radicchio, cored and shredded finely

salt and freshly ground black pepper
1 cup heavy cream
½ cup vegetarian Parmesan, finely grated
6 ounces gorgonzola dolcelatte, cubed
fresh sage leaves, to garnish

Preheat the oven to 400°F. Grease a 9 x 11-inch ovenproof dish.

Cook the pasta in a large pan of boiling salted water, according to the package instructions, until al dente, then drain.

Meanwhile, melt the butter in a large frying pan and cook the mushrooms and garlic for about 5 minutes until softened. Stir in the sage and radicchio and remove the pan from the heat. Season with salt and freshly ground pepper.

In a large bowl, stir together the cream, half of the Parmesan and the dolcelatte. Add the mushroom mixture and pasta. Season to taste with salt and freshly ground black pepper. Spoon into the ovenproof dish, sprinkle with the remaining Parmesan, and bake for about 20 minutes until golden and bubbling. To serve, sprinkle with some fresh sage.

DESSERT

RHUBARB, APPLE, AND OAT CRUMBLE

Preheat the oven to 400°F. Peel, quarter, and core **3 large cooking apples** and cut into chunks. Slice **4-5 washed and trimmed sticks of rhubarb** and slice into similar size pieces to the apple. Combine the fruit in a large bowl, add **½ teaspoon ground cinnamon** and **2-3 tablespoons sugar**, and mix well. Scoop the fruit into an ovenproof dish. Sift **2¼ cups all-purpose flour** into another bowl and add **12 tablespoons diced unsalted butter**. Rub the the butter into the flour until it resembles fine breadcrumbs. Add **6 tablespoons unrefined sugar**, **1 cup rolled oats**, and **a pinch of salt**, and mix thoroughly. Sprinkle the crumble evenly over the prepared fruit and place the dish on a baking sheet. Cook the crumble on the middle shelf of the oven for 45 minutes or until the fruit is bubbling and the top is golden. Serve with **heavy cream**. Serves 4-6

WEEK 13

BREAKFAST

WELSH RAREBIT

Preheat the broiler and toast **4 large slices of bread** on one side. Mix together **2 tablespoons softened butter, 1 teaspoon English mustard, salt** and **freshly ground black pepper,** vegetarian **Worcestershire sauce, 1¹/2 cups grated Cheddar,** and **2 tablespoons organic milk.** Spread the mixture over the untoasted sides of the bread and broil for 2–3 minutes until browned. Serve immediately. Serves 4

PACKED LUNCH

LEEK AND POTATO SOUP

Cut **3 large potatoes** into ¹/2-inch cubes and slice **1 leek** into 2-inch rounds. Heat some **olive oil** in a saucepan over medium heat, stir in the potato and leek, and cook for 2 minutes. Add **2¹/2 cups vegetable stock** and bring to a boil over high heat. When it is boiling, turn down the heat to low, and simmer for 20 minutes. When the vegetables are cooked, take the saucepan off the heat. With a ladle, carefully place 3 ladlefuls of the soup in a blender and purée for 10 seconds, then pour the blended soup into a big bowl. Repeat the blending until the saucepan is empty. Pour the blended soup back into the saucepan and reheat gently. Add **²/3 cup semi-skimmed organic milk, salt,** and **freshly ground black pepper,** and simmer for 2 minutes more. Serves 4

LUNCH

SPICY TOFU WITH GINGER

JOSEPHINE FAIRLEY

Tofu is very good at taking on the flavors of whatever it is marinated in. In this instance, it becomes infused with the enlivening taste of ginger. Tamari is a rich, dark variety of soy sauce.

³/4 cup grated ginger
   (I use a food processor for grating)
5 garlic cloves, finely chopped
¹/3 cup tamari soy sauce
¹/3 cup olive oil
1¹/4 cups red or white wine (I use leftover wine
   rather than open something new)
1¹/2 teaspoons turmeric
4 tablespoons ginger cordial
   (you could also use ginger beer)
2 pounds firm tofu

TO SERVE
brown rice
salad
broccoli
organic sourdough bread

SERVES 4

Combine the grated ginger together with all the other ingredients apart from the tofu in a food processor and pulse until smooth.

Cut the tofu into rectangular 1-inch cubes. (The smaller the cube, the more the sauce gets into the middle of the tofu; however, too small and they'll become mushy when cooking.)

Pour the sauce over the cubed tofu in a casserole with a lid, and leave to infuse in the fridge for anything between 4 to 24 hours. (The longer the better is my experience.)

Bake in the oven at 350°F for around 35 minutes, then remove the lid and cook for another 10 minutes.

Serve with brown rice and salad or green vegetable like broccoli. A good hunk of organic sourdough bread also soaks up the sauce beautifully!

SIDE
ROASTED HERBY MUSHROOMS

Preheat the oven to 350°F. Put **12 ounces baby bella mushrooms** in a baking dish, stalk side up. Sprinkle with **1 teaspoon freshly chopped rosemary leaves, 1 teaspoon fresh thyme leaves, a pinch of sea salt,** and **freshly ground black pepper.** Drizzle with **2 tablespoons olive oil** and **2 teaspoons lemon juice.** Bake for 30 minutes or until the mushrooms are tender. Serves 4

DINNER
PIZZA TWO WAYS

LAURA BAILEY

SERVES 4

You are making two pizzas here, one topped with red onion and mozzarella, the other with butternut squash and feta. They make a lovely pair. You wouldn't call butternut squash a standard pizza topping, but it turns out to be an inspired one.

FOR THE PIZZA DOUGH
2½ cups bread flour
½ teaspoon instant yeast
a large pinch of salt
1 tablespoon all-purpose flour
½ cup water

FOR THE TOPPING
¼ butternut squash, peeled and thinly sliced into crescent shapes
1 garlic clove, finely sliced
2 large red onions, cut into 24 wedges
⅓ cup water
2 tablespoons balsamic vinegar
3 tablespoons soft brown sugar
pesto
4 ounces mozzarella
4 ounces feta

Preheat the oven to 350°F.

To make the pizza dough, combine all the dry ingredients in the bowl of an electric mixer with the dough hook attachment. Slowly add the water. Allow the ingredients to combine and continue kneading the dough on a low speed for about 10 minutes. Leave the dough in the mixer bowl, cover it with plastic wrap, and leave in a warm place for about an hour.

Place the butternut squash and garlic in a baking dish. Drizzle with olive oil and sprinkle with some salt. Cook in the preheated oven for 15-20 minutes. When the squash is cooked, remove from the oven and increase the heat to 400°F.

Heat some olive oil in a saucepan, add the onions, and brown for about 5 minutes or so. Add the water, balsamic vinegar, and soft brown sugar. Bring to a boil, put a lid on the saucepan, and reduce the heat. Simmer until most of the liquid has evaporated. You should finish up with sweet, sticky, deep purple onions.

Divide the dough in two. Dust a work surface with flour, and roll each one out to about 12-14-inch rounds. They should be nice and thin. Place each pizza base on a baking sheet.

Spread a fine layer of pesto on each base. On 1 base, add the caramelized onion—you won't need all of it—then tear the mozzarella and place on the pizza. On the other base, add the butternut squash and crumble the feta over the top. Season with a little salt and freshly ground black pepper, and bake in the oven for about 10-12 minutes. Serve with a handful of arugula on each and some toasted pine nuts on the butternut squash pizza.

DESSERT
VICTORIA SPONGE CAKE

Heat oven to 375°F. Grease two 8-inch cake pans and line with parchment paper. In a large bowl, beat **14 tablespoons butter, 1¾ cups superfine sugar, 4 organic eggs, 1¾ cups self-rising flour, 1 teaspoon baking powder,** and **⅓ cup organic milk** until you have a smooth batter. Divide the mixture between the pans, smooth the surface, then bake for about 20 minutes until golden. Invert onto a rack, and cool completely. For the filling, beat **7 tablespoons softened butter** until smooth, then gradually beat in **1 cup sifted confectioner's sugar** and **½ teaspoon vanilla extract.** Spread over the bottom of 1 of the layers, then top with **some strawberry jam,** and sandwich the second layer on top. Dust with a little **confectioner's sugar** before serving. Makes 8 slices

WEEK 01

BREAKFAST
CINNAMON CREPES

Mix 1³/4 cups all-purpose flour, 1 tablespoon baking powder, and 1 tablespoon sugar then add 1 organic egg and up to 1 cup organic milk until you have a thick batter. Rest the batter in the fridge for 30 minutes. Melt some butter in a nonstick pan, then drop in spoonfuls of the batter. When little holes appear in the surface, flip and cook until golden on each side. Sprinkle with ground cinnamon and drizzle with some honey, if you wish. Serves 4

PACKED LUNCH
BLACK OLIVE, ENDIVE, AND ORANGE SALAD

Take 2 good endive heads and remove any damaged outer leaves before cutting them into slices about ¹/2-inch across. Make a dressing by mixing 3 tablespoons extra virgin olive oil with 1 tablespoon white wine vinegar, salt, and freshly ground black pepper, and pour this over the endive in a small bowl, tossing well. Peel and remove the pith from 1 large blood orange then divide into segments and cut each segment in 2. Add to the salad, along with ¹/2 cup pitted black kalamata olives. Toss well and serve. Serves 2

LUNCH
ALE AND PUFF PASTRY PIE
THE VEGETARIAN SOCIETY

SERVES 4

Being vegetarian, even if it's only for one day a week, doesn't mean you have to forsake the joys full-flavored dishes. The light ale in this dish does wondrous things to the mushrooms at its heart. It is also an incredibly easy pie to make.

3 tablespoons margarine
2 large bunches scallions, with the bottom
 3 inches chopped
1 pound small baby bella mushrooms, cut into
 2-inch pieces
1 tablespoon cornstarch
¹/2 teaspoon yeast extract (or a few dashes
 of soy sauce)
1 cup light ale
1 sheet ready-rolled puff pastry organic milk
organic milk or soy milk

Preheat an oven to 400°F.

Melt 2 tablespoons margarine in a large nonstick frying pan. Sauté the chopped scallions briefly. Add the mushrooms to the pan. Continue to sauté for 5 minutes until starting to color, stirring to prevent sticking.

Remove from the heat and sprinkle with the cornstarch. Once back on the heat, add the yeast extract (or soy sauce) and ale. Cook for another 5 minutes or until the mushrooms begin to soften. Use more ale if the mixture seems too dry.

Divide the mixture into four small ovenproof dishes, then cut out four pastry circles to place on top, leaving some room to rise. Brush with milk or soya milk and make a small hole in the top to let the steam escape. Bake for 20 minutes until golden.

SIDE
PARSNIP GRATIN

Preheat the oven to 400°F. To make the sauce melt **2 tablespoons butter** in a saucepan, add **1/2 cup all-purpose flour** and mix to a smooth paste. Cook for 2 minutes, stirring continuously. Remove the saucepan from the heat and gradually blend in **1¹/2 cups organic milk**. Return to the heat and bring gently to a boil, stirring continuously until the sauce thickens. Stir in **5 tablespoons crème fraîche** and season with **salt** and **freshly ground black pepper**. Place **2 cups cooked parsnip chunks** in an ovenproof dish and cover with the sauce. Sprinkle with **2 cups fresh breadcrumbs** and **2 tablespoons freshly grated Parmesan**, and bake for 25–30 minutes or until the top is golden brown. Serves 4

DINNER
SPELT RISOTTO WITH BUTTERNUT SQUASH, SPINACH, CHESTNUTS, AND GOAT CHEESE

SERVES 4

Spelt is an ancient form of wheat, tastier and more nutritious than its inbred cousins. Quite a lot of people with wheat intolerance are fine with it. This healthy risotto is a great way to get acquainted with it.

1 butternut squash, peeled, seeded
   and cut into chunks
8 sage leaves, chopped
4 garlic cloves, whole and lightly bruised
4 tablespoons olive oil
1 tablespoon unsalted butter
4 shallots, chopped
1¹/4 cups pearled spelt

2/3 cup dry white wine
2¹/2 cups hot vegetable stock
2 handfuls of baby leaf spinach
10 chestnuts, cooked, peeled, and
   roughly chopped
salt and freshly ground black pepper
hard goat cheese or pecorino

Preheat the oven to 375°F.

Put the butternut squash in a roasting pan, add the chopped sage and whole, bruised garlic cloves, season, and toss in 2–3 tablespoons of olive oil. Roast for about 25 minutes until tender and starting to brown at the edges.

Meanwhile, start making the risotto. Heat the remaining oil and the butter in a large sauté pan over medium heat. Add the chopped shallots and cook until tender but not colored. Add the spelt and stir to coat in the shallots and butter. Continue to cook for 1 minute until the spelt starts to smell slightly nutty. Pour the white wine into the pan, stirring all the time. Allow most of the wine to evaporate and then add the stock a ladleful at a time, stirring frequently, until all of the stock has been absorbed and the spelt is tender.

Add the roasted butternut squash to the pan along with the baby leaf spinach and chestnuts. Stir to combine, and season well with salt and freshly ground black pepper. Using a vegetable peeler, shave the goat cheese over the risotto and serve immediately.

DESSERT
CHOCOLATE MARZIPAN DATES

Pit **12 fresh dates** by scoring 1 side of the date and stuff with **2–3 ounces marzipan**. Dip the dates in **3 ounces melted dark chocolate** and roll in **1/4 cup chopped hazelnuts**. Place on a piece of parchment paper and chill in the refrigerator until set. Makes 12

WEEK 02

BREAKFAST

ENGLISH BREAKFAST MUFFINS

Dissolve **1 package dried yeast** and **1/2 teaspoon sugar** in **a little tepid organic milk**. Sift **2 cups all-purpose flour** into a bowl, add **a pinch of salt,** and make a well in the center. Pour in the yeast mixture and combine until it forms a dough. Cover the bowl and leave somewhere warm until the dough has doubled in size, about 30 minutes. Dust a work surface with flour, and roll out the dough to a thickness of about **1/2 inch**. Cut into 8 rounds, each about 2–3 inches in diameter. Place a nonstick pan on very low heat and add **1 tablespoon oil**. Cook the muffins for 5–7 minutes on each side until lightly golden brown. To serve, cool slightly, then split in half and lightly toast. Makes 8

PACKED LUNCH

CURRIED EGG, ALMOND, AND BROWN RICE STIR FRY

Cook **1 1/4 cups long grain brown rice** in lightly salted water for 30–35 minutes or until just tender. Drain, rinse under cold water, and drain again. Heat **4 tablespoons sunflower oil** in a wok or large frying pan over high heat. Shred **1 small cabbage** and add it to the wok or pan with **1 finely chopped garlic clove** and stir-fry for 3 minutes or until the cabbage begins to soften. Stir in **2/3 cup shelled almonds**, the rice, **1 teaspoon Madras curry powder**, and **1 teaspoon ground turmeric,** and cook for 2 minutes more. Chop and mix in **6 hard-boiled organic eggs**. Serves 4

LUNCH

BEET, RED ONION, AND ENDIVE SALAD

STELLA McCARTNEY

SERVES 4

Endive is grown in the dark to produce tight, pale heads that are bitter but in a good way. The pears and feta in this recipe take the edge off it, as do the beets.

5 golfball-size beets, trimmed of stalk and leaves
salt and freshly ground black pepper
3 tablespoons olive oil
1 tablespoon red wine vinegar
1 cup pecans
2 tablespoons clear honey
2 red onions, cut into wedges
3 garlic cloves, whole and unpeeled
2 ripe pears, quartered, cored, and sliced

2 heads endive, trimmed into separate leaves
large handful of wild arugula
1 heaping cup feta, crumbled

FOR THE DRESSING
3 tablespoons walnut oil
juice of 1/2 lemon
1 rounded teaspoon Dijon mustard

Preheat the oven to 350°F. Place a large piece of foil in a small roasting pan, put the beets in the middle, season, and drizzle with half of the olive oil and the red wine vinegar. Wrap the foil over and seal tightly. Roast the beets for 1 hour or until tender when tested with the point of a sharp knife. Remove from the roasting pan, unwrap, and cool.

Put the pecans in the roasting pan and drizzle with the honey. Stir to coat then roast for about 10 minutes until sticky and glazed. Remove from the roasting pan and cool the nuts on a plate. Put the onions on a baking sheet, add the garlic cloves, drizzle with the remaining olive oil, and roast for about 30 minutes until tender and starting to caramelize.

To make the dressing, squeeze the roasted garlic cloves from their skins into a small bowl, add the remaining ingredients and gently whisk until just combined. Peel the beets and cut into wedges. In a large serving bowl, layer the beets, onion, pears, endive, wild arugula, crumbled feta, and honey roast pecans. Generously drizzle with the dressing and serve immediately.

SIDE
ROASTED ACORN SQUASH

Preheat the oven to 350°F. Allow **¼ acorn squash** per person. Cut each squash in half and remove the seeds and fibers. Place in a greased ovenproof dish and drizzle with **1 tablespoon balsamic vinegar, 2 tablespoons honey,** and **1 tablespoon lemon juice** for each serving. Cook in the oven for 40 minutes until tender, turning over halfway. Serves 2

DINNER
LEEK AND RICOTTA TART

The French for leek is poireau, which is related to the word for pear (poire). The two come from very different families, but there's definitely a connection in their sweet softness when cooked. The combination of pine nuts and raisins with leeks may well be new to you but it's certainly a successful one.

4 largish leeks, trimmed and roughly chopped
2 tablespoons olive oil
2 garlic cloves, finely chopped
8 ounces ricotta
2 tablespoons toasted pine nuts
3 tablespoons raisins, softened in warm water
1 organic egg
salt and freshly ground black pepper

FOR THE PASTRY
7 tablespoons butter
1½ cups all-purpose flour
3 tablespoons water
pinch of salt

SERVES 4

Make the pastry by crumbling the butter into the flour and then adding water to make a dough. Add the salt and sprinkle with extra flour. Wrap in plastic wrap and chill in the fridge for 30 minutes.

Preheat the oven to 375°F.

Steam the leeks gently for about 10 minutes and drain. In a heavy-bottomed frying pan, heat the oil and gently cook the garlic. Then add the leeks and stir to coat well with oil; cook for about 5 minutes, stirring occasionally. Remove from the heat.

In a bowl, mix the ricotta with the pine nuts and raisins, and bind with the egg. Add the leeks, mix well, and season, then set aside to cool. Gently roll out the pastry to fit an 8-inch tart tin. Prick the base and bake blind for 10–15 minutes. Fill the tart with the leek and ricotta mixture, and return to the oven to cook for another 30 minutes or until risen and golden.

DESSERT
EASY CHOCOLATE FUDGE CAKE

Preheat the oven to 350°F. Grease a 1 quart baking dish. Sift **1 cup all-purpose flour** into a mixing bowl and add **1 teaspoon baking powder, 2 tablespoons cocoa powder,** and **½ cup sugar.** Make a well in the center, pour in **7 tablespoons melted butter, 2 organic eggs, 1 teaspoon vanilla extract,** and **1–2 tablespoons organic milk,** and beat until well combined. Stir in **½ cup chopped pecans,** and pour into the prepared pan. In another bowl, combine **½ cup firmly packed soft brown sugar, 2 tablespoons cocoa powder,** and **⅓ cup hot water.** Stir well and pour over the cake batter. Place in the oven and bake for 40 minutes. During baking, the cake will rise to the top and underneath there will be a delicious chocolate sauce. Serve hot with **cream.** Serves 4

WEEK 03

BREAKFAST

HASH BROWNS

Grate **1 large unpeeled potato** onto a clean towel. Bring up the edges of the towel, then squeeze over the sink to remove any excess water in the potatoes. Put into a bowl and add **1 tablespoon all-purpose flour** and **1 tablespoon Dijon mustard**. Season with **salt** and **freshly ground black pepper** and mix together. Divide the mixture into 8 balls and flatten between your hands. Heat a large frying pan with **1 tablespoon butter** and **1 tablespoon sunflower oil**, then add the potato patties to the pan. Cook for 2–3 minutes on each side, over medium heat, until golden. Stack a couple of hash browns on each serving plate and top with **a freshly poached organic egg** or **a couple of spoonfuls of crème fraîche**. Serves 4

PACKED LUNCH

PAPPARDELLE WITH TUSCAN KALE

Heat a large saucepan of salted water and bring to a boil. Add **4 ounces pappardelle** and cook for 6–8 minutes, until al dente. Meanwhile, heat **1 tablespoon olive oil** in a medium saucepan and, when hot, add **2 finely chopped garlic cloves**. Add **1½ cups roughly chopped kale (stalks removed)** and stir to wilt in the oil. Season with **salt** and **freshly ground black pepper**. Add **¼ cup white wine** and boil for 2–3 minutes until reduced. Add **2 tablespoons crème fraîche** and **2 tablespoons freshly grated Parmesan** and heat through. Drain the pasta, stir into the sauce, and serve immediately with some **extra Parmesan** in a bowl. Serves 2

LUNCH

JERUSALEM ARTICHOKE SOUP

SERVES 4

Not to be confused with globe artichokes, which are another kettle of fish entirely, the Jerusalem kind are the tubers of a member of the sunflower family. They are nutty and earthy and full of flavor.

1 pound Jerusalem artichokes
2 tablespoons olive oil
2 large onions, chopped
1 large garlic clove, minced
2 cups vegetable stock
strip of orange peel
salt and freshly ground black pepper
4 tablespoons heavy cream

Scrub the artichokes, discard any hard knobs, and roughly chop. Heat the oil in a heavy-bottomed pan and add the onions. Cook until translucent, add the garlic, continue cooking for a couple of minutes, and add the artichokes. Toss well to coat with oil and pour in the vegetable stock. Bring to a boil, add the orange peel, and season with salt and freshly ground black pepper. Cover and simmer for 15–20 minutes, until cooked. Remove from the heat, discard the peel, and purée in a food processor. Return to the pan, adjust the seasoning, stir in the cream, and serve.

SIDE

WINTER COLESLAW

VIVIENNE WESTWOOD

Cut **1 small white cabbage** in half, finely shred, and put in a large bowl. Add **1 thinly sliced red onion** and **1 coarsely grated carrot** and mix well. In a separate bowl, whisk together **3 tablespoons good-quality mayonnaise**, **1 tablespoon cider vinegar**, and **1 tablespoon honey**, then stir in **2 teaspoons toasted caraway seeds**. Stir the dressing into the cabbage mix and chill for at least an hour. Serves 4

DINNER

LENTIL, CHICKPEA, CHEDDAR, AND ONION BURGERS

Guilt-free fast food! Perfect in a toasted bun, these deliciously spicy burgers will become firm family favorites and are guaranteed to convert even the most committed of carnivores.

3 tablespoons olive oil
1 large onion, chopped
2 cloves garlic, minced
1 teaspoon ground cumin
1/4 teaspoon cayenne pepper
14-ounce can lentils, drained and rinsed
14-ounce can chickpeas, drained and rinsed
1 tablespoon tahini paste
2 tablespoons freshly chopped parsley
1 large organic egg, beaten
2 cups fresh breadcrumbs
1 cup grated Gruyère
1 cup feta, crumbled
salt and freshly ground black pepper
all-purpose flour, for dusting

TO SERVE
burger buns
shredded lettuce
sliced tomatoes
sliced red onions
sliced avocados
sour cream
ketchup
mayonnaise
pickles and relishes

SERVES 4

Heat 1 tablespoon of olive oil in a frying pan, add the chopped onion, and cook over medium heat until tender but not colored. Add the garlic, ground cumin, and cayenne, and cook for another 30 seconds. Remove from the heat.

Put the lentils and chickpeas into the bowl of a food processor and pulse until coarsely chopped. Add the onion mixture, tahini paste, and parsley, and pulse again until combined and nearly smooth. Spoon into a large bowl and add the beaten egg, breadcrumbs, and both of the cheeses. Mix using your hands and season well with salt and freshly ground black pepper.

Shape the mixture into patties and lightly dust in flour. Heat the remaining olive oil in a large frying pan, slide the burgers into the pan, and cook until golden on both sides.

Serve in toasted buns with lettuce, tomatoes, onions, and avocados, and a spoon of sour cream, ketchup, or mayonnaise, and pickles of your choice.

DESSERT

CAPPUCCINO CUPCAKES

Preheat the oven to 350°F. Line a 12-hole muffin pan with paper liners. In a large mixing bowl, cream **5 tablespoons unsalted butter** and **3/4 cup soft light brown sugar** together until pale and creamy. Add **2 organic eggs** one at a time, mixing all the time. The mixture might look split at this stage but don't worry, that's normal. Sift **3/4 cup all purpose flour** and **3/4 cup self-rising flour** together into a bowl. Mix **1 tablespoon instant espresso powder** and **1/3 cup organic milk** in a separate bowl. Fold in one-third of the flour mixture and beat well, then add half of the coffee mixture and beat well again. Repeat the process, beating well between each addition. Spoon the mixture into the liners until two-thirds full. Bake for 20–25 minutes until golden brown and springy to the touch. Transfer to a wire rack to cool. For the topping, whip **1 cup cream** and **1/4 cup confectioner's sugar** together to soft peaks. Spoon the cream into a piping bag fitted with a star nozzle and pipe swirls over the cupcakes. Decorate each cupcake with a **chocolate-covered espresso bean** and dust with **sweetened cocoa powder**. Makes 12

WEEK 04

BREAKFAST

CLASSIC IRISH SODA BREAD

This is delicious served warm, spread with butter and jam. Preheat the oven to 375°F and dust a baking sheet with flour. Sift **2¼ cups all-purpose flour, 2¼ cups whole-wheat flour, 2 teaspoons baking soda,** and **a pinch of salt** into a large bowl. Rub in **2 tablespoons butter**. Make a well in the center and pour in **1⅓ cups buttermilk**, and mix it quickly into the dry ingredients using a knife. If the dough seems too dry, add a little more buttermilk. Bring the dough gently together using your hands and shape into a ball roughly 8 inches in diameter. Place on the baking sheet and make two deep incisions across the top using a sharp serrated knife. Bake in the oven for 35–40 minutes. When done, the loaf should sound hollow when tapped on the bottom. Transfer to a wire rack to cool, covering it with a cloth to keep the crust soft. Any bread that isn't eaten fresh can be toasted the next day. Serves 4

PACKED LUNCH

PUMPKIN SOUP

Heat oven to 400°F. Peel and cut a **2-pound pumpkin** into large cubes, about 2 inches across, then toss in a large roasting pan with **1 tablespoon olive oil**. Roast for 30 minutes, turning once during cooking, until golden and soft. While the pumpkin cooks, melt **1 tablespoon butter** with **1 tablespoon olive oil** in a large saucepan, then add **2 diced onions, 1 thinly sliced garlic clove, 2 tablespoons coarsely chopped ginger,** and **2 finely chopped red chiles**. Cover and cook on very low heat for 15–20 minutes until the onions are completely soft. Add the pumpkin to the pan, add **3 cups hot vegetable stock** and **4 tablespoons crème fraîche**, then purée with a stick blender until smooth. Return to the pan, gently reheat, then season to taste with **salt** and **freshly ground black pepper**. Serve the soup in bowls with swirls of **crème fraîche**. Serves 6

LUNCH

MISO BROTH

SERVES 2

Miso is a wonderful savory substance made by fermenting soy beans with wheat, barley, or rye. Miso soup is practically Japan's national dish.

2 teaspoons sesame oil
2½ cups mushrooms (enoki or shiitake), sliced
½ carrot, peeled and sliced into matchsticks
1 red chile, sliced
1 tablespoon shredded fresh ginger
good handful of choy sum or baby leaf spinach, shredded

5 scallions, trimmed and finely sliced on the diagonal
2 tablespoons yellow miso paste
4 ounces tofu, drained and cut into small dice
tamari or soy sauce to taste

Heat the sesame oil in a wok or large frying pan and add the mushrooms and carrot. Quickly cook the veggies for a minute until just softened then add the chile and ginger and cook for another 10 seconds.

Throw the choy sum or baby leaf spinach and scallions into the wok and cook until the leaves are only just wilted. Remove from the pan and divide between 2 bowls.

Bring 2⅓ cups water to a boil in a large pan. In a small bowl, mix the miso with a couple of tablespoons of the water and then add the paste to the pan. Stir to combine and add a little more miso if needed. Divide the drained and diced tofu between the bowls and cover with the miso broth. Add tamari or soy sauce to taste and serve immediately.

SIDE
BUBBLE AND SQUEAK

Mash **1 pound peeled and boiled potatoes** with **2 tablespoons butter** and season with **salt and freshly ground black pepper**. Mix **3 cups chopped cooked cabbage or Brussels sprouts** into the mash with **1 tablespoon freshly chopped parsley**. Shape the potato mix into 4 rounds and flatten slightly with the palm of your hand. Heat **3 tablespoons oil** in a frying pan and fry the cakes for 4 minutes on each side, or until golden. Serve with **roasted vine** or **cherry tomatoes** and **tomato chutney**. Serves 4

DINNER
VEGETABLE PUFF PIE

This classically British pie cries out for mashed potato as an accompaniment. You'll certainly want something to mop up the juices.

4 tablespoons butter, plus 1 tablespoon
¼ cup plus 2 tablespoons all-purpose flour, plus extra for dusting
1½ cups organic milk
1 cup grated Cheddar
1 tablespoon freshly chopped parsley
1 teaspoon English mustard powder

1 carrot, thinly sliced
4 ounces button mushrooms, halved
1 leek, trimmed and finely sliced
3 cups broccoli, chopped into small florets
8 ounces ready-to-roll puff pastry
1 beaten organic egg to glaze
1 tablespoon sesame seeds

Preheat the oven to 400°F.

Melt 4 tablespoons butter in a saucepan, add the flour, and cook for 1 minute. Remove from the heat and gradually whisk in the milk. Return to the heat and bring to a boil, stirring continuously until the sauce thickens. Stir in the cheese, parsley, and mustard powder.

SERVES 4

In another pan, heat the remaining butter, add the carrots and the mushrooms, and cook until tender. Meanwhile, cook the leek for 5 minutes in a pan of salted boiling water and then add the broccoli and cook until tender. Drain.

Combine the vegetables with the sauce, mix well, and place the mixture in a lightly greased large pie dish.

Dampen the rim of the pie dish. Roll out the pastry on a lightly floured work surface. Cut off a strip of pastry and place it on the rim of the dish and brush it with water.

Lay the pastry lid over the top and press the edges together to seal. Trim and flute the edges. Make a hole in the top of the pie to let out the air while cooking, and use the trimmings to decorate the pie. Glaze with the beaten egg and sprinkle with sesame seeds.

Cook in the preheated oven for 30 minutes until golden brown.

DESSERT
CHOCOLATE BREAD AND BUTTER PUDDING

Preheat the oven to 375°F. You will need an ovenproof dish 7 inches long and 2 inches deep. In a medium saucepan, bring **2 cups organic milk** and **¾ cup heavy cream** to a boil over moderate heat. Meanwhile, mix together in a bowl **4 organic egg yolks** and **½ cup sugar**. Add the organic milk and cream mixture, stir well to combine, then strain into a pitcher, adding **a few drops of vanilla extract**. Layer **¼ sliced baguette** in the bottom of the ovenproof dish, and sprinkle with **⅓ cup golden raisins** and **2 ounces roughly chopped plain chocolate**. Dip **¼ sliced baguette** in **4 tablespoons melted butter** and lay the slices on top of the raisins. Cover with the cream mixture and leave to soak for 30 minutes, pushing the bread beneath the surface of the cream. Place the dish in a bain-marie (a roasting pan containing boiling water to reach to halfway up the sides of the ovenproof dish). Bake the pudding for 1 hour until golden brown. In a small saucepan heat together **4 tablespoons apricot jam** and **2 tablespoons orange juice**. Brush liberally over the bread and butter pudding and serve immediately. Serves 4–6

WEEK 05

BREAKFAST
GRANOLA

Preheat the oven to 350°F. Roughly chop **1¹/2 cups mixed nuts such as almonds, pecans, and hazelnuts,** and put into a large bowl. Add **4 cups rolled oats, ¹/2 cup sunflower seeds, ¹/2 cup pumpkin seeds, ¹/2 cup flaxseeds,** and **¹/2 cup flaked coconut,** and mix well. Add **¹/2 cup sunflower oil** and **¹/3 cup honey,** and mix thoroughly to combine. Pour the mixture into a large roasting pan and spread into an even layer. Bake for 20 minutes or until golden and crisp, stirring frequently so that the mixture toasts evenly. Remove from the oven and add **¹/2 cup roughly chopped dried cherries, cranberries, or blueberries.** Leave to cool before scooping into storage jars. Serve with **fresh berries, organic milk,** or **plain yogurt.** Makes 12 servings

PACKED LUNCH

CHEESE AND ONION SANDWICH

Mix together **¹/4 cup soft goat cheese** with **2 tablespoons cream cheese.** Heat a little **olive oil** in a pan and add **half a sliced red onion.** Allow the onion to sweat. When it starts to wilt, add **¹/4 teaspoon sugar, a pinch of salt,** some **freshly ground black pepper,** and **1 teaspoon balsamic vinegar.** Cook for another 3–4 minutes. Spread the goat cheese mixture over a slice of **whole-wheat bread** and top with the red onion and **a handful of arugula leaves.** Place another slice of bread on top and season with **salt** and **freshly ground black pepper.** Serves 1

LUNCH

CHICKPEA CURRY

SKYE GYNGELL

SERVES 4

Chickpeas are high in protein. Soaking them overnight reduces the cooking time, while the baking soda in this recipe helps soften them.

3 cups dried chickpeas, soaked overnight
1 teaspoon baking soda
1 teaspoon mustard seeds
1 teaspoon fennel seeds
1 teaspoon cumin seeds
1 teaspoon coriander seeds
5 cardamom pods
1 tablespoon vegetable oil
2 red onions, sliced

1 small bunch of cilantro, roots included
1 red chile
3 garlic cloves, chopped
4 carrots, peeled and diced
3 tablespoons maple syrup
juice of 2 limes
3 tablespoons soy sauce
2 small cans of good-quality tomatoes
4 tablespoons unsalted butter

Drain and place the chickpeas in a large pot of cold water. Add a teaspoon of baking soda. Cook over medium heat for around 45 minutes or until tender. Drain and set aside.

To make the base of the curry, warm up the spices in a small pan, being careful not to burn them, as this will result in a bitter taste. Grind using a mortar and pestle. Add the vegetable oil to a pot large enough to hold all the ingredients comfortably and place over medium heat. When the oil is warm, add the onions and soften for 5 minutes. Chop the cilantro and the chile very finely and add to the pot along with the garlic and the spices.

Add the diced carrots and cook for 10 minutes. Then add the maple syrup, lime juice, and soy sauce, stirring well to combine the flavors, and cook for another few minutes. Add the tomatoes and turn up the heat slightly. Cook for 15 minutes to thicken the sauce. At this point it should taste hot, sweet, and slightly sharp. Keep the pan over the heat until the carrots are cooked through but still firm. At this point, add the chickpeas and the butter and serve.

SIDE

POTATOES WITH HAZELNUTS AND ROSEMARY

SIMON ROGAN

Take about **1 tablespoon tiny rosemary leaves** from the bunch and set aside. Boil **1 pound Yukon gold potatoes** with **a stem of rosemary leaves**. Meanwhile, simmer **1/4 cup hazelnuts** in water for 4 minutes, drain, peel, and pat dry. Gently cook the hazelnuts in **a little hazelnut oil** until golden brown, season with **salt** and **freshly ground black pepper**, cool, and crush into smaller pieces. When the potatoes are cooked, peel, slice, and fry in a generous amount of hazelnut oil until they are golden brown. Remove and drain on paper towels, wipe clean the pan, and add another **2 tablespoons of hazelnut oil** with **1/3 cup crème fraîche**. Reduce until the sauce is the right consistency, add the rosemary leaves, and return the golden potato slices. Season with **salt** and **freshly ground black pepper**. Serve sprinkled with the fried hazelnut pieces. Serves 4

DINNER

ROASTED VEGETABLES AND MISO DRESSING WITH SESAME SEEDS

SERVES 4

Miso is rich in what the Japanese call umami—a lipsmacking savory tang often described as the fifth fundamental flavor (the others are sweet, salty, sour, and bitter). It's used to make a tasty Miso Broth (see Winter, Week 4, Lunch); today you're going to exploit one of miso's other virtues— it's great in dressings for salads and vegetables.

3 medium carrots, peeled and cut in
    half lengthwise
1 butternut squash, peeled, seeded and cut
    into wedges
3 small-medium parsnips, peeled and halved
    (or quartered if they are large)
2 tablespoons olive oil
3 cups broccoli, trimmed
2 tablespoons honey
1 tablespoon mixed black and white
    sesame seeds

FOR THE DRESSING
3 tablespoons toasted sesame oil
2 teaspoons freshly grated ginger
1 garlic clove, minced
1 heaping teaspoon yellow miso paste
1 tablespoon rice vinegar

Preheat the oven to 375°F.

Prepare the vegetables, then combine the carrots, squash, and parsnips in a large bowl and toss with 1–2 tablespoons olive oil. Arrange the veggies in a roasting pan in a single layer and cook on the middle shelf of a preheated oven for about 25 minutes or until tender and starting to brown at the edges. Add the broccoli to the pan, drizzle the vegetables with 1 tablespoon of the honey, and sprinkle with the sesame seeds. Return to the oven and cook for another 5 minutes to caramelize.

While the vegetables are cooking, prepare the dressing. Spoon the remaining tablespoon of honey into a small bowl, add the other dressing ingredients, and whisk lightly to combine. Arrange the warm honey-roasted vegetables on a platter, drizzle with the dressing, and serve.

DESSERT

PECAN PIE

Lightly flour a work surface and roll out **1 pound pie dough** to a thickness of 1/4 inch. Line a 9-inch pie dish with the pastry and trim the excess, leaving a 1-inch overhang. Using your fingers, take the overhang and roll it under itself, allowing the rolled edge to rest on the edge of the pie dish. Crimp the edge with your fingers, then chill for 30 minutes or until firm. Preheat the oven to 350°F. Line the prepared pastry with parchment paper and a layer of baking beans, and bake for 15 minutes. Remove the parchment paper and beans and bake for 10 minutes more or until the pie begins to turn golden in color. Meanwhile, make the filling by whisking together **6 tablespoons melted butter, 1 cup loosely packed dark brown sugar, 1 cup golden corn syrup, 4 organic eggs, 1 teaspoon vanilla extract,** and **1/4 teaspoon salt** in a medium bowl. Scatter the pie base with **11/4 cups chopped pecans**, pour the filling over the top, and sprinkle with another **1/2 cup chopped pecans**. Bake in the oven for 50 minutes to 1 hour or until the filling is set. Cool before serving. Serves 8–10

WEEK 06

BREAKFAST

POTATO FARLS

Cut **1 medium potato** into chunks and cook in boiling water until tender. Drain well and press through a potato ricer or mash. Measure out **1/2 cup** and cool. Sift **5 tablespoons all-purpose flour** and **1/2 teaspoon baking powder** onto the cooled mash. Mix **1 organic egg** and **1/4 cup organic milk** and add to the potato mix. Mix until smooth. Heat a large nonstick frying pan over medium heat. Add **1/2 teaspoon sunflower oil** and **a little butter**. Add **1 tablespoon of batter** for each farl and cook 4 at a time. Cook for about 1 minute until the underside is golden brown and small bubbles appear. Flip the farls and cook until golden. Remove from the pan and keep warm while you cook the remaining farls in the same way, adding a tiny bit of oil and butter to the pan as and when needed. Serve topped with **grated mature Cheddar** or crumbled **blue cheese** and drizzle with **honey**. Makes 6-8

PACKED LUNCH

PILAU RICE WITH CASHEWS

Heat **2 tablespoons oil** in a large saucepan, add **4 finely chopped shallots** and cook for 5 minutes, stirring occasionally, without browning. Stir in **1 teaspoon ground cumin**, **1 teaspoon ground coriander**, **1/2 teaspoon chile powder**, **6 cardamom pods**, **1-inch cinnamon stick**, and a few gratings of **fresh nutmeg**, and cook for 2 minutes, ensuring that the spices do not burn. Add **2 minced garlic cloves** and **1 1/4 cups basmati rice** and cook for 5 minutes, stirring constantly. Pour in **2 cups vegetable stock**, season with **salt**, cover, and simmer for 15 minutes, stirring occasionally, until the rice is tender and the stock has been absorbed. Transfer to a warmed serving plate, sprinkle with **1/2 cup roasted cashew nuts**, and garnish with **a handful of cilantro leaves**. Serves 3-4

LUNCH

CAULIFLOWER KORMA

As any fan of Indian cooking knows, korma is a mild, creamy kind of curry. Cauliflower and brazil nuts share those qualities, making for a fantastic, simple to prepare lunch.

3 tablespoons vegetable oil
1 medium onion, sliced
1 garlic clove, minced
1 red chile, seeded and finely chopped
2 teaspoons medium hot curry powder
1 cup brazil nuts, shelled

1/2 cup creamed coconut made up to 1 1/2 cups with water
1 small cauliflower, cut into small florets
1 cup broccoli, cut into small florets
2 zucchini, cut into small chunks

SERVES 4

Heat the oil in a frying pan and cook the onion, garlic, chile, and curry powder for 5 minutes.

Grind half the brazil nuts in a food processor, then add them to the coconut liquid and pour the liquid into the frying pan. Combine and remove from the heat.

Bring a pan of water to a boil and parboil the vegetables: boil the cauliflower for 3 minutes, the broccoli for 2 minutes, and the zucchini for 1 minute. Drain.

Add all the vegetables to the korma sauce and simmer for 4 minutes, stirring in the remaining nuts just before serving.

SIDE
SPICY BEET SALAD

Cook **8–9 trimmed beets** in a steamer for 20–30 minutes until tender. Peel and slice them when cool, reserving the liquid that accumulates on the plate. Toss them in the **juice of ½ lemon** and coat with **½ teaspoon ground cumin, ½ teaspoon ground cinnamon, ½ teaspoon ground paprika, 1 tablespoon orange flower water,** and **2 tablespoons olive oil,** together with the liquid. Season with **salt** and **freshly ground black pepper,** cover, and chill. To serve, toss with **2 tablespoons freshly chopped parsley** and arrange on individual plates on a bed of **mixed lettuce leaves**—colored varieties mixed with green leaves work well. Serves 4

DINNER
VEGETABLE AND TOFU STIR-FRY WITH SOBA NOODLES

Soba is the Japanese name for buckwheat noodles, which are thin and brown, and tastier and more substantial than most other kinds. This fresh, crunchy stir-fry shows them off to good advantage.

½ head Napa cabbage leaves, cut into ½-inch ribbons
4 ounces shiitake mushrooms, halved
1 bunch scallions, cut into 2-inch lengths
4 ounces baby corn, sliced in half
4 ounces snow peas, sliced in half
9 ounces soba noodles
1 tablespoon toasted sesame oil

1 tablespoon soy sauce
4 tablespoons vegetable oil
9 ounces firm tofu, drained and cut into 1-inch cubes
2 tablespoons rice flour
1 garlic clove, minced
1 cup bean sprouts
2 tablespoons shoyo (Japanese soy sauce)

SERVES 4

Prepare the vegetables and set them aside in small piles.

Bring a large saucepan of water to a boil and cook the noodles according to the instructions on the package, until just tender. Drain well and toss in the sesame oil and soy sauce.

Meanwhile, heat half the oil in a wok or large frying pan, dust the tofu cubes in rice flour, and fry in the hot oil until golden. Remove from the pan. Add the remaining oil to the wok, add the garlic and fry for a few seconds, and then add the mushrooms, scallions, and baby corn. Stir-fry over high heat for 3 minutes.

Add the Napa cabbage leaves, snow peas, and bean sprouts, and sprinkle in the shoyo. Continue to stir-fry for another 2–3 minutes until the vegetables are just tender. Return the tofu to the pan, stir to combine, and heat through.

To serve, divide the noodles among 4 warmed serving plates and top with the stir-fried vegetables and tofu. Garnish with chives, if desired.

DESSERT
CHOCOLATE TRUFFLES

This recipe uses raw egg, which should be avoided by the elderly, pregnant, and very young. Melt **6 ounces semi-sweet chocolate** in a bowl over a pan of hot water. Add **1 organic egg yolk, 2 tablespoons butter** and **1 teaspoon coffee extract,** and leave in a cool place for 30–40 minutes until set. Mold into small egg shapes with your fingers, and roll in **1 tablespoon cocoa** powder to coat evenly. Makes 20

WEEK 07

BREAKFAST

CHOCOLATE CROISSANT

Preheat the oven to 350°F. Slice **1 croissant** in half lengthwise, but don't go all the way through—it should open like a book. Sprinkle the bottom half of the croissant with **1 tablespoon chopped milk chocolate**. Close up, put on a baking sheet, and grate **a little chocolate** over the top. Bake in the oven for 5 minutes or until the chocolate has melted. Serve warm. Serves 1

PACKED LUNCH

CHEESE AND CARROT CHUTNEY SANDWICH

The chutney will need to be made in advance but is well worth it. In a bowl, mix together **1 pound grated carrots, 1 teaspoon grated ginger, 1 cup cider vinegar, 1 finely chopped red chile, 1 teaspoon crushed fennel seeds,** and **a pinch of salt.** Cover and set aside for 24 hours. Pour the mixture into a pan, add **1/3 cup water** and bring to a boil, then reduce the heat to low and simmer for 10 minutes. Stir in **11/2 cups brown sugar**, increase the heat, and boil the mixture until it becomes thick, about 30 minutes. Remove from the heat and spoon into sterilized jars.
To make your sandwich, take **2 slices of whole-wheat bread** and spread with butter. Put a few slices of **mild Cheddar** over one of the buttered slices, then spread with 1 tablespoon of the carrot chutney. Top with **a handful of arugula leaves** and the remaining slice of bread. Serves 1

LUNCH

ONION BHAJIS WITH TOMATO AND CHILE SAUCE

DARINA ALLEN

SERVES 4

Onion bhajis are a very popular appetizer in Indian restaurants. They seem tricky to make, but these ones are anything but. They are served with a feisty sauce that transforms what is usually thought of as a snack into a satisfying meal.

FOR THE TOMATO AND CHILE SAUCE
1 heaping teaspoon green chiles, seeded and chopped
1 red pepper, seeded and cut in 2-inch dice
1/2 x 14-ounce can of chopped tomatoes
1 garlic clove, minced
1 teaspoon sugar
1 teaspoon soft brown sugar
1 tablespoon white wine vinegar
2 tablespoons water

1 cup all-purpose flour
2 teaspoons baking powder
1 teaspoon chili powder
2 organic eggs, beaten
1/2 cup water
4 onions, thinly sliced in rings
2 tablespoons snipped fresh chives
salt and freshly ground pepper
sunflower oil

First make the sauce. Put the chiles, pepper, tomatoes, and garlic into a stainless-steel saucepan with the sugars, vinegar, and water. Season and simmer for 10 minutes until reduced by half.

Sift the flour, baking powder, and chili powder into a bowl. Make a well in the center, add the eggs, gradually add in the water, and mix to make a smooth batter. Stir in the thinly sliced onions and chives. Season well with salt and freshly ground pepper.

Just before serving, heat the oil to 325°F.

Fry teaspoons of the batter in the sunflower oil for about 5 minutes on each side until crisp and golden, then drain on paper towels. Serve hot or cold with the tomato and chile sauce.

SIDE

CHEESY KALE GRATIN

Preheat the oven to 375°F. Remove the stalks from **9 ounces kale** and shred finely. Plunge into boiling water for 30-60 seconds, then refresh under cold water. Set aside. Melt **2 tablespoons butter** in a saucepan, stir in **¹/₄ cup plain flour,** and cook for 2 minutes. Remove the pan from the heat and gradually blend in **1¹/₂ cups organic whole milk,** stirring well. Place back on the heat and bring gently to a boil, stirring continuously until thickened and smooth. Crumble in **4 ounces goat cheese.** Add **¹/₂ teaspoon mustard powder** and **salt** and **freshly ground black pepper,** and mix well. Place the kale in an ovenproof dish, then cover with the sauce. Combine **³/₄ cup breadcrumbs** and **1 tablespoon caraway seeds,** then spread evenly over the surface. Bake in the oven for 20-25 minutes or until the topping is golden brown. Serves 4-6

DINNER

LEEK, POTATO, AND FETA PIZZETTA

SERVES 4

A pizzetta is simply a small pizza. The puff pastry in this recipe is a shortcut but it produces a highly satisfactory result.

1 medium potato, cut 2-inch slices
2 tablespoons olive oil
4 leeks, trimmed and finely sliced
sea salt and freshly ground black pepper
1 pound puff pastry
4 ounces feta
1 tablespoon fresh thyme leaves

Preheat the oven to 400°F.

Boil the potato slices until tender, about 10 minutes, then drain thoroughly.

Meanwhile, heat the oil in a large frying pan, add the leeks, and cook on medium heat until softened, about 7-8 minutes. Add the potatoes to the pan and season with salt and freshly ground black pepper, stir to combine, and cook for another 1-2 minutes.

On a lightly floured surface, roll out the puff pastry in a circle roughly 10 inches in diameter, to a thickness of about 2 inches. Place the pastry on a large baking sheet and, using a sharp knife, lightly score a border 2 inches in from the edge.

Spoon the leek and potato mixture over the pastry, leaving the 2-inch border. Crumble the feta over the top, sprinkle with the thyme, then bake in the oven for 30 minutes until the edges of the pastry are golden. If the top is browning, cover with foil then return to the oven.

DESSERT

BAKED PEARS

Preheat the oven to 350°F. Put **¹/₂ cup whole almonds** in a small roasting pan and toast in the oven for 5 minutes. Leave to cool slightly and then roughly chop the almonds and put them in a bowl. Crumble **6 soft amaretti cookies** and add to the chopped almonds with the **zest of 1 lemon** and **a pinch of ground cinnamon.** In another small bowl, cream together **6 tablespoons softened unsalted butter** and **1 tablespoon sugar** until pale and light. Add **1 organic egg yolk** and **a teaspoon of vanilla extract,** and beat again until smooth before adding the crumbled cookie mixture. Peel **4 ripe pears** using a vegetable peeler, and toss in the **juice of 1 lemon** to prevent them from discoloring. Halve the pears and remove the cores using a teaspoon, and arrange in a greased ovenproof dish cut side up. Stuff the pears with the filling mixture, and sprinkle with the remaining lemon juice. Drizzle with **4-6 tablespoons Marsala** and a couple of tablespoons of water, cover loosely with foil, and bake on the middle shelf of the preheated oven for about 25 minutes or until tender. The cooking time will depend on the ripeness of the pears. Serve 2 pear halves per person with the buttery Marsala pan juices poured over the top and with a scoop of good-quality **vanilla ice cream** or **heavy cream.** Serves 2

WEEK 08

BREAKFAST
FRENCH TOAST

Beat **4 organic eggs** lightly with a fork in a bowl. Stir in **1 teaspoon sugar**, **a pinch of salt**, and **1 cup organic milk**. Melt a pat of **butter** in a nonstick frying pan set over medium-low heat. Cut **8 slices of white bread** and dip them, one at a time, into the egg mixture. Soak only as many slices as you will be cooking at one time. Place the bread in the frying pan and cook gently until golden brown, then turn and brown the other side. Serve hot with **butter** and **syrup**. Serves 2

PACKED LUNCH
BLACK-EYED BEAN CASSEROLE WITH CILANTRO

Soak **1 1/4 cups black-eyed beans** in water overnight, drain, and boil in plenty of water until tender, approximately 45 minutes. Heat **2 tablespoons sunflower oil** in a pan and cook **1 finely chopped onion** until golden brown. Add **2 finely chopped garlic cloves** just as the onions are browning. Add **1 tablespoon paprika**, **1 bird's eye chile** (seeded and finely chopped) and **1 cup diced carrots** and cook slowly until the carrots are al dente. Pour in a **14-ounce can chopped tomatoes** and the drained black-eyed beans, and simmer gently for 5 minutes. Add an **11-ounce can of corn**, **a dash of tabasco**, and **salt** and **freshly ground black pepper**, and continue to simmer for 6–7 minutes, making sure that it does not dry out. Remove from the heat and sprinkle with **a handful of finely chopped cilantro**. Make a topping by mixing together **1/2 cup sour cream**, approximately **1/3 cup roughly chopped cilantro**, and **1 tablespoon lime juice**. Season to taste before serving. Serves 4

LUNCH
TORTILLA DE PATATAS
OMAR ALLIBHOY

SERVES 4

This is the classic Spanish tortilla, slowly fried on one side then turned over and fried on the other. Leaving the cooked potatoes in the egg mix for a while before using them helps soften them and unites them with the rest of the dish.

2 pounds good potatoes, finely chopped
(1 inch thick)
1 Spanish onion, finely chopped (1 inch thick)
olive oil, for frying
10 organic eggs, beaten
a pinch of table salt
aïoli to serve

Fry the potatoes and onion in the olive oil over high heat till golden (around 12–15 minutes) stirring them from time to time so they cook evenly. Drain them and mix them with the eggs and season with a pinch of salt. If you have the time, let the mix soak for at least 30 minutes.

To make the tortilla, place a nonstick pan over medium heat and drizzle in a bit of olive oil. Pour the tortilla mix into the pan and lower the heat to minimum. After 5 minutes, cover the pan with a plate (always wider than the pan) and, holding it tight with your hand, flip the tortilla onto the plate then slide it back into the pan so the uncooked side is down (Note: if it is the first time you're going to flip a tortilla, you had better practice with the plate and an empty pan first). The cooking time depends on the size and depth of the pan in relation to the amount of tortilla mix. I recommend eating the tortilla when still runny in the middle. Serve with aïoli.

SIDE

STUFFED ONIONS

For the stuffing, preheat the oven to 325°F. Rub **6 slices of day-old whole-wheat bread** into crumbs with your hands. Place the breadcrumbs in a shallow baking pan and bake in the oven until golden, approximately 10–15 minutes. Take out and cool. In a large saucepan, heat enough oil to cook **4 finely chopped ribs of celery** and **a few finely chopped sage leaves, a handful of thyme leaves,** and **a stem of rosemary leaves** over moderate heat, until the celery is soft. Add **1½ cups shelled and coarsely chopped chestnuts** and cook another minute. Add a **14-ounce can lentils** and the breadcrumbs to the chestnut mix. Stir in **a handful of freshly chopped parsley, salt,** and **freshly ground black pepper.** Let the stuffing cool completely. For the onions, chop off the tops and bottoms of **4 large red onions,** then peel. Use your hands to rub **a little oil** over surface of onions. Sprinkle with **freshly ground black pepper** and roast at 350°F for 20 minutes or until they start to soften. Take them out of the oven, and when cool enough to handle, push out the centers, leaving a hollow shell to hold the stuffing. Chop up the rest of the onion and add to the stuffing. Fill the hollow onions with the stuffing. Replace the onion tops and bake in the oven for 30 minutes. Serves 4

DINNER

VEGETABLE SATAY

SERVES 4

The almonds here are a pleasing alternative to the peanuts on which most satays are based. The savory sweetness of the sauce is matched by the same quality in the caramelized vegetables.

1 tablespoon sesame oil
1 tablespoon vegetable oil
1 red chile, seeded and finely chopped
2 garlic cloves, minced
1 inch ginger, finely grated
½ teaspoon turmeric
1 teaspoon tamarind paste
½ cup ground almonds

2 tablespoons peanut butter
1 cup coconut milk
juice and zest from 1 lime
1 teaspoon sea salt
1–2 sweet potatoes
2–3 carrots
2–3 turnips

Heat the sesame and vegetable oils in a frying pan and cook the chile, garlic, ginger, turmeric, and tamarind paste. Add the ground almonds, peanut butter, coconut milk, lime juice and zest, and salt and simmer for 2–3 minutes. Remove from the heat and let cool.

For the vegetables, preheat the oven to 350°F. Peel the vegetables and cut into 1-inch cubes. Marinate in the sauce for 5 minutes. Transfer the vegetables to a baking sheet, cover with foil, and bake for 25–30 minutes, until tender but barely colored. Set aside to cool. Spear the vegetables onto skewers and cook, on a hot grill pan, over high heat until colored. Warm the remaining sauce and serve separately.

DESSERT

CHOCOLATE AND CHESTNUT CAKE

Preheat the oven to 350°F. Grease the inside of an 8-inch springform pan and line the base with a disk of buttered parchment paper. Dust with **1 tablespoon cocoa powder** and shake out the excess. Put **7 ounces precooked peeled chestnuts** into a small frying pan, add **2 tablespoons sugar** and **⅓ cup organic whole milk,** and cook over low to medium heat for 5 minutes until the chestnuts start to soften. Remove from the heat, pour into the bowl of a food processor, and purée until smooth. Add **1 teaspoon vanilla extract** and cool. Place **8 tablespoons unsalted butter** and **5 ounces chopped dark chocolate** in a heatproof bowl and melt either in the microwave on low or over a pan of barely simmering water. Stir until smooth, remove from the heat, and cool slightly. Cream **3 large organic eggs** and **¾ cup sugar** until thick, pale, and doubled in volume. Mix in the chestnuts until thoroughly combined. Add the melted chocolate mixture, and fold until smooth. Carefully pour the batter into the prepared pan, spread level, and bake on the middle shelf of the preheated oven for about 30 minutes until risen and the top has formed a light crust. Remove the cake from the oven, put the pan on a wire cooling rack, and cool to room temperature. The cake will sink and the crust might crack as it cools, but this is part of the cake's appeal. Dust with **cocoa powder** and serve with **crème fraîche.** Serves 4

WEEK 09

BREAKFAST

WINTER FRUIT SALAD

Take **1 cup dried apricots** and **1 cup prunes** and soak them overnight covered in boiling water. Put into a saucepan in the morning and add **2 tablespoons currants** and the **zest of a small lemon**. Mix in **2 tablespoons honey** and cover with water. Bring the pan to a boil and simmer for about 25–30 minutes. Cool and refrigerate. Before serving for breakfast the next day, add **2/3 cup orange juice** and **2 sliced bananas**. Serve with **Greek yogurt** if you like. Serves 4–6

PACKED LUNCH

GREEN PEA PILAU

Heat **1/3 cup vegetable oil** in a large saucepan over medium heat and finely chop **1 small onion**. Cook the chopped onion, **broken cinnamon stick**, **1 teaspoon freshly chopped ginger**, **1/2 teaspoon chile powder**, **a pinch of ground turmeric**, **1/2 teaspoon cumin seeds**, and **1 teaspoon salt** for 10 minutes. Add **2 1/2 cups water** and bring to a boil. Add **2 cups long grain rice**, cover, lower the heat, and simmer for 15 minutes. Add **1 3/4 cups frozen peas** and cook for another 5 minutes, until all the liquid has been absorbed and the rice is tender and fluffy. Serves 6

LUNCH

SPICED WHOLE-WHEAT COUSCOUS WITH SWEET POTATO AND PISTACHIOS

STELLA McCARTNEY

SERVES 4

Whole-wheat couscous is nuttier and a little more nutritious than the white, bran-free variety. It complements sweet potato perfectly and vice versa. This is a typical North African dish; za'tar is a spice mix used extensively in the region's cuisine.

3 small sweet potatoes
4 tablespoons olive oil
2 tablespoons pumpkin seeds
1 1/2 cups giant whole-wheat couscous
1 2/3 cups light vegetable stock or water
handful of raisins, preferably organic
1 rounded teaspoon za'tar
1/2 cup unsalted pistachios, chopped

TO SERVE
1 lemon
2 tablespoons extra virgin olive oil
salt and freshly ground black pepper
2 tablespoons freshly chopped cilantro
2 tablespoons freshly chopped
   flat-leaf parsley
1 tablespoon freshly chopped mint

Preheat the oven to 400°F.

Scrub the sweet potatoes under cold water and cut each into 6 wedges. Put into a roasting pan, drizzle with 2 tablespoons olive oil, season with salt and freshly ground black pepper, and roast in the oven for about 20-25 minutes or until the sweet potato is tender and starting to caramelize at the edges. Add the pumpkin seeds to the pan for the last 5 minutes of cooking time.

While the sweet potato is cooking prepare the couscous. Heat 2 tablespoons olive oil in a large sauté pan, add the couscous, and cook gently for 2–3 minutes until starting to brown. Add half of the stock or water to the pan and continue to cook for about 15 minutes, stirring frequently until the couscous is tender and has absorbed the liquid. Add the remaining stock or water to the pan as and when needed. Remove from the heat and add the raisins, za'tar, and chopped pistachios to the pan, season with salt and freshly ground black pepper, and cool slightly.

Mix together the juice from half the lemon and the extra virgin olive oil and pour over the warm sweet potato when it comes out of the oven. Gently stir the freshly chopped herbs and roasted sweet potato wedges into the couscous and serve with extra lemon wedges for squeezing over.

SIDE
COLCANNON

Mash **1 pound peeled and cooked** potatoes and season with **salt** and **freshly ground black pepper** before stirring in the **slices of 1 cooked leek** and juices in which they were cooked. Then add **3 cups sliced and cooked cabbage** and mix thoroughly over a low heat. Arrange on a warmed serving dish and make a well in the center. Keep warm. Partly melt **4 tablespoons butter**, and pour it into the well. Serve immediately. Serves 4

DINNER
GLAMORGAN SAUSAGES

The McCartney family knows a fair bit about vegetarian sausages—Linda's are the UK's best-selling brand—but people in Wales have been making this excellent cheese-based variety for at least 150 years. Describing them as sausages may be stretching a point as they don't have skins, but however you classify them, they are extremely good. The ideal cheese to use is Caerphilly, which is delightfully fresh and crumbly, but you can use Cheddar.

SERVES 4

2 tablespoons butter
1 large onion, finely chopped
1 leek, trimmed and finely sliced
1 garlic clove, minced
2 cups fresh white breadcrumbs
1/2 teaspoon dry mustard powder
2 tablespoons freshly chopped parsley

4 ounces Welsh cheese, such as Caerphilly, crumbled or grated, or Cheddar
salt and freshly ground black pepper
2 large organic eggs, beaten
2 tablespoons all-purpose flour
2 tablespoons vegetable oil

Melt the butter in a small frying pan and gently cook the onions and leeks for 3–4 minutes until just softened. Add the minced garlic and cook for another 30 seconds. Transfer the vegetables to a bowl and mix with the breadcrumbs, mustard, parsley, cheese, and a good sprinkling of salt and freshly ground black pepper.

Bind the mixture together with the beaten eggs. Divide into 8 and form into sausage shapes or small patties. Lightly roll into the flour.

Heat the oil in a frying pan and gently fry the sausages or cakes for 3–4 minutes on each side until golden brown. Drain on kitchen paper and serve immediately.

DESSERT
PEAR CAKE

Preheat the oven to 325°F. Grease and line the base of an 8-inch round pan. Grind **1 cup blanched hazelnuts** in a food processor until fairly fine. Add **1¼ cups self-rising flour** and mix. Add **12 tablespoons butter** chopped into small pieces and pulse until it forms crumbs. Add **½ cup plus 2 tablespoons sugar** and **2 beaten large organic eggs** and mix briefly. Peel, core, and chop **2 small ripe pears** and stir into the mixture by hand. Spoon the mixture into the pan and smooth the top. Peel, core, and slice **3 small ripe pears** and sprinkle onto the top of the cake. Press down lightly and bake for 50–60 minutes until firm to the touch. Cool in the pan for 10 minutes, then turn out of the pan and cool on a wire rack. Serves 8

WEEK 10

BREAKFAST

DRIED APRICOT COMPOTE

Put **2 tablespoons freshly squeezed lemon juice**, **1/3 cup freshly squeezed orange juice**, and **2 tablespoons honey** in a small pan and bring gently to a boil. Then add **1 1/2 cups dried apricots** and **1 cup raisins**. Reduce the heat and simmer until tender—about 10 minutes. Remove the fruits and boil the liquid for a couple of minutes to reduce it. Put the fruits back into the sauce, together with **1 cup chopped toasted walnuts**, and serve either warm or refrigerate and serve chilled. Serves 4

PACKED LUNCH

FARRO, SUN-DRIED TOMATOES, AND FETA

MINDY FOX

Bring a medium saucepan of salted water to a boil. Add **1 1/2 cups dried farro** and cook for about 18 minutes until tender but still firm to the bite. Drain and transfer to a bowl. Add **3 tablespoons good-quality extra virgin olive oil**, then finely grate **the zest of 1 lemon** into the bowl, holding the zester close to catch any flavorful oil from the rind. Toss to combine. Add **3 ounces sheep's milk feta**, **1 tablespoon sun-dried tomato spread** (or finely chopped sun-dried tomatoes in oil), **1 tablespoon roughly chopped parsley**, and **a few generous pinches of flaky coarse sea salt**. Stir to combine. Allow the flavors to meld for a couple of minutes, then taste and adjust the amounts of sun-dried tomato spread and salt to your liking. Serve warm or at room temperature. Serves 4

LUNCH

POTATO AND PEA SAMOSAS

SERVES 4

Samosas can take almost any filling you can dream up, but this potato and pea combination proves that simple is often best. Make sure you make a large batch.

1 pound potatoes, peeled and cut into 1/2-inch dice
1 cup frozen peas, cooked and drained
1/2 teaspoon cumin seeds
1/2 teaspoon coriander seeds
seeds from 4 cardamom pods
1/2 teaspoon black onion seeds
2 tablespoons sunflower oil
1 onion, finely chopped
1 fat garlic clove, minced

1/2 tablespoon freshly grated ginger
1 large green chile, seeded and finely chopped
1/2 teaspoon turmeric powder
1/4 teaspoon chile powder
1 heaping tablespoon mango chutney
salt and freshly ground black pepper
2 tablespoons chopped cilantro
10 ounces filo pastry
melted butter, to brush

Cook the potatoes in boiling salted water until tender. Add the peas and cook for a further 30 seconds. Drain and set aside. Tip the cumin, coriander, and cardamom into a frying pan and toast over a medium heat for 1 minute. Coarsely grind the onion seeds using a mortar and pestle.

Heat the oil in a large frying pan, add the onion and cook until soft. Add the garlic, ginger, and chile, and cook for 30 seconds then add the spices. Continue to cook for 1 minute, then add the diced potatoes and peas. Mix well and cook for 3–4 minutes, stirring frequently. Remove from the heat, add the chutney and chopped cilantro, and season well.

Preheat the oven to 375°F. Lay a sheet of filo pastry on the work surface and brush with melted butter. Lay another pastry sheet on top and cut into strips 3 inches wide, then brush with the melted butter. Put a spoonful of the potato mixture onto the top left-hand corner of each strip. Fold over to make a triangle and continue folding down the length of the strip to completely encase the filling. Repeat with the remaining filling and pastry. Arrange on baking sheets and bake for 25 minutes until golden and crisp. Serve with pickles and relishes.

SIDE
TANGY ROOTS

Preheat the oven to 350°F. Place **1 chopped parsnip** and **1 trimmed and chopped leek** in a roasting pan, add **1 tablespoon fresh thyme leaves** and **salt** and **freshly ground black pepper**. Dot with **4 tablespoons butter** and cook in the preheated oven for 10 minutes, stirring once. Add **2 diced carrots** and cook for another 30 minutes, until just tender. Add **1½ cups peeled and cooked chestnuts**, **½ shredded curly cabbage**, **1 tablespoon orange marmalade**, and **½ cup vegetable stock** and cook for another 10 minutes. Serve hot. Serves 4

DINNER
VEGETABLE LASAGNE

SERVES 4

Vegetable lasagne is a student staple but it can be a whole lot better than that implies. The key is to take a bit of care and follow a decent recipe like this one.

3 tablespoons olive oil
1 eggplant, cut into rounds ½-inch thick
1 large zucchini, cut into slices
8-ounce ball mozzarella, drained
8–10 dry lasagne sheets
2 tablespoons freshly grated vegetarian
    Parmesan

FOR THE CHEESE SAUCE
3 tablespoons butter
2 tablespoons all-purpose flour
2 cups organic milk
1 cup grated Gruyère

FOR THE TOMATO SAUCE
1–2 tablespoons olive oil
1 onion, finely chopped
2 garlic cloves, finely chopped
1 tablespoon tomato paste
14-ounce can tomatoes
salt and freshly ground black pepper
1 cup cherry tomatoes, halved
1 teaspoon sugar
2 tablespoons freshly chopped basil leaves

Preheat the oven to 400°F. Heat 1 tablespoon of olive oil in a large frying pan over high heat, add the eggplant slices in a single layer, and sauté until golden brown on both sides. Repeat with the remaining eggplant and the zucchini, adding more oil to the pan as needed.

Prepare the tomato sauce. Heat the olive oil in a saucepan, add the onion, and cook until soft but not colored. Add the garlic and continue to cook for 1 minute. Add the tomato paste with both the tomatoes and the sugar, and season with salt and freshly ground black pepper. Cook over low to medium heat for 20 minutes until the sauce has reduced and thickened slightly. Check the seasoning, add the basil, remove from the heat, and cool slightly.

Prepare the cheese sauce. Melt the butter in a saucepan. Stir in the flour and cook for 2 minutes. Slowly add the milk to the pan, stirring constantly. Bring to a boil and simmer very gently for 3–4 minutes, stirring constantly, until the sauce has thickened, coats the back of a spoon, and is smooth and glossy. Remove from the heat and stir in the Gruyère.

Spoon half of the tomato sauce into the base of an 8 x 12-inch ovenproof dish. Scatter with half of the eggplant and zucchini. Tear half of the mozzarella into pieces and spread on top of the vegetables, and top with a layer of lasagne sheets. Repeat this layering one more time. Spoon the cheese sauce over the final lasagne layer, sprinkle with grated Parmesan, and bake for about 30 minutes until golden and bubbling.

DESSERT
CREME BRULEE

Preheat the oven to 300°F. Mix **6 organic egg yolks** with **3 tablespoons sugar**. Heat **2½ cups heavy cream** and **1 vanilla pod** to just below boiling, then leave for 30 minutes to infuse. Reheat and whisk into the egg mixture. Strain the custard into 4 small ramekins. Place the ramekins in a small roasting pan and pour hot water into the pan to come halfway up the ramekins. Bake for 20–30 minutes until the custards are just set but still wobbly in the center. Cool, then chill for at least 2 hours (preferably overnight). To finish, sprinkle the top of each custard with a layer of **sugar**, about 1 tablespoon per ramekin, then place under an extremely hot broiler until the surface is golden and caramelized. Serves 4

WEEK 11

BREAKFAST

TOFU SCRAMBLE WITH SPINACH

Drain and slice **1 block of tofu** into 1-inch cubes, then, crumble it slightly. Sauté **1/2 diced onion** and the crumbled tofu in **oil** for 3–5 minutes, stirring often. Add **2 tablespoons vegetable oil**, **1 tablespoon soy sauce**, **1/2 teaspoon turmeric**, and **salt** and **freshly ground black pepper**, and reduce the heat to medium and allow to cook for 5 minutes, stirring frequently and adding more oil if necessary. Add **1 cup spinach** and let it wilt for 2 minutes. Serve topped with **grated cheese** or wrapped in a **warmed tortilla** with **1 teaspoon of salsa** for a breakfast burrito. Serves 2

SIDE

SMOKY POLENTA FRIES

YOTAM OTTOLENGHI

Line a shallow baking sheet with plastic wrap. Bring **1 1/3 cups vegetable stock** to a boil in a saucepan. Slowly add **1/2 cup quick-cook polenta** while stirring with a wooden spoon. Cook on a low heat for 5 minutes, stirring all the time. Remove from the heat and mix in **2 tablespoons butter**, **1/2 cup grated scarmorza affuicata cheese** (or mozzarella) and **salt** and **freshly ground black pepper** to taste. Once the cheese and butter have melted into the mix, transfer it to the lined baking sheet. Use a wet spatula to level the polenta to an even 2 inches. Cover the surface with plastic wrap and leave to cool completely, then chill for at least 30 minutes. Meanwhile, make a tomato sauce. Place a large nonstick frying pan on high heat. Once hot, add **12 ounces plum tomatoes** and leave for about 15 minutes, stirring occasionally. The tomato skins need to blacken well; don't remove them from the heat too early. Transfer the hot tomatoes to a mixing bowl and break them with a spoon. Pick out the skins and discard. Heat **2 tablespoons olive oil** in a small pan, add **1/2 thinly sliced medium onion**, and cook on medium heat for 3 minutes, just to soften. Add the onion and oil to the tomatoes, then add **2 minced garlic cloves**, **a pinch of red pepper flakes**, **1/4 teaspoon sugar**, and **salt** to taste. When the sauce comes to room temperature, stir in **2 tablespoons chopped parsley** if you like. Once set, remove the polenta from the baking sheet and cut it into fries, roughly 1/2 inch thick and 2 inches long. Fill a medium saucepan with enough vegetable oil to come 1 inch up its sides, and heat well. Toss the chips in **all-purpose flour** until well coated, shake off the excess, and carefully place in hot **vegetable oil**. Fry for about 3 minutes to a golden-brown color, and transfer to paper towels. Don't make too many fries at a time. Serve the hot fries with the tomato sauce on top or in a bowl on the side. Serves 4

LUNCH

RICH AND CREAMY CELERIAC GRATIN

Celeriac has a slightly nutty, milder, and sweeter taste than celery—ideal for making a rich and creamy gratin.

2 tablespoons butter
2 pounds celeriac, peeled and thinly sliced
4 garlic cloves, finely chopped
2 fresh red chiles, finely chopped

1 large stem rosemary leaves, finely chopped
1 cup grated Cheddar
salt and freshly ground black pepper
1 2/3 cups cream

SERVES 4

Preheat the oven to 375°F. Butter a large gratin dish. Cover the base of the gratin dish with a layer of celeriac. Sprinkle with some of the garlic, chile, rosemary, and cheese, and season with salt and pepper. Repeat the layers until everything has been used up, ending with celeriac but reserving a little of the cheese to go on the top. Pour over just enough cream to reach the last layer—it shouldn't cover the celeriac. Sprinkle with the reserved cheese, dot with butter, and bake for 40–50 minutes, until crisp and golden and the celeriac can be easily pierced with a fork.

SIDE

CITRUS BASMATI RICE

Cook **1 1/2 cups basmati rice** for 15–20 minutes or according to the package instructions until cooked through. Stir in the **zest and juice of 1 lime**, **zest and juice of 1 lemon**, **2 tablespoons finely chopped cilantro**, and **1/3 cup plain yogurt**, adding **salt** and **freshly ground black pepper** to taste. Serve immediately, garnished with **lime wedges** and some **cilantro leaves**. Serves 4

DINNER

PUMPKIN AND TOFU LAKSA

SERVES 4

Laksa is a Malaysian dish consisting of noodles served in a spicy, coconut milk-based broth. The silky tofu in this recipe moderates the heat, as do the matchsticks of cucumber sprinkled over the top of the dish to serve.

9 ounces pumpkin of your choice, seeded and cut into 1/2-inch dice

sea salt

4 tablespoons vegetable oil

9 ounces tofu, cut into 4 equal pieces

2 1/2 cups coconut milk

3 tablespoons soy sauce

2 teaspoons sugar

7 ounces rice noodles

2 1/2 cups bean sprouts

1 cucumber, seeded and cut into matchsticks

3–4 scallions, trimmed and cut into matchsticks

1 small bunch cilantro, leaves only

FOR THE SPICE PASTE

2 garlic cloves, minced

1 red chile, finely chopped

1 tablespoon finely grated fresh ginger

3–4 scallions, finely chopped

1 teaspoon turmeric

1 stalk lemongrass

3 lime leaves, chopped

juice of 1 lime

Put the pumpkin in a saucepan, cover with water, add a pinch of salt, and bring to a boil. Reduce the heat, cover with a lid, and simmer for 10 minutes until the pumpkin is tender and can be pierced easily with a fork. Drain, reserving the cooking liquid, and keep warm.

Put all the ingredients for the spice paste in a blender, together with 1–2 tablespoons water, and pulse until you have a smooth, but not too thick, purée.

Heat 1 tablespoon oil in a frying pan set over medium heat, add the tofu, and fry until golden, about 3–4 minutes. Remove from the pan and set aside.

Heat 2 tablespoons oil in a saucepan, add the spice paste, and fry for 2–3 minutes. Then add the coconut milk, tofu, soy sauce, and sugar, followed by the reserved pumpkin liquid. Bring to a boil, reduce the heat, and simmer for 10–15 minutes until the liquid has thickened slightly.

Meanwhile, put the noodles in a bowl, cover with boiling water, and let them soak for 10 minutes, stirring them occasionally so they don't stick together. Drain thoroughly, toss in the remaining oil, and divide among four warmed bowls. Top each with bean sprouts and pumpkin cubes and a piece of tofu. Ladle in the coconut liquid and scatter with the cucumber, scallions, and cilantro.

DESSERT

BROWNIES

Preheat the oven to 325°F. Grease and line a 8 x 12 inch baking pan with parchment paper. Put **1 cup walnut halves** onto a baking sheet and toast in the oven for 5 minutes, leave to cool, then roughly chop. Melt **11 tablespoons diced unsalted butter** and **8 ounces chopped dark chocolate** together in a heatproof bowl either in the microwave on a low setting or over a pan of barely simmering water. Remove from the heat, stir until smooth, and cool slightly. In another bowl beat together **4 large beaten organic eggs**, **2 1/2 cups sugar**, and **1 teaspoon vanilla extract**. Add the melted chocolate and butter mixture and stir gently until combined. Sift **1 cup all-purpose flour** and **a pinch of salt** into the bowl and fold into the batter along with the chopped nuts. Pour into the prepared pan, spread level, and bake on the middle shelf of the preheated oven for 25 minutes until the top has formed a light crust and the underneath is still slightly squishy. Cool in the pan and then cut into squares to serve. Makes 9 squares

WEEK 12

BREAKFAST

TOASTED BAGEL WITH HUMMUS

PAUL McCARTNEY

My favorite breakfast—not only quick and easy, but also very nutritious. Split **a bagel** in half and lightly toast. Spread one half with **1/2 teaspoon Marmite or Vegemite**, and the other with **1 tablespoon hummus** (either store-bought or see Spring, Week 3, Lunch), then sandwich together. Delicious!

PACKED LUNCH

BLOOD ORANGE, AVOCADO, AND WHITE BEAN SALAD

ALLEGRA McEVEDY

Using a small sharp knife, cut the top and bottom off **2 blood oranges** and place them on a cutting board. Working from top to bottom, and following the shape of the orange, cut the peel off in sections. Pick up your naked orange and, over a little bowl, cut between the white dividers so that the orange segments fall into the bowl. Once you have cut out all the segments, give the remaining pulp a good squeeze so that all the juice falls into the bowl. Chop up the stalky ends of **a large handful of watercress** until you get to the leaves, and put both parts in a big bowl with the orange segments (but retain the juice), **1 sliced avocado**, **1 grated carrot**, **a heaping cup cooked white beans**, and **a handful of mint leaves**. Measure out 5 tablespoons of the orange juice into a small bowl (you can drink any remaining juice) with **3 tablespoons extra virgin olive oil** and **1 tablespoon red wine vinegar**. Season with **salt and freshly ground black pepper**, give it a quick whisk with a fork, then spoon it over the salad. Serves 2

LUNCH

CLASSIC FRENCH ONION SOUP

SERVES 4

This is the definitive French soup, rich, filling, and addictive. Slow-cooking the onions gives them tremendous depth of flavor and gives the soup its lovely amber color. The cheese-topped croûtons are simply fantastic.

1 tablespoon sunflower oil	2$^{1}/_{2}$ cups vegetable stock
2 tablespoons butter	sea salt and freshly ground black pepper
1 pound onions, thinly sliced	4 thick slices baguette
1/2 cup white wine	1 cup Gruyère, grated

Melt the oil and butter in a heavy-bottomed saucepan, add the onions, and cook, stirring occasionally, until the edges of the onions begin to turn dark. Reduce the heat to very low and continue to cook the onions for 30 minutes until they are a rich brown color.

Raise the heat, pour in the wine, and deglaze the pan, scraping the base and edges well. Pour in the stock, season with salt and freshly ground pepper, bring to a simmer, and cook very gently for about 45 minutes.

When ready to serve, toast the slices of baguette, sprinkle thickly with the Gruyère, and place under a broiler until the cheese is melted. Place each piece of toast in 4 individual bowls, ladle in the soup, and serve.

SIDE/SNACK

CRISP AND GOLDEN POORIS

Place 1¼ cups all-purpose whole-wheat flour and ½ teaspoon salt in a bowl, add ⅓ cup water, and mix to a fairly soft dough. Knead for 4–5 minutes, until soft but no longer sticky. Put the dough on a lightly floured surface, and work and roll it with your hands until you have a long snake of dough, about 1 inch in diameter. Cut off a piece of dough about 1 inch long, and wrap the remaining dough in plastic wrap. Work the small piece of dough between your palms until it forms a small, neat ball. Coat with **flour**, then roll out until you have a small, flat patty about 3 inches in diameter. Continue cutting and shaping the dough in this way, always keeping the pieces of dough covered with plastic wrap when not being worked. Heat **1 cup vegetable oil** in a wok or large frying pan until hot enough to brown a cube of bread in 30 seconds, and deep fry the pooris, 1 or 2 at a time, making sure you don't overcrowd the pan. Cook each batch for 2–3 minutes, until lightly browned, turning them once and splashing them with hot oil to make them puff up. Drain on paper towels before serving warm. Makes 14

DINNER

SWEET POTATO JALFREZI

SERVES 4

Jalfrezi is one of our favorite kinds of curry. It is quite hot, but in this recipe, the juiciness of the mango cools it down delightfully.

1–2 tablespoons vegetable oil
1 medium onion, chopped
1 garlic clove, minced
2 tablespoons Jalfrezi seasoning
2 cups vegetable stock
1⅓ cups passata

1 pound sweet potatoes, in ½ inch dice
1 pound cauliflower, broken into small florets
1 red pepper, seeded and in ½ inch strips
1 mango, peeled and roughly chopped
salt and freshly ground black pepper
2 tablespoons chopped cilantro

Heat the oil in a heavy-bottomed pan. Gently cook the onion and garlic until soft. Stir in the Jalfrezi seasoning and cook for 3 minutes. Stir in the stock, passata, sweet potatoes, cauliflower, and pepper. Bring to a boil, reduce the heat, and simmer until the vegetables are tender.

Season to taste. Stir in the mango and cilantro and serve immediately. Rice and slices of mango make an ideal accompaniment.

DESSERT

ALMOND SWEETS

Place ½ cup pitted dates, ½ cup dried apricots, ⅓ cup seedless raisins, and **2 tablespoons apple juice** in a food processor or blender, and pulse until smooth, scraping down the sides as necessary. Form the mixture into balls the size of a cherry, then roll them in **½ cup chopped and browned almonds** until completely coated. Makes 30

WEEK 13

BREAKFAST

CINNAMON RAISIN TOAST

Beat **4 organic eggs** lightly with a fork in a bowl. Stir in **1 teaspoon sugar**, **a pinch of salt**, and **1 cup organic milk**. Melt **a pat of butter** in a nonstick frying pan set over medium-low heat. Dip **8 slices of white bread**, one at a time, into the egg mixture. Soak only as many slices as you will be cooking at a time. Place the bread in the frying pan and cook gently until golden brown, then turn and brown the other side. Sprinkle with **a handful of raisins**, dust with **ground cinnamon**, and drizzle with some **honey** if you wish. Serves 2

PACKED LUNCH

ROASTED VEGETABLES AND GIANT WHOLEWHEAT COUSCOUS SALAD

Preheat the broiler. Halve and seed **3 red peppers** and place cut-side down on a baking sheet. Place under the broiler and char until the skins are blackened. Put the peppers in a plastic bag and seal. When cool enough to handle, remove the skins, cut into strips, drizzle with **1 tablespoon olive oil**, and set aside. Thinly slice **2 onions** and place on another baking sheet. Drizzle with **1 tablespoon olive oil**, season with **salt** and **freshly ground black pepper**, and broil, turning occasionally, until charred at the edges. Set aside. Bring a pan of water to a boil, add **1 cup whole-wheat couscous**, and simmer for 7 minutes. Drain then put into a bowl. Add the roasted peppers and onions and **1/2 cup sliced marinated artichoke hearts**. Whisk together **2 tablespoons olive oil** with **1 tablespoon balsamic vinegar** and stir into the couscous. Serves 2

LUNCH

WINTER MINESTRONE

STELLA McCARTNEY

Don't be fooled by the name—the character of this thick, wholesome soup is more North African than Italian. It has a lot in common with the European version though, with the farro playing a similar role to the vermicelli noodles found in many recipes.

2/3 cup farro semiperlato (or pearled spelt)
4 tablespoons olive oil, plus extra to serve
1 large onion, finely chopped
1 leek, finely chopped
1 rib celery, finely chopped
2 medium carrots, peeled and finely chopped
1 medium turnip, peeled and finely chopped
3 garlic cloves, minced

pinch of dried red pepper flakes
14-ounce can tomatoes
1 quart vegetable stock
14-ounce can cannellini beans, drained and rinsed
1 bunch kale, shredded
salt and freshly ground black pepper
freshly grated vegetarian Parmesan to serve

SERVES 4

Rinse the farro in a sieve under cold running water, put into a bowl, cover with cold water, and soak for 20 minutes while you prepare the soup base. Heat the olive oil in a large saucepan. Add the chopped veggies and cook over low-medium heat for 10–15 minutes until tender but not colored. Add the garlic and red pepper flakes and cook for another minute.

Pour the tomatoes into the pan, add the stock, and bring to a boil. Drain the farro and add to the pan. Reduce the heat to a gentle simmer, cover, and cook the soup for 25 minutes until the vegetables are tender and the farro is cooked. Add the cannellini beans and cook for 2–3 minutes more. You may need to add extra stock if the soup is too thick. Add the kale and cook for 3–4 minutes until tender.

Season to taste with salt and freshly ground black pepper. Serve in bowls with a drizzle of olive oil, a sprinkle of grated Parmesan, and slices of toasted sourdough bread.

SIDE

SPICED PARSNIPS

Preheat the oven to 425°F. Cook **5-6 peeled and chopped parsnips** in boiling water for 2 minutes, then drain and toss in **2 tablespoons melted butter or oil**. Mix together **3 tablespoons soft brown sugar**, **1 teaspoon ground cinnamon**, and **1 teaspoon lemon zest**. Roll the buttered parsnips in the sugar mixture and bake in the oven for 20 minutes until golden. Serves 4

DINNER

VEGETARIAN SHEPHERD'S PIE

SERVES 4

There probably aren't that many vegetarian shepherds, unless they are responsible for sheep that are bred solely for their wool. Those who exist needn't feel disadvantaged compared to their carnivorous colleagues—they can make shepherd's pies just as good based on Puy lentils and green split peas.

³/4 cup Puy lentils
¹/4 cup green split peas
6 tablespoons butter
1 red onion, chopped
2 carrots, chopped
2 ribs celery, chopped
1 garlic clove, finely chopped
1 tablespoon fresh thyme leaves
¹/4 teaspoon ground mace
¹/4 teaspoon cayenne pepper
¹/3 cup vegetable stock

sea salt and freshly ground black pepper
3 medium tomatoes, sliced
1¹/2 pounds potatoes
1 small onion, finely chopped
1 cup Cheddar, grated
2 tablespoons organic milk

FOR THE TOMATO SAUCE
2 tablespoons butter
1 cup tomatoes, skinned and chopped
1 tablespoon tomato ketchup

Preheat the oven to 375°F.

Wash and pick over the lentils and split peas, put in a pan, cover with 1 cup water, and bring to a boil. Reduce the heat, cover, and simmer gently until the lentils and peas have absorbed most of the water and are soft, about 40–45 minutes.

Melt 2 tablespoons butter in a frying pan set over medium heat and cook the red onion, carrots, celery, and garlic until softened. Stir into the lentils and split peas. Add the thyme, mace, cayenne pepper, and vegetable stock, and season with salt and freshly ground black pepper. Spoon into a 1 quart baking dish and arrange the slices of tomato in a layer on the top.

Peel and boil the potatoes until tender, then mash with 2 tablespoons butter. Soften the onion in the remaining 2 tablespoons butter and stir into the mash, along with the grated cheese and milk. Season with salt and freshly ground black pepper and spoon on top of the tomatoes. Place in the oven and bake for 30 minutes until golden.

To make the tomato sauce, melt the butter in a saucepan, then add the tomatoes and ketchup. Simmer on a low heat until thickened, about 15 minutes. Served spooned over the pie.

DESSERT

CHRISTMAS PUDDING TRIFLE

TRISTAN WELCH

Bring **²/3 cup organic milk** and **1 cup heavy cream** to a boil with **a little nutmeg**. While the milk and cream are heating, beat **6 organic egg yolks** and **³/4 cup sugar**. Break up and divide an English **Christmas pudding** into four ramekins. Once the milk and cream have boiled, pour into the egg yolks and sugar, constantly mixing. Once mixed, pour the custard into the ramekins through a sieve. Bake in the oven at 225°F for 45 minutes. Once baked, chill in the fridge for a couple of hours. Top the ramekins with **8 crushed amaretti cookies**, then **1 cup heavy cream** whipped with **a dash of brandy**, and then **a sprinkle of toasted almonds** to finish. Serves 4

A

acorn squash, roasted 182
Aikens, Tom 16
alcohol-free piña colada 35
ale and puff pastry pie 177
Alexander, Stephanie 28
alfalfa sprouts: green club sandwich 113
Allen, Darina 201
Allibhoy, Omar 205
almond milk: fruity quinoa 139
almonds: almond cake 36
    almond sweets 222
    baked pears 202
    Bircher muesli with apple 151
    cassata 48
    cherry shortbread 32
    curried egg, almond, and brown rice 21
    eggplant and dried apricot pastilla 90
    florentines 152
    fruit and nut breakfast bars 51
    lemon, almond, and pear cake 132
    lemon and pistachio biscotti 44
    linguine with almonds and Caciocavallo 48
    raspberry and almond bars 60
    tomato, feta, almond, and date baklava 148
    vegetable satay 206
    watercress soup with toasted almonds 63
    wild rice and apricots 131
amaretti cookies: baked pears 202
    cassata 48
    Christmas pudding trifle 226
    fruity amaretti 98
Anderson, Pamela 113
apples: apple cake 136
    apple syllabub 156
    baked apples with yogurt 131
    Bircher muesli with apple 151
    rhubarb, apple, and oat crumble 168
    Waldorf salad 27
    warm halloumi, apple, and radish salad 114
apricot jam: breakfast brioche 55
    chocolate bread and butter pudding 190
apricots (dried): almond sweets 222
    apricot and oat fingers 113
    Bircher muesli with apple 151
    cranberry and apricot oat bars 144
    dried apricot compote 213
    eggplant and dried apricot pastilla 90
    fruit and nut breakfast bars 51
    fruit, seed, and nut muesli 69
    wild rice and apricots 131
    winter fruit salad 209

artichoke hearts: paella verduras 110
    roasted vegetable and giant whole-wheat couscous salad 225
    spring ragout of artichoke hearts, fava beans, peas, and turnips 28
artichokes see globe artichokes; Jerusalem artichokes
arugula: and creamy mustard 40
    beet, red onion, endive salad 181
    Boston lettuce, soft-boiled egg, roast tomatoes, capers, and Parmesan 86
    green club sandwich 113
    pizza two ways 172
    spring vegetable tarte fine 16
    sweet potato gnocchi with arugula pesto 15
    white bean and arugula salad 31
asparagus: asparagus, egg, and cress sandwich 77
    asparagus risotto 60
    asparagus tart 44
    soft-boiled eggs with asparagus spears 15
    cannelloni bean and asparagus gratin 56
    cheese and asparagus croquettes 64
    chickpea with red chard and asparagus 93
    paella verduras 110
    spring vegetable stew 20
    spring vegetable tarte fine 16
avocados: avocado on toast 147
    blood orange, avocado, and white bean salad 221
    green club sandwich 113
    guacamole 102
    quesadillas with avocado, sour cream, and salsa 74
    salad of wild rice, charred corn, spiced pecans, avocados, and feta 106
    tricolor ciabatta 97

B

bagels: toasted bagel with hummus 221
Bailey, Laura 172
baklava, tomato, feta, almond, and date 148
balsamic, acorn squash and 188
bamboo shoots: crispy spring rolls 24
    Thai vegetable curry 152
bananas: banana and honey muffins 105
    banana yogurt pot 117
    banoffee pie 28
    best ever banana bread 20
    fabulous fiber muffins 27
    fried bananas with pecans and maple syrup 59
    nectarine smoothie 73

peanut butter and banana cupcakes 64
    strawberry and banana smoothie 23
    winter fruit salad 209
    yogurt, banana, and rye toast 89
banoffee pie 28
barley flakes: fruit, seed, and nut muesli 69
    granola 193
    granola and berries 85
basil: basil and mushroom tart 139
    basil-scented braised fennel 98
    fresh tomato and basil soup 73
Batali, Mario 48
bayd mahsmi 94
beans: black-eyed bean casserole with cilantro 205
    blood orange, avocado, and white bean salad 221
    cannellini bean and asparagus gratin 56
    cannellini bean and rosemary hummus 85
    Carribean rice and beans 127
    eggplant, potato, and pepper stew 164
    huevos rancheros 43
    Mexican bean salad 69
    refried bean tacos 82
    roasted butternut squash and zucchini 128
    spicy tomato and bean salad 35
    Tuscan bean vegetable soup 147
    white bean and arugula salad 31
    winter minestrone 225
bean sprouts: crispy spring rolls 24
    pad thai noodles 55
    pumpkin and tofu laksa 218
    Thai vegetable curry 152
    vegetable and tofu stir-fry with soba noodles 198
beer: ale and puff pastry pie 177
Beer, Maggi 124
beet: beet, red onion, endive salad 181
    spicy beet salad 198
Bell, Annie 44
berries: granola and berries 85
    summer berry muffins 93
    see also raspberries, strawberries, etc
bhajis: onion bhajis with tomato and chile sauce 201
Bircher muesli with apple 151
blackberries: fruity quinoa 139
black currant ice cream 102
black-eyed beans: black-eyed bean casserole with cilantro 205
    Mexican bean salad 69
blood orange, avocado, and white bean salad 221
blue cheese pâté 63
blueberries: blueberry pancakes 19

fruity quinoa 141

oatmeal with blueberries 31

bok choy: stir-fry with spring vegetables and
noodles 52

borlotti beans: roasted butternut squash and
zucchini 128

bran flakes: fabulous fiber muffins 27

brandy: tiramisù 118

brazil nuts: cauliflower korma 197

fruit, seed, and nut muesli 69

bread: asparagus, egg, and cress sandwich 77

avocado on toast 147

bruschetta broccoli di rape 27

Caesar salad 31

carrot and hummus crunch on sourdough
43

cheese and carrot chutney sandwich 201

cheese and onion sandwich 193

stuffed onions 206

chocolate bread and butter pudding 190

cinnamon raisin toast 225

classic French onion soup 221

classic Irish soda bread 189

crisp and golden pooris 222

French toast 205

garlic bread 48

good old-fashioned macaroni and cheese
43

green club sandwich 113

grilled vegetable bloomer 117

herb bread 160

hot mozzarella sandwich 39

hummus and flatbread 23

melon gazpacho 90

Mexican cornbread 74

potato and Gruyère focaccia 114

Stilton pâté with Melba toast and cherry
tomatoes 109

tangy cauliflower relish and cheese
sandwich 59

tricolor ciabatta 97

vegetarian croque Madame 23

veggie sausage sandwich 143

Welsh rarebit 171

yellow squash and garlic bruschetta 77

yogurt, banana, and rye toast 89

breadcrumbs: parsnip gratin 178

stuffed tomatoes with Gruyère 97

breakfast bars 25

breakfast brioche 55

breakfast frittata 155

brioche, breakfast 55

broccoli: bruschetta broccoli di rape 27

cauliflower korma 197

creamy broccoli soup 47

lemon broccoli 156

pasta with broccoli, sun-dried tomatoes,
and olives 151

penne with broccoli, mascarpone, and
dolcelatte 140

roasted vegetables and miso dressing
with sesame seeds 194

stir-fry with spring vegetables and
noodles 52

super vegetable salad 36

vegetable puff pie 190

lentil stew with pan-fried halloumi and
pomegranate 102

brownies 218

bruschetta: bruschetta broccoli di rape 27

yellow squash and garlic bruschetta 77

Brussels sprouts: bubble and squeak 190

bubble and squeak 190

bulgar wheat: Middle Eastern tabbouleh salad
15

burgers, lentil, chickpea, Cheddar, and onion
186

burrito: spicy burrito with salsa and guacamole
163

butter: fenugreek butter 52

garlic bread 48

herb bread 160

buttermilk: blueberry pancakes 19

classic Irish soda bread 189

summer berry muffins 93

butternut squash: pizza two ways 172

roasted butternut squash and zucchini 128

roasted butternut squash with pine nuts
and goat cheese 163

roasted vegetables and miso dressing
with sesame seeds 194

spelt risotto with butternut squash,
spinach, chestnuts, and goat cheese 178

C

cabbage: bubble and squeak 190

colcannon 210

curried egg, almond, and brown rice 181

stir-fry cabbage 148

summer coleslaw 82

sweet and sour Chinese cabbage 24

tangy roots 214

winter coleslaw 186

Caesar salad 31

cakes: almond cake 36

apple cake 136

best ever banana bread 20

brownies 218

cappuccino cupcakes 186

carrot cake 160

chocolate and chestnut cake 206

gingerbread cake 144

gluten-free cranberry polenta cake 124

lemon drizzle bake 164

peanut butter and banana cupcakes 64

pear cake 210

raspberry and almond bake 60

Victoria sponge cake 172

zucchini cupcakes 82

Caldesi, Katie 167

cannellini beans: cannellini bean and
asparagus gratin 56

cannellini bean and rosemary hummus 85

winter minestrone 225

capers: jacket fries with tartare-style sauce 106

panzanella 117

penne with broccoli, mascarpone, and
dolcelatte 140

cappuccino cupcakes 186

caramel: banoffee pie 28

caramelized grapefruit 39

crème brûlée 214

caraway seeds: carrot and hummus crunch on
sourdough 43

carrots: black-eyed bean casserole with
cilantro 205

carrot and hummus crunch on sourdough
43

carrot cake 160

carrot soup 81

cheese and carrot chutney sandwich 201

chickpea curry 193

chickpea tagine with harissa 156

crispy spring rolls 24

fresh spring rolls 41

roasted vegetables and miso dressing
with sesame seeds 194

spring vegetable stew 20

summer coleslaw 82

super vegetable salad 36

tangy roots 214

vegetable satay 206

vegetarian shepherd's pie 226

Vietnamese style rolls 39

winter coleslaw 186

winter minestrone 225

cashews: granola 193

pilau rice with cashews 197

cassata 48

cassava chips 78

casseroles see stews and casseroles

cauliflower: cauliflower korma 197

crunchy cauliflower and macaroni 51

Sicilian cauliflower pasta 64

split pea dhal and cauliflower curry 132

sweet potato jalfrezi 222

tangy cauliflower pickle and cheese sandwich 59

vegetable pilau 47

celery: creamy celery soup with Stilton 131

panzanella 117

Waldorf salad 27

chard: chickpea with red chard and asparagus 93

cheese: baked zucchini, feta, and tomatoes 60

baked mushroom, mascarpone, and polenta 167

baked penne with dolcelatte and radicchio 168

beet, red onion, endive salad 181

blue cheese pâté 63

Caesar salad 31

cheese and asparagus croquettes 64

cheese and carrot chutney sandwich 203

cheese and chive potato jackets 159

cheese and onion sandwich 193

cheesy kale gratin 202

classic French onion soup 221

creamy celery soup with Stilton 131

crunchy cauliflower and macaroni 51

easy egg florentine 140

eggplant parmigiana 70

eggplant, potato, and pepper stew 164

farro with spicy sun-dried tomatoes and feta 213

fatoush salad with grilled halloumi 59

fava bean salad with cheese chips 73

feta and couscous salad with pomegranate 118

fig and goat cheese salad 123

fregola sarda pasta with tomatoes 105

French bean, Roquefort, and walnut salad 89

Glamorgan sausages 210

good old-fashioned macaroni and cheese 43

Greek salad 109

grilled figs with ricotta 101

hot mozzarella sandwich 39

huevos rancheros 43

leek and goat cheese quiche 155

leek and ricotta tart 182

leek, potato, and feta pizzetta 202

lentil, chickpea, Cheddar, and onion burgers 186

lentil stew with pan-fried halloumi and pomegranate 102

linguine with almonds and Caciocavallo 48

macerated strawberries with mascarpone on rye 118

Mexican cornbread 74

mozzarella and tomato salad 85

mozzarella pasta 93

pasta with fresh spring herbs 51

pear, walnut, and Stilton salad 151

penne with broccoli, mascarpone, and dolcelatte 140

pepper pockets 101

pizza two ways 172

porcini and celery risotto 40

potato and Gruyère focaccia 114

Puy lentils and roasted red peppers with cheese 159

quesadillas with avocado, sour cream, and salsa 74

refried bean tacos 82

risotto with artichokes 98

roasted butternut squash with pine nuts and goat cheese 163

roasted vegetable pizza 94

salad of wild rice, charred corn, spiced pecans, avocado, and feta 106

sautéed eggplant and mozzarella 144

smoky polenta chips 217

spelt risotto with butternut squash, spinach, chestnuts, and goat cheese 178

spinach, ricotta, Parmesan gnocchi with tomato sauce 56

spinach tart 32

Stilton pâté with Melba toast and cherry tomatoes 109

stuffed tomatoes with Gruyère 97

tagliatelle with mushroom sauce 160

tangy cauliflower pickle and cheese sandwich 59

tomato, feta, almond, and date baklava 148

tricolor ciabatta 97

vegetable lasagne 214

vegetable puff pie 190

vegetarian croque Madame 23

vegetarian shepherd's pie 226

warm halloumi, apple and radish salad 114

Welsh rarebit 171

zucchini, potato, and dill frittata 69

see also cream cheese; mascarpone

cheesecake; limoncello and ricotta 24

red currant 90

cherries (dried): cherry shortbread 32

granola and berries 85

cherries (glacé): florentines 152

chervil: spring vegetable tarte fine 16

chestnuts: stuffed onions 206

chocolate and chestnut cake 206

spelt risotto with butternut squash, spinach, chestnuts, and goat cheese 178

tangy roots 214

chickpeas: chickpea curry 193

chickpea with red chard and asparagus 93

hummus and flatbread 23

lentil, chickpea, Cheddar, and onion burgers 186

spicy falafel with tahini sauce 19

chile sauce: refried bean tacos 82

chiles: black-eyed bean casserole with cilantro 205

carrot and hummus crunch on sourdough 43

cauliflower korma 197

chickpea curry 193

chickpea with red chard and asparagus 93

easy spiced dhal with poppadoms 123

green pea curry 86

Mexican cornbread 74

onion bhajis with tomato and chile sauce 201

pad thai noodles 55

papaya salad 78

potato and pea samosas 213

pumpkin and tofu laksa 218

pumpkin soup 189

salad of wild rice, charred corn, spiced pecans, avocado, and feta 106

spicy burrito with salsa and guacamole 163

spicy tomato and bean salad 35

split pea dhal and cauliflower curry 132

stir-fry with spring vegetables and noodles 52

sweet and sour tofu 152

Thai vegetable curry 152

vegetable satay 206

warm halloumi, apple, and radish salad 114

watercress soup with toasted almonds 63

Chinese cabbage, sweet and sour 24

Chinese leaves: crispy spring rolls 24

vegetable and tofu stir-fry with soba noodles 198

chives: cheese and chive potato jackets 159

chocolate: brownies 218

cassata 48

chocolate and chestnut cake 206

chocolate bread and butter pudding 190

chocolate croissant 201

chocolate marzipan dates 178

chocolate truffles 198

double chocolate crackle cookies 40
easy chocolate fudge pudding 182
florentines 152
Christmas pudding trifle 226
chutney, carrot 201
ciabatta: panzanella 117
tricolor ciabatta 97
yellow squash with garlic bruschetta 77
cilantro: black-eyed bean casserole with
cilantro 205
chickpea curry 193
citrus basmati rice 218
crunchy beans with fenugreek butter 52
easy spiced dhal with poppadoms 123
eggplant and dried apricot pastilla 90
fatoush salad with grilled halloumi 59
guacamole 102
Mexican cornbread 74
pad thai noodles 55
pumpkin and tofu laksa 218
spiced wholewheat couscous with sweet
potato and pumpkin seeds 209
Thai vegetable curry 152
Vietnamnese style rolls 39
cilantro cress: carrot soup 81
cinnamon: cinnamon pancakes 177
cinnamon raisin toast 225
toasted rye bread with cinnamon honey
butter 123
citrus basmati rice 218
classic French onion soup 221
classic Irish soda bread 189
club sandwich, green 113
cobnut dressing, whole artichoke with 164
coconut: carrot cake 160
cauliflower korma 197
coconut milk: alcohol-free pina colada 35
Carribean rice and beans 127
pumpkin and tofu laksa 218
split pea dhal and cauliflower curry 132
Thai vegetable curry 152
vegetable satay 206
coffee: cappuccino cupcakes 186
tiramisù 118
colcannon 210
coleslaw: summer coleslaw 82
winter coleslaw 186
cookies: cherry shortbread 32
double chocolate crackle cookies 40
lemon and pistachio biscotti 44
see also amaretti cookies
corn on the cob: salad of wild rice, charred
corn, spiced pecans, avocado, and
feta 106
Thai vegetable curry 152

vegetable and tofu stir-fry with soba
noodles 198
cornbread, Mexican 74
cottage cheese: pasta with fresh spring
herbs 51
Cotton, Fearne 82
couscous: chickpea tagine with harissa 156
feta and couscous salad with
pomegranate 118
red and yellow pepper salad 147
roasted vegetable and whole-wheat
couscous salad 225
spiced whole-wheat couscous with sweet
potato and pumpkin seeds 209
cranberries: cranberry and apricot oat bars
144
gluten-free cranberry polenta cake 124
granola and berries 85
cream: apple syllabub 156
baked penne with dolcelatte and
radicchio 168
banoffee pie 28
chocolate bread and butter pudding 190
Christmas pudding trifle 226
creamy celery soup with Stilton 131
crème brûlée 214
panna cotta 128
pavlova with raspberries 114
pistachio meringues 106
red currant cheesecake 90
spinach tart 32
strawberries with mascarpone and cream
70
tiramisù 118
two onion quiche 63
scones 37
see also sour cream
cream cheese: cheese and onion sandwich 193
peanut butter and banana cupcakes 64
red currant cheesecake 90
Stilton pâté with Melba toast and cherry
tomatoes 109
zucchini cupcakes 82
crème brûlée 214
crème fraîche: asparagus tart 44
eggplant with tomatoes and crème
fraîche 81
parsnip gratin 178
potatoes with hazelnuts and rosemary 194
pumpkin soup 189
cress: asparagus, egg, and cress sandwich 77
carrot soup 81
crisp and golden pooris 222
croissant, chocolate 201
croque Madame, vegetarian 23

croquettes, cheese and asparagus 64
crumble: penne with broccoli, mascarpone,
and dolcelatte 140
rhubarb, apple, and oat crumble 168
cucumber: bayd mahsmi 94
cucumber and yogurt dip 131
fatoush salad with grilled halloumi 59
Vietnamese style rolls 39
Greek salad 109
Middle Eastern tabbouleh salad 15
panzanella 117
pumpkin and tofu laksa 218
cupcakes: cappuccino cupcakes 186
peanut butter and banana cupcakes 64
currants: winter fruit salad 209
curries: cauliflower korma 197
chickpea curry 193
curried egg, almond, and brown rice 181
green pea curry 86
split pea dhal and cauliflower curry 132
sweet potato jalfrezi 222
Thai vegetable curry 152

D

D'Acampo, Gino 24
dates: almond sweets 222
chocolate marzipan dates 178
fruit and nut breakfast bars 51
tomato, feta, almond, and date baklava
148
Demetre, Anthony 81
dhal: easy spiced dhal with poppadoms 123
split pea dhal and cauliflower curry 132
dips: baba ghanoush 136
cucumber and yogurt dip 131
guacamole 102
spiced pea dip 36
tahini dip 135
double chocolate crackle cookies 40
dried fruit: cassata 48
fruit, seed, and nut muesli 69
drinks: alcohol-free pina colada 35
mango lassi 74
nectarine smoothie 73
strawberry and banana smoothie 23
dulche de leche: banoffee pie 28

E

easy chocolate fudge pudding 182
easy egg florentine 140
easy spiced dhal with poppadoms 123
eggplant: eggplant and dried apricot pastilla
90
baba ghanoush 136

eggplant casserole with pomegranate 124
eggplant parmigiana 70
eggplant, potato, and pepper stew 164
eggplant with tomatoes and crème fraîche 81
grilled vegetable bloomer 117
ratatouille 89
roast vegetable tart 155
roasted vegetable pizza 94
sautéed eggplant and mozzarella 144
Thai vegetable curry 152
vegetable lasagne 214
eggs: asparagus, egg, and cress sandwich 77
bayd mahsmi 94
blue cheese pâté 63
boston lettuce, soft-boiled egg, roast tomatoes, capers, and Parmesan 86
breakfast brioche 55
breakfast frittata 155
cinnamon raisin toast 225
curried egg, almond, and brown rice 181
easy egg florentine 140
egg and spinach 161
French toast 205
fresh pea and fava bean omelet 105
huevos rancheros 43
laban bil bayd 44
oeuf en cocotte 109
rösti with mushrooms 127
scrambled eggs with mushrooms 135
soft-boiled eggs with asparagus spears 17
spaghetti omelet 35
spicy burrito with salsa and guacamole 165
tortilla de patatas 205
vegetarian croque Madame 23
zucchini omelet 83
zucchini, potato, and dill frittata 69
Elia, Maria 148
endive: baked penne with dolcelatte and radicchio 168
beet, red onion, endive salad 181
black olive, endive, and orange salad 177
French bean, Roquefort, and walnut salad 89
English breakfast muffins 181

F

fabulous fiber muffins 27
Fairley, Josephine 171
falafel: spicy falafel with tahini sauce 19
farls, potato 197
farro: farro, sun-dried tomatoes, and feta 213
winter minestrone 225

fatoush salad with grilled halloumi 59
fava beans: fava bean salad with cheese chips 73
fresh pea and broad bean omelette 105
globe artichokes with fava beans and oregano 32
paella verduras 110
spring ragout of artichoke hearts, fava beans, peas, and turnips 28
spring vegetable stew 20
stir-fry with spring vegetables and noodles 52
fennel: basil-scented braised fennel 98
fennel sautéed with peppers 135
fenugreek butter, green beans with 52
feta cheese: baked zucchini, feta, and tomatoes 60
beet, red onion, endive salad 181
farro, sun-dried tomatoes, and feta 213
feta and couscous salad with pomegranate 118
Greek salad 109
leek, potato, and feta 'pizzetta' 202
pizza two ways 172
salad of wild rice, charred sweet corn, spiced pecans, avocado, and feta 106
tomato, feta, almond, and date baklava 148
figs: fig and goat cheese salad 123
grilled figs with ricotta 101
filo pastry: eggplant and dried apricot pastilla 90
spinach filos 70
tomato, feta, almond, and date baklava 148
Firth, Livia 151
flapjacks, dried cranberry and apricot 144
flatbread, hummus and 23
florentines 152
focaccia, potato, and Gruyère 114
Fox, Mindy 213
fregola sarda pasta with tomatoes 105
French beans: French bean, Roquefort, and walnut salad 89
papaya salad 78
see also green beans
French toast 205
fresh pea and fava bean omelet 105
fresh tomato and basil soup 73
fries: cheese fries 73
jacket fries with tartare-style sauce 106
smoky polenta fries 217
frittata: breakfast frittata 155
zucchini, potato, and dill frittata 69
fruit: fruit and nut breakfast bars 51

fruit, seed, and nut muesli 69
fruity quinoa 139
granola and berries 85
summer berry muffins 93
winter fruit salad 209
see also apples, strawberries etc
fudge pudding, easy chocolate 182

G

garlic: bruschetta broccoli di rape 27
eggplant and dried apricot pastilla 90
garlic bread 48
laban bil bayd 44
panzanella 117
roast vegetable tart 155
stir-fry with spring vegetables and noodles 52
yellow zucchini and garlic bruschetta 77
Gates, Stefan 55
gazpacho, melon 90
gherkins: tartare-style sauce 106
ginger: eggplant and dried apricot pastilla 90
gingerbread cake 144
pumpkin soup 189
spicy tofu with ginger 171
Glamorgan sausages 210
globe artichokes: globe artichokes with fava beans and oregano 32
risotto with artichokes 98
whole artichoke with hazelnut dressing 164
gluten-free cranberry polenta cake 124
gnocchi: spinach, ricotta, Parmesan gnocchi 56
sweet potato gnocchi with arugula pesto 15
goat cheese: baked penne with dolcelatte and radicchio 168
cheese and onion sandwich 193
cheesy kale gratin 202
fig and goat cheese salad 123
fregola sarda pasta with tomatoes 105
leek and goat cheese quiche 155
potato salad with goat cheese dressing 126
Puy lentils and roasted red peppers with goat cheese 159
roasted butternut squash with pine nuts and goat cheese 163
spelt risotto with butternut squash, spinach, chestnuts, and goat cheese 178
golden raisins: apple cake 136
chocolate bread and butter pudding 190
fabulous fiber muffins 27

fruit, seed, and nut muesli 69
granola 193
honey-roasted nuts and seeds 168
zucchini cupcakes 82
gooseberry fool 56
granita, watermelon 94
granola 193
granola and berries 85
grapefruit: caramelized grapefruit 39
carrot soup 81
gratins: cannellini bean and asparagus gratin 56
cheesy kale gratin 202
parsnip gratin 178
rich and creamy celeriac gratin 217
Greek salad 109
green beans: crunchy beans with fenugreek butter 52
paella verduras 110
split pea dhal and cauliflower curry 132
super vegetable salad 36
see also French beans
green club sandwich 113
green pea curry 86
green pea pilau 209
grilled field mushrooms 20
ground rice: best ever banana bread 20
Gruyère cheese: classic French onion soup 221
lentil, chickpea, Cheddar, and onion burgers 186
oeuf en cocotte 109
potato and Gruyère focaccia 114
roast vegetable pizza 94
spring vegetable tarte fine 16
stuffed tomatoes with Gruyère 97
vegetarian croque Madame 215
vegetable lasagne 214
guacamole 102
Gyngell, Skye 193

H

halloumi cheese: lentil stew with pan-fried halloumi and pomegranate 102
fatoush salad with grilled halloumi 59
halloumi with strawberry sauce 120
warm halloumi, apple and radish salad 114
Hansen, Anna 106
harissa, tagine with 156
Harrelson, Woody 47
hash browns 185
hazelnuts: carrot soup 81
florentines 152
fruit and nut breakfast bars 51
pear cake 210

penne with broccoli, mascarpone, and dolcelatte 140
potatoes with hazelnuts and rosemary 194
summer coleslaw 82
herb bread 160
honey: apricot and oat fingers 113
banana and honey muffins 105
beet, red onion, endive salad 181
dried apricot compote 213
eggplant and dried apricot pastilla 90
fruit and nut breakfast bars 51
fruity amaretti 98
granola 193
grilled peaches with Greek yogurt 110
honey-roasted nuts and seeds 168
mango lassi 74
toasted rye bread with cinnamon honey butter 123
winter fruit salad 209
yogurt, banana, and rye toast 89
huevos rancheros 43
hummus: cannellini bean and rosemary hummus 85
carrot and hummus crunch on sourdough 43
green club sandwich 113
hummus and flatbread 23
toasted bagel with hummus 221

I

ice cream: cassata 48
black currant 102

J

jacket fries with tartare-style sauce 106
jalfrezi, sweet potato 222
jam: breakfast brioche 55
chocolate bread and butter pudding 190
Victoria sponge cake 172
Jerusalem artichoke soup 185

K

kale: cheesy kale gratin 202
stir-fried kale 124
korma, cauliflower 197

L

laban bil bayd 44
laksa, pumpkin and tofu 218
lasagne, vegetable 214
lassi, mango 74
leeks: boston lettuce, soft-boiled egg, roast tomatoes, capers, and Parmesan 88

colcannon 210
creamy broccoli soup 47
leek and goat cheese quiche 155
leek and potato soup 171
leek and ricotta tart 182
leek, potato, and feta pizzetta 202
tangy roots 214
vegetable puff pie 190
winter minestrone 225
lemon: citrus basmati rice 218
crêpes with lemon and sugar 47
eggplant casserole with pomegranate 124
globe artichokes with fava beans and oregano 32
guacamole 102
hummus and flatbread 23
lemon, almond, and pear cake 132
lemon and lime tart 52
lemon and pistachio biscotti 44
lemon broccoli 156
lemon drizzle bake 164
pancakes with lemon and sugar 49
lemongrass: sweet and sour tofu 152
lemon thyme: shallots glazed with orange 140
lentils: eggplant casserole with pomegranate 124
lentil, chickpea, Cheddar, and onion burgers 186
lentil stew with pan-fried halloumi and pomegranate 124
lentils with tahini dip 135
Puy lentils and roasted red peppers with goat cheese 159
stuffed onions 206
vegetarian shepherd's pie 226
lettuce: Boston lettuce, soft-boiled egg, roast tomatoes, capers, and Parmesan 86
Caesar salad 31
fatoush salad with grilled halloumi 59
roasted butternut squash and zucchini 128
spicy beet salad 198
super vegetable salad 36
Vietnamese style rolls 39
warm halloumi, apple, and radish salad 109
watercress and lettuce salad 111
limes: chickpea curry 193
citrus basmati rice 218
crunchy beans with fenugreek butter 52
guacamole 102
lemon and lime tart 52
mango and lime 97
melon, lime, and mint soup 55

papaya salad 78
limoncello and ricotta cheesecake 24
linguine with almonds and Caciocavallo 48
Locatelli, Giorgio 73
Loubet, Bruno 90
Louie, Laura 47

M

macaroni: crunchy cauliflower and macaroni 51
    good old-fashioned macaroni and cheese 43
    pasta with fresh spring herbs 51
macerated strawberries with mascarpone on rye 118
McCartney, Paul 36, 82, 221
McCartney, Stella 82, 123, 160, 181, 209, 225
McEvedy, Allegra 221
Malgieri, Nick 114
mangoes: mango and lime 97
    mango lassi 74
    sweet potato jalfrezi 222
maple syrup: fried bananas with pecans and maple syrup 59
marinated olives 28
marmalade: marmalade muffins 127
    tangy roots 214
Marsala: baked pears 202
    tiramisù 118
marzipan: chocolate marzipan dates 178
mascarpone: baked mushroom, mascarpone, and polenta 167
    macerated strawberries with mascarpone on rye 118
    penne with broccoli, mascarpone, and dolcelatte 140
    strawberries with mascarpone and cream 70
    tiramisù 118
mayonnaise: jacket fries with tartare-style sauce 106
    winter coleslaw 186
Maxwell, Andrew 109
Melba toast, Stilton pâté with cherry tomatoes and 109
melon: melon and strawberries 77
    melon gazpacho 90
    melon, lime, and mint soup 55
    peach salad 81
    watermelon granita 94
meringues: pavlova with raspberries 114
    pistachio meringues 106
Mexican bean salad 69
Mexican cornbread 74
Middle Eastern tabbouleh salad 15

milk: alcohol-free pina colada 35
    baked mushroom, mascarpone, and polenta 167
    carrot soup 81
    chocolate bread and butter pudding 190
    Christmas pudding trifle 226
    cinnamon raisin toast 225
    creamy celery soup with Stilton 131
    nectarine smoothie 73
    parsnip gratin 178
    oatmeal with blueberry compote 31
minestrone, winter 225
mint: eggplant and dried apricot pastilla 90
    eggplant casserole with pomegranate 124
    feta and couscous salad with pomegranate 118
    laban bil bayd 44
    melon and strawberries 77
    melon, lime, and mint soup 55
    Middle Eastern tabbouleh salad 15
miso: miso broth 189
    roasted vegetables and miso dressing with sesame seeds 194
morels: asparagus risotto 60
mozzarella cheese: cheese and asparagus croquettes 64
    eggplant parmigiana 70
    hot mozzarella sandwich 39
    mozzarella and tomato salad 85
    mozzarella pasta 93
    sautéed eggplant and mozzarella 144
    tricolor ciabatta 97
    vegetable lasagne 214
muesli: Bircher muesli with apple 151
    fruit, seed, and nut muesli 69
muffins: banana and honey muffins 105
    English breakfast muffins 181
    fabulous fiber muffins 27
    marmalade muffins 127
    onion and walnut muffins 167
    summer berry muffins 93
mushrooms: ale and puff pastry pie 177
    asparagus risotto 60
    baked mushroom, mascarpone, and polenta 167
    baked penne with dolcelatte and radicchio 168
    basil and mushroom tart 139
    creamy mushroom soup 145
    crispy spring rolls 24
    crunchy cauliflower and macaroni 51
    grilled shiitake mushrooms 20
    quesadillas with avocado, soured cream, and salsa 74

roasted herby mushrooms 172
roasted mushrooms, tomatoes, and pine nuts 163
roasted vegetable pizza 94
rosti with mushrooms 127
scrambled eggs with mushrooms 135
tagliatelle with mushroom sauce 160
Thai vegetable curry 152
vegetable and tofu stir-fry with soba noodles 198
vegetable puff pie 190
walnut and mushroom risotto 136
mustard: arugula and creamy mustard 40

N

Napa cabbage: vegetable and tofu stir-fry with soba noodles 198
nectarine smoothie 73
noodles: pad thai noodles 55
    pumpkin and tofu laksa 218
    stir-fry with spring vegetables and noodles 52
    vegetable and tofu stir-fry with soba noodles 198
    Vietnamese style rolls 39
nuts: roasted honey nuts and seeds 168
    see also almonds, walnuts, etc

O

oatmeal with blueberry compote 31
oats: apricot and oat fingers 113
    Bircher muesli with apple 151
    cranberry and apricot oat bars 144
    fruit and nut breakfast bars 51
    fruit, seed, and nut muesli 69
    granola 193
    oatmeal with blueberry compote 31
    rhubarb, apple, and oat crumble 168
oeuf en cocotte 109
okra: Thai vegetable curry 152
olives: baba ghanoush 136
    black olive, endive, and orange salad 177
    carrot soup 81
    eggplant, potato, and pepper stew 164
    fregola sarda pasta with tomatoes 105
    Greek salad 109
    marinated olives 28
    mozzarella and tomato salad 85
    panzanella 117
    penne with broccoli, mascarpone, and dolcelatte 140
    pepper pockets 101
omelets: fresh pea and fava bean omelet 105
    spaghetti omelet 35

onions: asparagus risotto 60
baked mushroom, mascarpone, and polenta 167
bayd mhamsi 94
beet, red onion, endive salad 181
cheese and onion sandwich 193
chickpea tagine with harissa 156
chickpea with red chard and asparagus 93
classic French onion soup 221
eggplant and dried apricot pastilla 90
Glamorgan sausages 210
grilled vegetable bloomer 117
Jerusalem artichoke soup 185
lentil, chickpea, Cheddar, and onion burgers 186
onion and walnut muffins 167
onion bhajis with tomato and chile sauce 201
panzanella 117
paella verduras 110
pizza two ways 172
pumpkin soup 189
risotto with artichokes 98
roasted vegetable tart 155
roasted vegetable and giant wholewheat couscous salad 225
salad of wild rice, charred corn, spiced pecans, avocado, and feta 106
stuffed onions 206
tagliatelle with mushroom sauce 160
tomato, feta, almond, and date baklava 148
tortilla de patatas 205
vegetable pilau 47
vegetarian shepherd's pie 226
Waldorf salad 27
winter minestrone 225
orange: black olive, endive, and orange salad 177
blood orange, avocado, and white bean salad 221
carrot cake 160
chocolate bread and butter pudding 190
dried apricot compote 213
feta and couscous salad with pomegranate 118
fruity amaretti 98
grilled peaches with Greek yogurt 110
melon, lime, and mint soup 55
orange marinated tofu skewers 113
raspberry and almond tart 60
shallots glazed with orange 140
winter fruit salad 209
orecchiette pasta: pasta with broccoli 151
Ottolenghi, Yotam 217
oyster sauce: pad thai noodles 55

P
pad thai noodles 55
paella verduras 110
pancakes: blueberry pancakes 19
cinnamon pancakes 177
crêpes with lemon and sugar 47
Scotch pancakes with maple syrup 45
spiced pumpkin pancakes 143
panna cotta 128
panzanella 117
papaya salad 78
pappardelle with cavolo nero 185
parsnips: parsnip gratin 178
parsnip soup 167
roasted vegetables and miso dressing with sesame seeds 194
spiced parsnips 226
tangy roots 214
pasta: baked penne with dolcelatte and radicchio 168
crunchy cauliflower and macaroni 51
fregola sarda pasta with tomatoes 105
good old-fashioned macaroni and cheese 43
linguine with almonds and Caciocavallo 48
mozzarella pasta 95
pappardelle with kale 185
pasta with broccoli 151
pasta with fresh spring herbs 51
penne with broccoli, mascarpone, and dolcelatte 140
Sicilian cauliflower pasta 66
tagliatelle with mushroom sauce 162
vegetable lasagne 214
pastilla, eggplant and dried apricot 90
pastries: eggplant and dried apricot pastilla 90
leek, potato, and feta pizzetta 202
spinach filos 70
tomato, feta, almond, and date baklava 148
see also pies; quiches; tarts
pâte brisée 139
pâtés: blue cheese pâté 63
Stilton pâté with Melba toast and cherry tomatoes 109
pavlova with raspberries 114
peaches: fruity amaretti 98
grilled peaches with Greek yogurt 110
peach salad 81
peanut butter and banana cupcakes 64
peanuts: pad thai noodles 55
pears: baked pears 202

beet, red onion, endive salad 181
lemon, almond, and pear cake 132
pear cake 210
pear, walnut, and Stilton salad 151
pears poached with star anise 148
peas: fennel sautéed with peppers 135
fresh pea and fava bean omelet 105
green pea curry 86
green pea pilau 209
paella verduras 110
potato and pea samosas 213
spiced pea dip 36
spring ragout of artichoke hearts, fava beans, peas, and turnips 28
spring vegetable stew 20
spring vegetable tarte fine 16
vegetable pilau 47
watercress soup 63
peas (split): easy spiced dhal with poppadoms 123
split pea dhal and cauliflower curry 132
vegetarian shepherd's pie 226
pecans: beet, red onion, endive salad 181
easy chocolate fudge pudding 182
fried bananas with pecans and maple syrup 59
fruit, seed, and nut muesli 69
fruity quinoa 139
pecan pie 194
salad of wild rice, charred corn, spiced pecans, avocado, and feta 106
penne: baked penne with dolcelatte and radicchio 168
mozzarella pasta 93
penne with broccoli, mascarpone, and dolcelatte 140
peperonata 157
peppers: chickpea tagine with harissa 156
eggplant, potato, and pepper stew 164
fatoush salad with grilled halloumi 59
fennel sautéed with peppers 135
grilled vegetable bloomer 117
melon gazpacho 90
Mexican bean salad 69
onion bhajis with tomato and chile sauce 201
grilled peaches with Greek yogurt 110
paella verduras 110
pepper pockets 101
potato salad 128
Puy lentils and roasted red peppers with goat cheese 159
ratatouille 89
red and yellow pepper salad 147
roast vegetable tart 155

roasted vegetable and whole wheat couscous salad 225

roasted vegetable pizza 94

sweet potato jalfrezi 222

tagine with harissa 158

Thai vegetable curry 152

Vietnamese style rolls 39

Pernod: pears poached with star anise 148

pesto: grilled vegetable bloomer 117

sweet potato gnocchi with arugula pesto 15

Peyton, Oliver 164

pies: ale and puff pastry pie 177

banoffee pie 28

vegetable puff pie 190

pilau: green pea pilau 209

pilau rice with cashews 197

vegetable 47

pina colada, alcohol-free 35

pine nuts: blue cheese pâté 63

eggplant, potato, and pepper stew 164

fregola sarda pasta with tomatoes 105

leek and ricotta tart 182

roasted butternut squash with pine nuts and goat cheese 163

roasted mushrooms, tomatoes, and pine nuts 163

Sicilian cauliflower pasta 64

pineapple: alcohol-free pina colada 35

pineapple fritters 78

Pink 70

pistachio nuts: feta and couscous salad with pomegranate 118

grilled peaches with Greek yogurt 110

lemon and pistachio biscotti 44

pistachio meringues 106

spiced whole-wheat couscous with sweet potato and pistachios 209

pita breads: fatoush salad with grilled halloumi 59

Pizarro, José 110

pizza: pizza two ways 172

roasted vegetable pizza 94

pizzetta, leek, potato, and feta 202

plum crumble 140

polenta: baked mushroom, mascarpone, and polenta 167

gluten-free cranberry polenta cake 124

Mexican cornbread 74

smoky polenta chips 217

super vegetable salad 36

pomegranate molasses: eggplant casserole with pomegranate 124

lentil stew with pan-fried halloumi and pomegranate 102

pomegranate seeds: feta and couscous salad with pomegranate 118

mango lassi 74

pooris, crisp and golden 222

poppy seeds: summer coleslaw 82

porcini mushrooms: porcini and celery risotto 40

tagliatelle with mushroom sauce 160

potatoes: breakfast frittata 155

bubble and squeak 190

cheese and asparagus croquettes 64

cheese and chive potato jackets 159

colcannon 210

creamy broccoli soup 47

creamy celery soup with Stilton 131

eggplant, potato, and pepper stew 164

hash browns 185

jacket fries with tartare-style sauce 106

leek and potato soup 171

leek, potato, and feta pizzetta 202

potato and Gruyère focaccia 114

potato farls 197

potato and pea samosas 213

potato salad with goat cheese dressing 128

potatoes with hazelnuts and rosemary 194

rosti with mushrooms 127

split pea dhal and cauliflower curry 132

spring vegetable stew 20

tortilla de patatas 205

vegetarian shepherd's pie 226

scones 63

zucchini, potato, and dill frittata 69

Potts Dawson, Arthur 128

puff pastry: ale and puff pastry pie 177

pumpkin: pumpkin and tofu laksa 220

pumpkin soup 191

spiced pumpkin pancakes 145

pumpkin seeds: Bircher muesli with apple 151

fruit and nut breakfast bars 51

honey-roasted nuts and seeds 168

spiced whole wheat couscous with sweet potato and pistachios 209

Puy lentils and roasted red peppers with goat cheese 159

quesadillas with avocado, sour cream, and salsa 74

quiches: leek and goat cheese quiche 155

see also tarts

quince: poached quince with vanilla 159

quinoa: fruity quinoa 139

quinoa and roasted tomato salad 19

radicchio: baked penne with dolcelatte and radicchio 168

French bean, Roquefort, and walnut salad 89

radishes: fatoush salad with grilled halloumi 59

summer coleslaw 82

warm halloumi, apple, and radish salad 114

raisins: almond sweets 222

carrot cake 160

cinnamon raisin toast 225

dried apricot compote 213

florentines 152

fruit, seed, and nut muesli 69

leek and ricotta tart 182

Sicilian cauliflower pasta 64

spiced whole wheat couscous with sweet potato and pumpkin seeds 209

wild rice and apricots 131

Randall, Theo 40

rarebit, Welsh 171

raspberries: pavlova with raspberries 114

pistachio meringues 106

raspberry and almond bars 60

ratatouille 89

red and yellow pepper salad 147

red kidney beans: Carribean rice and beans 127

red currant cheesecake 90

refried beans: huevos rancheros 43

refried bean tacos 82

relish, tangy cauliflower 59

rhubarb: rhubarb, apple, and oat crumble 168

rhubarb sorbet 16

rice: asparagus risotto 60

Carribean rice and beans 127

citrus basmati rice 218

curried egg, almond, and brown rice 181

green pea pilau 209

paella verduras 110

pilau rice with cashews 197

porcini and celery risotto 40

risotto with artichokes 98

vegetable pilau 47

walnut and mushroom risotto 136

see also wild rice

ricotta: fruity amaretti 98

grilled figs with ricotta 101

leek and ricotta tart 182

spelt risotto with butternut squash, spinach, chestnuts, and goat cheese 178

spinach, ricotta, Parmesan gnocchi 56

R

Q

risotto: asparagus risotto 60
porcini and celery risotto 40
risotto with artichokes 98
walnut and mushroom risotto 136
Rogan, Simon 194
root vegetables: tangy roots 214
Roquefort cheese: French bean, Roquefort, and walnut salad 89
rosti with mushrooms 127
rye bread: macerated strawberries with mascarpone on rye 118
toasted rye bread with cinnamon honey butter 123
yogurt, banana, and rye toast 89
rye flakes: granola 193

S

salads: bayd mahsmi 94
beet, red onion, endive salad 181
black olive, endive, and orange salad 177
blood orange, avocado, and white bean salad 221
Caesar salad 31
fatoush salad with grilled halloumi 59
fava bean salad with cheese chips 73
feta and couscous salad with pomegranate 118
fig and goat cheese salad 123
French bean, Roquefort, and walnut salad 89
Greek salad 109
melon and peach salad 81
Mexican bean salad 69
Middle Eastern tabbouleh salad 15
mozzarella and tomato salad 85
panzanella 117
papaya salad 78
pear, walnut, and Stilton salad 151
potato salad 128
quinoa and roasted tomato salad 19
red and yellow pepper salad 147
roasted butternut squash and zucchini salad 128
roasted vegetable and whole wheat couscous salad 225
salad of wild rice, charred corn, spiced pecans, avocado, and feta 106
spicy beet salad 198
spicy tomato and bean salad 35
summer coleslaw 82
super vegetable salad 36
Waldorf salad 27
warm halloumi, apple, and radish salad 114

watercress and lettuce salad 109
white bean and arugula salad 31
winter coleslaw 186
salsa 102
quesadillas with avocado, sour cream and salsa 74
spicy burrito with salsa and guacamole 163
samosas, potato and pea 213
Sandler, Nick 43
sandwiches: asparagus, egg, and cress sandwich 77
cheese and carrot chutney sandwich 201
cheese and onion sandwich 193
green club sandwich 113
hot mozzarella sandwich 39
tangy cauliflower relish and cheese sandwich 59
vegetarian croque Madame 23
veggie sausage sandwich 143
satay, vegetable 206
sausages: Glamorgan sausages 210
veggie sausage sandwich 143
scallions: ale and puff pastry pie 177
fatoush salad with grilled halloumi 59
Mexican cornbread 74
Middle Eastern tabbouleh salad 15
pumpkin and tofu laksa 218
quesadillas with avocado, sour cream, and salsa 74
salsa 102
spicy burrito with salsa and guacamole 163
spring vegetable stew 20
spring vegetable tarte fine 16
stir-fry with spring vegetables and noodles 52
summer coleslaw 82
super vegetable salad 36
vegetable and tofu stir-fry with soba noodles 198
scones 63
seeds: roasted butternut squash and zucchini salad 128
see also pumpkin seeds, sunflower seeds, etc
semolina: sweet potato gnocchi with arugula pesto 15
sesame seeds, roasted vegetables, and miso dressing with 194
shallots glazed with orange 140
shepherd's pie, vegetarian 226
sherry: tiramisù 118
shiitake mushrooms: vegetable and tofu stir-fry with soba noodles 198
shortbread, cherry 32

Sicilian cauliflower pasta 64
skewers: grilled peaches with Greek yogurt 110
orange marinated tofu 113
vegetable satay 206
smoky polenta chips 217
smoothie; nectarine smoothie 73
strawberry and banana smoothie 23
snow peas: summer coleslaw 82
vegetable and tofu stir-fry with soba noodles 198
soba noodles, vegetable and tofu stir-fry with 198
soda bread, classic Irish 189
soft-boiled eggs with asparagus spears 15
sorbets: rhubarb sorbet 16
super smooth strawberry sorbet 86
sorrel: spring vegetable tarte fine 16
soups: carrot soup 81
classic French onion soup 221
creamy broccoli soup 47
creamy celery soup with Stilton 131
fresh tomato and basil soup 73
Jerusalem artichoke soup 185
leek and potato soup 171
melon gazpacho 90
melon, lime, and mint soup 55
miso broth 189
parsnip soup 167
pumpkin soup 189
Tuscan bean vegetable soup 147
watercress soup with toasted almonds 63
winter minestrone 225
sourdough bread: carrot and hummus crunch on sourdough 43
veggie sausage sandwich 145
sour cream: black-eyed bean casserole with cilantro 205
Mexican cornbread 74
peanut butter and banana cupcakes 64
quesadillas with avocado, sour cream, and salsa 74
Tuscan bean vegetable soup 147
soy sauce: chickpea curry 193
rosti with mushrooms 127
spicy tofu with ginger 171
sweet and sour tofu 152
vegetable and tofu stir-fry with soba noodles 198
Spacey, Kevin 102
spaghetti omelet 35
spaghetti: pasta with fresh spring herbs 51
spaghetti omelet 35
spelt risotto with butternut squash, spinach, chestnuts, and goat cheese 178
spiced parsnips 226

spiced pea dip 36
spiced pumpkin pancakes 143
spiced whole wheat couscous with sweet
        potato and pistachios 209
spicy beet salad 198
spicy falafel with tahini sauce 19
spicy tofu with ginger 171
spicy tomato and bean salad 35
spinach: easy egg florentine 140
        egg and spinach 161
        pepper pockets 101
        roasted butternut squash and zucchini
        salad 128
        spelt risotto with butternut squash,
        spinach, chestnuts, and goat cheese 178
        spinach filos 70
        spinach, ricotta, Parmesan gnocchi 56
        spinach tart 32
        spring vegetable tarte fine 16
        tofu scramble with spinach 217
split peas see peas (split)
sponge cake, Victoria 172
spring ragout of artichoke hearts, fava beans,
        peas, and turnips 28
spring rolls: crispy spring rolls 24
        Vietnamese style rolls 39
spring vegetable stew 20
spring vegetable tarte fine 16
squash: pizza two ways 172
        roasted butternut squash 182
        roasted butternut squash and zucchini
        salad 128
        roasted butternut squash with pine nuts
        and goat cheese 163
        roasted vegetables and miso dressing
        with sesame seeds 194
        spelt risotto with butternut squash,
        spinach, chestnuts, and goat cheese 178
star anise, pears poached with 148
stews and casseroles: black-eyed bean
        casserole with cilantro 205
        chickpea tagine with harissa 156
        eggplant casserole with pomegranate 124
        eggplant, potato, and pepper stew 164
        lentil stew with pan-fried halloumi and
        pomegranate 102
        spring vegetable stew 20
Stilton cheese: creamy celery soup with Stilton
        131
        pear, walnut and Stilton salad 151
        Stilton pâté with Melba toast and cherry
        tomatoes 109
stir-fry with spring vegetables and noodles 52
strawberries: fruity amaretti 98
        macerated strawberries with mascarpone

on rye 118
        melon and strawberries 77
        pistachio meringues 106
        strawberries with mascarpone and cream
        70
        strawberry and banana smoothie 23
        super smooth strawberry sorbet 86
strawberry jam: Victoria sponge cake 172
sugar snaps: Thai vegetable curry 152
summer berry muffins 93
sunflower seeds: Bircher muesli with apple 151
        fruit and nut breakfast bars 51
        fruit, seed, and nut muesli 69
        granola 193
        honey-roasted nuts and seeds 168
super smooth strawberry sorbet 86
super vegetable salad 36
sweet and sour Chinese cabbage 24
sweet and sour tofu 152
sweet potatoes: chickpea tagine with harissa
        156
        spiced whole wheat couscous with sweet
        potato and pumpkin seeds 209
        sweet potato gnocchi with arugula pesto
        15
        sweet potato jalfrezi 222
        vegetable satay 206
sweet corn: black-eyed bean casserole with
        cilantro 205
        Mexican cornbread 74
        salad of wild rice, charred sweet corn,
        spiced pecans, avocado, and feta 106
        Thai vegetable curry 152
        vegetable and tofu stir-fry with soba
        noodles 198
sweets: almond sweets 222
        chocolate truffles 198
Swiss chard: chickpea with red chard and
        asparagus 93
syllabub, apple 156

T

tabbouleh: Middle Eastern tabbouleh salad 15
tacos, spicy refried bean 82
tagine: chickpea tagine with harissa 156
tagliatelle: tagliatelle with mushroom sauce 160
tahini: hummus and flatbread 23
        lentils with tahini dip 135
tamarind paste: pad thai noodles 55
tangy roots 214
Tanner, James 101
tartare-style sauce, jacket fries with 106
tarts: asparagus tart 44
        basil and mushroom tart 139
        leek and ricotta tart 182

lemon, almond, and pear cake 132
        lemon and lime tart 52
        pecan pie 194
        spinach tart 32
        spring vegetable tarte fine 16
        see also quiches
teabreads: best ever banana bread 20
Thai vegetable curry 152
tiramisù 118
toast: avocado on toast 147
        cinnamon raisin toast 225
        Stilton pâté with Melba toast and cherry
        tomatoes 109
        Welsh rarebit 171
        yogurt, banana, and rye toast 89
tofu: grilled peaches with Greek yogurt 110
        orange marinated tofu skewers 113
        pumpkin and tofu laksa 218
        spicy tofu with ginger 171
        super vegetable salad 36
        sweet and sour tofu 152
        tofu scramble with spinach 217
        vegetable and tofu stir-fry with soba
        noodles 198
tomatoes: baked zucchini, feta, and tomatoes
        60
        black-eyed bean casserole with cilantro
        205
        Boston lettuce, soft-boiled egg, roast
        tomatoes, capers and Parmesan 86
        chickpea tagine with harissa 156
        eggplant casserole with pomegranate 124
        eggplant parmigiana 70
        eggplant, potato, and pepper stew 164
        eggplant with tomatoes and crème fraîche
        81
        farro with spicy sun-dried tomatoes and
        feta 213
        fatoush salad with grilled halloumi 59
        fregola sarda pasta with tomatoes 105
        fresh tomato and basil soup 73
        grilled peaches with Greek yogurt 110
        Greek salad 109
        guacamole 102
        melon gazpacho 90
        Middle Eastern tabbouleh salad 15
        mozzarella and tomato salad 85
        mozzarella pasta 93
        onion bhajis with tomato and chile sauce
        201
        orange marinated tofu skewers 113
        panzanella 117
        paella verduras 110
        papaya salad 78
        quesadillas with avocado, sour cream, and